Leanne is really courageous to write about the NAEC. We've been like the forgotten people and she's highlighted that and provided some balance. Being part of the NAEC rejuvenated my way of thinking and doing, inspired me to relearn my language, and to initiate a lot of things. I'm happy I was part of the National Aboriginal Education Committee, that's where it all started. The only way is through education. It's all come back to me, from Leanne's work, what the NAEC has given me. It's a big past and she's highlighted the whole of it. They deserve to be remembered.

UNCLE LAURIE PADMORE, DULGABARRA YIDINJI ELDER

In this beautifully written book we are taken on a journey that renders visible the hidden history of Aboriginal and Torres Strait Islander advocacy in education. This exciting book captures the very best of the formidable and indomitable spirit of those early education warriors who paved the way for many of us to follow. Dr Holt's contribution is no less.

DISTINGUISHED PROFESSOR AILEEN MORETON-ROBINSON, GOENPUL, QUANDAMOOKA; OFFICE OF INDIGENOUS EDUCATION AND ENGAGEMENT, RMIT UNIVERSITY

Culturally grounded knowledge and the principle of self-determination are pivotal to the creation of culturally affirming and intellectually enriching education, the sort that are essential tools in the fight for Aboriginal and Torres Strait Islander rights and freedoms. Holt's book *Talking Strong* is an important account of a seminal period in Aboriginal education history and policy development in Australia. Holt captures the essence of the transformative era of the NAEC and the narratives of triumph and trials shared by the key players places readers directly in the room of change and transformation. A must read.

PROFESSOR BOB MORGAN, GAMILARAAY; CONJOINT PROFESSOR, WOLLOTUKA INSTITUTE, UNIVERSITY OF NEWCASTLE

Talking strong

The National Aboriginal Education Committee and the development of Aboriginal education policy

ABORIGINAL STUDIES PRESS

First published in 2021
by Aboriginal Studies Press

An AIATSIS Research Publication

© Leanne Holt 2021

All rights reserved. No part of this book may be reproduced or transmitted in any form or by any means, electronic or mechanical, including photocopying, recording or by any information storage and retrieval system, without prior permission in writing from the publisher. The Australian *Copyright Act 1968* (the Act) allows a maximum of one chapter or 10 per cent of this book, whichever is the greater, to be photocopied by any educational institution for its education purposes provided that the educational institution (or body that administers it) has given a remuneration notice to Copyright Agency Limited (CAL) under the Act.

The opinions expressed in this book are the author's own and do not necessarily reflect the view of AIATSIS or ASP.

The author and publisher have made every effort to trace the original copyholders of materials used in this book. If anyone has any further information, please contact the publisher.

Aboriginal and Torres Strait Islander people are respectfully advised that this publication contains names and images of deceased persons and culturally sensitive information.

Aboriginal Studies Press is the publishing arm of the Australian Institute of Aboriginal and Torres Strait Islander Studies.

GPO Box 553, Canberra, ACT 2601
Phone: (61 2) 6246 1183
Fax: (61 2) 6261 4288
Email: asp@aiatsis.gov.au
Web: www.aiatsis.gov.au/asp/about.html

 A catalogue record for this book is available from the National Library of Australia

9781925302318 (pb)
9781925302394 (ePub)

Printed in Australia by SOS Print, Sydney
Design and typesetting by Greg Jorsz & Christine Bruderlin

FOREWORD

Talking Strong is what we do. Talking Strong takes us on a path that needed Aboriginal and Torres Strait Islander people to be talking strong, to start those baby steps.

Leanne Holt gives us *Talking Strong: The National Aboriginal Education Committee and the development of Aboriginal and Torres Strait Islander education in Australia* an engaging, well-researched volume, rich with anecdotes (some a bit embarrassing on my part) and some interesting information that has not seen the light of day before.

Pearl Duncan once said to me, 'We are so fortunate that we were born at the right time and have the opportunity to be involved in this almost magical experience.' For many of us, membership of the National Aboriginal Education Committee provided a path that perhaps we never would have dreamed of. Personally, I could see what others were achieving and realised the possibilities. While my passion was for curriculum development, fuelled by membership of the NAEC's curriculum subcommittee, Initial Teacher Education was a priority. While I had achieved my childhood hope of becoming a teacher, further study beckoned and I needed to gain a PhD in order to work in this area. It was through working in the higher education sector and membership of the National Aboriginal and Torres Strait Islander Higher Education Consortium that I met Leanne Holt, who at that time was located at The Wollotuka Institute, University of Newcastle.

When Leanne first mentioned that she was hoping to write a history of the National Aboriginal Education Committee, I was on one hand quite envious and on the other, delighted and excited that it would be done.

Participating in interviews with Leanne took me back to my first-ever encounter with the NAEC. At that time, I was a primary school teacher in Hobart, grappling with the inability to truth-tell in the school curriculum. It was 1977.

On one particular day, I was reading the *Mercury* newspaper over my morning coffee when I came across what to me was the most amazing story with a photograph of Phil Stewart, Patsy Cameron, Colin Bourke and Stephen Albert, a photograph that is shown on page 39.

There was a meeting in Hobart! Not just any meeting, but a meeting of the National Aboriginal Education Committee! Naturally, I hightailed it to the meeting venue as soon as school was over for the day and as Patsy Cameron recounted in this volume, 'That's when we first met Kaye Price. Kaye actually arrived at our accommodation that night ... she said, 'Hey, here I am. I'm an Aboriginal teacher. I'm number two.'

The Tasmanian Aboriginal Centre had not long been established and my best friend, Lennah West (Newson) and her mother, Auntie Ida, had invited me to become involved. Lennah often came to my classes to talk about things Aboriginal; she often told the students that, 'It doesn't matter how much milk you put in your tea, it's still a cup of tea.' The TAC nominated me for membership and you can imagine my principal's astonishment to receive a call from Federal Minister for Aboriginal Affairs Fred Chaney congratulating me on my appointment.

The NAEC was a watershed in Australian education, not just in relation to Aboriginal and Torres Strait Islander histories and cultures, but for Australia as a whole. For the first time, a wide range of people started to pay attention and we as educators received a great deal of support from members of the non-Indigenous population. As Leanne recounts, 'Developing relationships with non-Indigenous people was an important initiative because it would have been impossible for the NAEC to achieve its goals without their support and collaboration.' This support and collaboration remain a critical issue.

One of the most powerful things the NAEC did was to hold meetings at different locations across the country. Visible. Approachable. Community meetings at Yuendumu, Mer (Murray Island), Broome, Cape Barren Island. As Patsy says, 'Really early ... we decided that we wanted to get out into communities. We wanted to go out — not sit in Canberra and have meetings there in this big, flash place.' Similarly, the NAEC conferences provided the biggest opportunity for Aboriginal and Torres Strait Islander people to network, to share and gain insights into different ways of working. Eleanor Bourke remembers, 'Those networks were invaluable

'. . . Always meant you had a contact somewhere you could talk to if you were looking for some information. You could use the network and that's just priceless really.'

What was accomplished during the tenure of the NAEC would not have been possible without the tremendous talents and dedication of each member. Right from the beginning, members shared their vision and provided strength, confidence and wisdom that were the impetus for change. There have also been lasting friendships and the network is ever-expanding. In the last few months, I found myself meeting Hazel McKellar's daughter and working with one of Eddie Mabo's daughters.

There is no doubt in my mind that the establishment of the NAEC laid the foundation for the work that many Aboriginal and Torres Strait Islander people have carried out over the years. The solidarity and confidence paved the way for many more education achievements. As I work with others, Indigenous and non-Indigenous, on aspects of the Australian curriculum, I remain grateful for NAEC members' confidence in my ability to participate in the curriculum subcommittee and for their support for my horrified reaction to a resource that had been developed for teachers that stated, 'Aboriginal Dreaming stories are like fairy stories'. And so it began.

I will always be indebted to members of the NAEC for their teaching and my learning: in particular, to Eddie Mabo who taught me that humility is a virtue; May O'Brien who taught me to be patient; John Budby who tried to teach me that Tasmania is not the centre of the world; Didimain Uibo, who encouraged my laughter; Errol West who taught me the word 'sesquipedalianism'; Paul Hughes who taught me tenacity; and Peter Buckskin who taught me what friendship really means. And to the NAEC Secretariat, as it was there that I met my husband and best friend, John, forty years ago.

Talking Strong takes us on a journey through the years and demonstrates that Aboriginal and Torres Strait Islander people have been working diligently over this journey to change education so that it accommodates our languages, world views, cultures, science and technologies. This is being achieved slowly through the efforts of Aboriginal and Torres Strait

Islander people ourselves, with support from others who understand our values, but the NAEC laid the groundwork.

What Leanne Holt has done in this remarkable piece of work, is to place forever in the minds of all, the so very important catalyst for change that was the National Aboriginal Education Committee.

Dr Kaye Price AM

CONTENTS

Acronyms xiv
Acknowledgments xv
Connecting to Country. xvii
Contributors xix
Introduction: Aboriginal and Torres Strait Islander voices in education 1

Chapter 1. The dawning of a national approach to
Aboriginal and Torres Strait Islander education. 6
    The 1973 *Schools in Australia* report. 7
    Gaining a voice: the Aboriginal Consultative Group. 9
    May O'Brien 12
    Rex Granites 14
    The 1975 *Education for Aborigines* report 15
    The birth of the National Aboriginal Education Committee 17

Chapter 2. A voice in education: The first term of the NAEC, 1977–80 20
    The appointment and formation of the NAEC 21
    Stephen Albert. 22
    Lillian Holt 27
    Setting the national agenda 29
    Taking NAEC meetings to communities 31
    Patsy Cameron. 34
    Bob Morgan. 42

Chapter 3. Community collaboration: the Aboriginal Education
Consultative Groups. 45
    Development of the state and territory education groups 46
    Collaborative workshops 56
    Empowering connections. 57

Chapter 4. Redefining access to education 61
    Taking over the space: National Aboriginal
    Education Conferences 61
    Community-driven schooling: a study into the
    Townsville Black Community School. 66
    The 1979 *Education and Employment of Aboriginal and
    Torres Strait Islander Teachers* report 72

  A time for evolution. 78

Chapter 5. Taking our place in education: the second term of
the NAEC, 1980–83 79
  The second chairperson and members 80
  Peter Buckskin 84
  Laurie Padmore 87
  Specialist appointments. 89
  Pearl Duncan 91
  John Lester 93
  Didimain Uibo 95

Chapter 6. From consultation to involvement: raising our voices 96
  Fostering strong government relationships 97
  The strategy of Aboriginalisation 99
  The first consolidated national policy for Aboriginal and Torres
  Strait Islander education 102
  Colin Bourke 103

Chapter 7. Introducing Aboriginal and Torres Strait Islander
studies: A change in education 109
  The 1982 *Report to the Australian Education Council* 114

Chapter 8. Asserting a right to self-determination:
the third term of the NAEC, 1983–85 116
  The third chairperson and members 117
  Paul Hughes 118
  Kay Price 121
  Victor Forrest 123
  Wendy Ludwig 124
  John Heath 126
  A change in government makes Aboriginal and Torres Strait
  Islander education a priority 128
  The NAEC as principal adviser 131
  Increased power in determining funding priorities 135

Chapter 9. Setting strong priorities 138
  The 1984 *Technical and Further Education for*
  Aborigines and Torres Strait Islanders: Participation
  and Self-Determination report 139
  1000 Aboriginal teachers by 1990 142
  The 1985 *Support Systems for Aboriginal Students*
  in Higher Education Institutions report 147

  Towards an Aboriginal pedagogy and epistemology:
  the final NAEC conference 152

Chapter 10. Consolidating Aboriginal education policy:
the final term of the NAEC, 1986–89 155
  The fourth chairperson 156
  Errol West. 155
  The 1986 *Policy Statement on Teacher Education
  for Aborigines and Torres Strait Islanders* 158
  The 1986 *Policy Statement on Tertiary Education
  for Aborigines and Torres Strait Islanders* 163
  The Aboriginal and Torres Strait Islander Pedagogy Project . . . 167
  The 1989 *National Policy Guidelines for
  Early Childhood Education*. 168

Chapter 11. The NAEC's final story 173
  The 1988 *Report of the Aboriginal Education Policy Task Force* . 173
  The launch of the Aboriginal Education Policy. 177
  Criticism of the joint policy statement 179
  Recommendations for combating racism in higher education. . 182
  The final phase of the NAEC 183
  Eleanor Bourke 183

Chapter 12. The river continues to flow: a celebration
of leadership and legacy 186
  An empowered space in education 187
  The increase in participation in education 189
  Aboriginal and Torres Strait Islander employment 193
  Aboriginal and Torres Strait Islander leadership
  and mentorship. 194
  Aboriginal and Torres Strait Islander curriculum. 195
  National policy development 196
  Legacy and advice 199

Conclusion. 211

Appendix A. NAEC membership 213

Appendix B. Timeline of reports 217

References 218

Index. 225

List of figures

Figure 1. Karuah River, NSW, Worimi Country xvi
Figure 1.1. Members of the Aboriginal Consultative Group 10
Figure 1.2. May O'Brien and Carol Garlett, 2014 13
Figure 1.3. Letter from the Western Australian Department of Native Affairs to the Director of Education, 10 September 1951 13
Figure 1.4. Japanangka Rex Granites, 2014 14
Figure 2.1. Stephen Albert 23
Figure 2.2. The NAEC logo was designed by Kaye Price and featured on a badge worn by NAEC members 30
Figure 2.3. Patsy Cameron and the author at Patsy's home, Tasmania, 2013 34
Figure 2.4. Phil Stewart, Patsy Cameron, Colin Bourke and Stephen Albert meeting in Tasmania, August 1977 39
Figure 2.5. Bob Morgan 42
Figure 3.1. The NAEC members, 1980 47
Figure 3.2. Margaret Valadian, Kaye Price, Stephen Albert and Natascha McNamara at the DAA state superintendents meeting, Hobart, 1980 57
Figure 4.1. Logo of the 6th National Aboriginal Education Conference, 1981 65
Figure 5.1. Peter Buckskin, 2016 84
Figure 5.2. John Budby 89
Figure 5.3. Peter Buckskin, Laurie Padmore, Victor Forrest, Pat (Julia) Williamson, Mary Atkinson and Ted (Eric) Hampton at an NAEC meeting 90
Figure 5.4. John Lester, University of Newcastle, 2017 94
Figure 6.1. Colin Bourke with staff of Monash University where he was Director of the Centre for Research into Aboriginal Affairs from 1977–1981 104
Figure 8.1. Paul Hughes 118
Figure 8.2. Kaye Price, University of Tasmania, 2013 121
Figure 8.3. NAEC members, 1984 122
Figure 8.4. John Heath, 2018 126

Figure 9.1. John Heath, Bob Morgan, Errol West and
 Bill Daniels at Sydney Technical College, 1986 140
Figure 9.2. Figure 9.2. NAEC chairperson Paul Huges with Sue Hawley
 (centre) and executive officer Kaye Price, 1983 policy summit,
 Goulburn. 144
Figure 9.3. Students of Monash University's Orientation Scheme
 for Aborigines, 1987. 148
Figure 10.1. Errol West. 157
Figure 11.1. Paul Hughes (right), chairperson of National
 Education Policy Task Force, with Gerry Hand,
 Federal Minister for Aboriginal Affairs, 1988 174
Figure 11.2. Painting featured on the cover of the
 National Review of Education for Aboriginal and
 Torres Strait Islander Peoples: Final Report 178

List of tables

Table 1.1. School participation rates for Aborigines and Torres Strait
 Islander and total population, Australia, 1971 7
Table 9.1. Aboriginal and Torres Strait Islander teacher targets
 by state and territory, 1982. 143
Table 11.1. Education participation rates, 1986 177

Acronyms

ABSEG	Aboriginal Secondary Grants Scheme
ABSTUDY	Aboriginal Study Grants Scheme
ACG	Aboriginal Consultative Group
ACTAECG	Australian Capital Territory AECG
AECG	Aboriginal Education Consultative Group
AITEP	Aboriginal and Islander Tertiary Education Program
ATSIC	Aboriginal and Torres Strait Islander Commission
CAE	College of Advanced Education
CASWG	Commonwealth Aboriginal Studies Working Group
DAA	Department of Aboriginal Affairs
EEATSIT	Education and Employment of Aboriginal and Torres Strait Islander Teachers
MATSITI	More Aboriginal and Torres Strait Islander Teachers Initiative
NAC	National Aboriginal Committee
NAEC	National Aboriginal Education Committee
NITE	National Inquiry into Teacher Education
NSW	New South Wales
NSWAECG	NSW Aboriginal Education Consultative Group
NTAECG	Northern Territory AECG
SAAECG	South Australian AECG
TAFE	Technical and Further Education
TAFEWP	TAFE Working Party
TASAECG	Tasmanian AECG
VET	Vocational Education and Training
WAAECG	Western Australian AECG

Acknowledgments

This book is a result of the shared stories, knowledges and experiences of the past members of the NAEC and the late Susan Ryan, who have entrusted me to pass on their journey, which has led the way for Aboriginal education policy and the raising of Aboriginal voices — it is truly an honour.

Importantly, I acknowledge my family and friends, especially my husband, Lee, and two wonderful children, Tanisha and Jaiden; my parents, Judy and Brian Lilley, and sister, Korinne; your love, inspiration and patience have allowed me the time and space to complete the study and work that led to this book. Thank you for believing in me.

I also thank my colleagues across the academy for your continued mentorship and guidance, including the National Aboriginal and Torres Strait Islander Higher Education Consortium and Macquarie University communities, in particular Distinguished Professor Aileen Moreton-Robinson, Professors Peter Buckskin, Boni Robertson, Kaye Price and Bob Morgan, Cheryl Newton, Dr Joe Perry and Jen Gili for your unwavering support and encouragement.

I am grateful to the dedicated staff at the Australian Institute of Aboriginal and Torres Strait Islander Studies (AIATSIS) and Aboriginal Studies Press for their patience and assistance in transforming my thesis into a book. Also, to my supervisors, Associate Professor Erica Southgate, Professor Jenny Gore and Dr Michael Donovan, I appreciate your guidance throughout my PhD.

To all the people throughout my life who have inspired me, believed in me and contributed to my personal growth to get me where I am today, I thank you. To Aunty Colleen, who has provided me with friendship and inspiration, and who, at 88, continues to contribute strong knowledge and wisdom.

This book is dedicated to Indigenous peoples across the world who have fought to have their voices heard for the benefit of present and future

Indigenous generations who need to keep up the fight through being strong, proud and resilient – with big, strong voices.

Connecting to Country

I am a Worimi and Biripai woman (Lilley/Bugg) of coastal New South Wales (NSW). Although my ancestral links are from this nation, I have lived on Darkinjung country, on the NSW Central Coast, and have forged strong links with this Aboriginal community.

I am currently Pro Vice-Chancellor (Indigenous Strategy), Macquarie University, having worked in higher education for more than twenty years. In 2016, I completed my doctorate in education at The University of Newcastle. I am passionate about Aboriginal and Torres Strait Islander education and continue to draw on the knowledges and guidance of my family, colleagues, community and Elders.

Karuah River runs through Worimi Country from the mountains of Gloucester (NSW) and down to the mouth of the river at Karuah, before flowing out to the Pacific Ocean. The riverbanks are where my ancestors

Karuah River, NSW, Worimi Country (photo courtesy Louise Duff).

lived as fishermen and oyster farmers. My grandfather's spirit (ashes) was returned to the river once he passed over to the spirit world. I feel a connection to the river through the spirits of my ancestors as a significant place to me personally but also to the Worimi people. Throughout this book, the river forms the connections with my Country and the relationships of my Country, my knowledge, my journey and experiences. As it commences its journey, the fresh water gradually meets the salt water, which is fed from the ocean; it becomes a mix of fresh water and salt water (brackish).

The fresh water represents the Aboriginal and Torres Strait Islander peoples who have long journeyed through mountains, coastal lands and bushlands, bringing with them stories/education passed through generations. The river survives through flood and drought, like the strength of our people, who show resilience, sometimes varying their path according to environmental impacts, but always continuing to flow. Fresh water gives life, just as the members of the National Aboriginal Education Committee (NAEC) gave life to Indigenous education. Through sharing their experiences and expertise, they were able to forge a journey for us to continue.

The salt water represents non-Indigenous people who have travelled across the oceans to settle in Australia, bringing different viewpoints and forms of education. The salt water, while in the ocean, can sometimes be forceful and damaging, and not always easy for swimming; however, when it enters the river or estuary, it is calmer and easier to interact with. The salt water represents the government, particularly, in this instance, the Department of Education and the Department of Aboriginal Affairs, including the non-Indigenous ministers and public servants in the departments.

The joining of fresh water and salt water is a reflective environment that represents the sharing of cultures, experiences and stories based on respect and reciprocity to ensure a healthy future for both Indigenous and non-Indigenous people. The river itself represents a journey; it gives life and sustenance to living things; it represents our future.

Contributors

Members of the NAEC, as well as Susan Ryan, the Minister for Education from 1983 to 1987, participated in the development of this book. The contributors who shared stories are the life of this book and they hold and retain the ownership of their knowledge. The knowledges shared through yarning and storytelling occurred during numerous interviews between the contributors and me. Their voices are recorded in quotes throughout this book, alongside my own, as we share the space to illuminate the culture, dynamics and journey of the NAEC and related organisations.

Stephen Albert, NAEC Chairperson, 1977–81, Member, Western Australia, 1983–86
Interviewed, 23 November 2012 [NSW].
Stephen, a descendant of the Bardi people in Western Australia, was the inaugural chairperson of the NAEC. He was also well known as a musician and actor, and for his work in Aboriginal and Torres Strait Islander media, education and health.

Colin Bourke, NAEC Inaugural Member, Victoria, 1977–79
Interviewed, 19 June 2013 [Victoria].
Colin is a descendant of the Gamilaraay people in New South Wales and grew up in Yarrawonga, Victoria. He was an inaugural member of the NAEC and throughout his career held a number of senior positions in higher education, including being the first Aboriginal person to hold a deputy vice-chancellor role.

Eleanor Bourke, NAEC Member, Victoria, 1979–81, 1985–89, Deputy Chairperson, 1988–89
Interviewed, 19 June 2013 [Victoria].
Eleanor, a descendant of the Wergaia and Wamba Wamba peoples, was appointed to the NAEC in 1979 for two years and then reappointed in 1985, continuing through to the conclusion of the committee as the deputy chairperson in the final year.

Peter Buckskin, NAEC Member, South Australia, 1981–84, 1986–88
Interviewed, 6 November 2015 [South Australia].
Peter Buckskin, a descendant of the Narungga people in South Australia, was the youngest appointment to the NAEC. Peter went on to hold senior roles in both the Australian Public Service and in higher education. He was the chairperson of the National Aboriginal and Torres Strait Islander Higher Education Consortium from 2010 to 2018.

Patsy Cameron, NAEC Inaugural Member, Tasmania, 1977–79
Interviewed, 5 March 2013 [Tasmania].
Patsy grew up on Flinders Island in Tasmania. She was an inaugural member of the NAEC and is a writer, artist and scholar. Patsy has been a member of a number of government and community-based advisory committees, providing cultural and educational expertise towards the advancement of her communities.

Pearl Duncan, NAEC Member, 1979–83, Primary Specialisation
Interviewed, 29 September 2015 [Queensland].
Pearl Duncan, a descendant of the Gamilaraay people in New South Wales, was a specialist primary school appointment to the NAEC. Pearl spent most of her career as a primary teacher, moving to higher education at the end of her career.

Victor Forrest, NAEC Member, Western Australia, 1981–83, Research Officer, 1983–85
Interviewed, 22 January 2016 [NSW].
Victor, a descendant of the Nyungar/Yamajti peoples in Western Australia, was raised on the Mount Magnet Aboriginal reserve. Victor spent two years as an NAEC member before being appointed NAEC research officer in 1983. Victor also contributed to the opening of the Centre for Aboriginal Studies at Curtin University in 1983.

Rex Granites, NAEC Member, 1983–84, Traditional (Cultural) Specialisation

Interviewed, 7 August 2014 [NSW].

Rex Granites was a Warlpiri man from the Western Desert of the Northern Territory. Rex was an artist and was appointed to the NAEC on the basis of both his educational and traditional knowledge. As an ordained pastor, Elder, artist, translator and mentor, Rex worked with Aboriginal communities to ensure the physical and spiritual healing of his people.

John Heath, NAEC Member, New South Wales, 1985–88

Interviewed, 18 January 2016 [NSW].

John is a descendant of the Biripai people. Throughout John's career, he was a teacher, worked for ABSTUDY and held leadership roles in higher education. John was an inaugural executive member of the NSWAECG.

Lillian Holt, NAEC Member, 1985–88, Executive Officer, 1978–80, Tertiary Specialisation

Interviewed, 17 June 2013 [South Australia].

Lillian was born on Cherbourg Aboriginal Reserve in Queensland. At the age of seventeen, she was the first Aboriginal person employed by the ABC in Brisbane and the first Aboriginal principal of the College of Aboriginal Education in Adelaide, now known as Tauondi Aboriginal Community College.

Paul Hughes, NAEC Member, South Australia, 1977–81, Chairperson, 1983–86

Interviewed, 18 June 2013 [South Australia].

Paul is a descendant of the Yankunytjatjara/Narungga/Kaurna peoples in South Australia. Paul was appointed as the third chairperson of the NAEC. At the time of Paul's initial appointment to the NAEC, he was an executive officer for the South Australian Department of Education.

John Lester, NAEC Member, 1980–83, Primary Specialisation

Interviewed, 9 November 2015 [NSW].

John is a descendant of the Wonnarua people. John started his career as a teacher and later became the first Aboriginal principal of a TAFE college. John was also the first director of Aboriginal Education in the NSW Department of Education and held leadership positions within higher education.

Wendy Ludwig, NAEC Member, 1983–86, Adult Education Specialisation

Interviewed, 26 February 2016 [NSW].

Wendy is a descendant of the Kungarakany/Gurindji peoples in the Northern Territory. Wendy has strong expertise in vocational education, having been a head of faculty at TAFE for twelve years. Wendy also worked in leadership roles within higher education and at Batchelor Institute.

Robert (Bob) Morgan, NAEC Member, New South Wales, 1979–89

Interviewed, 18 March 2016 [NSW].

Bob is a descendant of the Gamilaraay people and was born and raised in Walgett, New South Wales. He was the longest serving member of the NAEC. Bob was the founding president of the NSWAECG and worked in senior positions in the public service and in higher education.

May O'Brien, NAEC Inaugural Member, Western Australia, 1977–81

Interviewed, 3 June 2014 [Western Australia].

May was a descendant of the Wongatha people in Western Australia. May became the first Aboriginal teacher in Western Australia and later was the first Aboriginal person to become a superintendent with the Department of Education in Western Australia.

Laurie Padmore, NAEC Member, Tasmania, 1981–84

Interviewed, 20 June 2012 [Tasmania].

Laurie is a descendant of the Dulguburra Yidinji people in the Atherton Tablelands, Queensland. He spent many years working in Aboriginal education with the Tasmanian Department of Education. He was nominated by the Tasmanian Aboriginal Education Consultative Group (Committee) to become a member of the NAEC.

Kaye Price, NAEC Member, Tasmania, 1979–81, Executive Officer, 1982–84

Interviewed, 19 January 2013 [Queensland].
Kaye is a descendant of the Aboriginal peoples of Tasmania. Kaye was a member of the NAEC prior to being appointed as its executive officer. Kaye commenced her career as a teacher and has also worked for the Department of Education and in leadership roles within higher education. She has remained passionate about Aboriginal and Torres Strait Islander education, publishing and editing a number of books and journals.

Susan Ryan, Minister for Education, 1983–87

Interviewed, 3 February 2016 [NSW].
The Hon. Susan Ryan was the Minister for Education and Youth Affairs from 1983 to 1987. Minister Ryan was very committed to Aboriginal and Torres Strait Islander education and worked very closely with the NAEC.

Didimain Uibo, NAEC Member, Northern Territory, 1980–84, Primary Specialisation

Interviewed, 4 November 2014 [Northern Territory].
Didimain is a descendant of the Nunggubuyu and Warnindilyakwa peoples from Numbulwar and Groote Eylandt in the Northern Territory. After studying, Didimain went back to her community to become a teacher and was later appointed principal at Numbulwar School, retaining this position for many years, which incorporated preschool, primary, high school and post-secondary students.

The interviews in this book

The interviews with contributors to this book were conducted as part of my doctoral research, which I completed in 2016. I consider the contributors as storytellers and as co-researchers in the research.

The interviews were inspirational and I feel a sense of privilege in having the opportunity to share the contributors' personal stories, achievements and challenges, and to bring them to a wider audience. All interviews were conducted face to face. They were audio-recorded and transcribed, with the permission of the contributors, who also checked them for accuracy. Minor copyedits have been made to the interviews for this current publication.

INTRODUCTION

Aboriginal and Torres Strait Islander voices in education

> If there is going to be harmony between our two societies then it will have to be through education. When white people have a better awareness of Aboriginals then maybe our kids will have a better time. (Stephen Albert, cited in Ohlsson 1977, p. 2)

Since time immemorial, education has been integral to the progress and sustainability of every society, including Aboriginal and Torres Strait Islander society. The effect of colonisation on the education of Indigenous people in Australia was catastrophic (Parbury 1991). Until the late 1960s, restrictions and disempowerment, brought about by the policies and laws of the colonisers, resulted in a dismal educational success rate.

In 1971, the population of Aboriginal and Torres Strait Islander peoples in Australia was estimated to be approximately 150,000. The majority of the Indigenous working population was employed in either agriculture or community service. At this time, approximately 40,000 Aboriginal and Torres Strait Islander students were in school education and about fifty-five Aboriginal and Torres Strait Islander people were attending universities across the country (ACG 1975). Stephen Albert, inaugural chairperson of the National Aboriginal Education Committee (NAEC), illuminates the long-term disempowerment of Aboriginal and Torres Strait Islander peoples in education:

> Since 1788, the Aborigines of Australia have been subjected in varying degrees to an education system which has aimed to rationalise their dispossession from the land, deprecate their culture and, in general, endeavour to make the indigenous people of this country lose their own rich cultural background and think, act and hold the same values as middle-class Europeans. (Albert 1978, p. 1)

Until the 1970s, colonial policies attempted to control, assimilate and 'civilise' Indigenous people; this resulted in removing access to a rigorous traditional education system while effectively denying access to Western education (Parbury 1991). The Australian Government Commission of Inquiry into Poverty stated that Aboriginal and Torres Strait Islander peoples had the lowest outcomes in all aspects of their lives, including living conditions, health and education, of any Australian peoples (Sackville 1975).

In 1969, while on the campaign trail to become prime minister, Gough Whitlam stated:

> When government makes opportunities for any of the citizens, it makes them for all citizens. We are all diminished as citizens when any of us are poor. Poverty is a national waste as well as individual waste. We are all diminished when any of us are denied proper education. The nation is the poorer — a poorer economy, a poorer civilisation, because of this human and national waste. (Naylor & James 2015, p. 3)

This statement reflects the impetus for change at the time, coinciding with one of the first significant initiatives by the Australian Government to encourage the participation of Aboriginal and Torres Strait Islander peoples in education. The introduction of the Aboriginal Study Grants Scheme (ABSTUDY) in 1969, followed a year later by the Aboriginal Secondary Grants Scheme (ABSEG), demonstrated an initial commitment by the government. The grant schemes marked a new beginning; over the next forty-five years, a plethora of policies, programs and initiatives were introduced, focusing on the advancement of Aboriginal and Torres Strait Islander peoples through education.

The 1970s were a turning point for Aboriginal and Torres Strait Islander education and policy, with the realisation that Aboriginal and Torres Strait Islander peoples had a right to a voice for their own self-determination and self-management (Maddison 2009). A number of committees, including the NAEC, were established to provide that voice to the Australian Government. This was the first time that Aboriginal and Torres Strait Islander voices were heard on a national level in relation to education policy, and it marked a clear starting point of access, participation and success for Aboriginal and Torres Strait Islander peoples within a Western education system.

Appointed by the Australian Government in 1977 following recommendations in the Education for Aborigines report (ACG 1975), the NAEC was the first government-appointed Aboriginal and Torres Strait Islander education committee in Australia that had a membership of all Aboriginal and Torres Strait Islander scholars, leaders and experts. The advice it gave was informed by Aboriginal and Torres Strait Islander voices from across the whole of Australia. The committee set agendas, policy positions and educational programs that would progress Aboriginal and Torres Strait Islander education priorities from this time forward.

The role of the NAEC was to provide advice and guidance to the Department of Education and the Department of Aboriginal Affairs on the development, implementation and funding of programs and policies. These programs and policies would contribute to educational outcomes for Aboriginal and Torres Strait Islander people from early childhood through to higher education (Ohlsson 1977).

According to a study by Altman, Biddle and Hunter (2005), the 1980s marked the most dramatic change in outcomes in Aboriginal and Torres Strait Islander policy, particularly in education. Throughout most of the 1980s, the NAEC was the principal advisory body to the Australian Government, with a key focus on community consultation and participation, access for Aboriginal and Torres Strait Islander people to all levels of education, Aboriginal teacher training, Aboriginal studies and development of a consolidated policy position.

Limited research has been undertaken on the progress of the national movement for Indigenous education over the past forty years, particularly as it relates to Indigenous-informed education policy. The existing literature has not given appropriate recognition to the NAEC as a significant committee that led the National Aboriginal Education Policy agenda, or to its substantial role in creating structures and foundations from a national Aboriginal and Torres Strait Islander perspective. The NAEC had a diverse membership encompassing Elders, expert knowledge holders, classroom teachers and leaders in education. Together, they were able to contribute broad knowledge and advice to the departments. Appendix A provides the full membership of the NAEC over its four terms from 1977 to 1989, and Appendix B lists the reports that the NAEC was instrumental in providing.

This book describes the significant contribution of Aboriginal and Torres Strait Islander people to the development of national Aboriginal and Torres Strait Islander education policy in Australia from 1975, when the NAEC was first recommended, through to 1989, when the NAEC was disbanded. Through Aboriginal and Torres Strait Islander voices and perspectives, it examines the roles of Aboriginal and Torres Strait Islander peoples in creating discussion, debate and cultural empowerment in Indigenous education to ensure the progression of education for Aboriginal and Torres Strait Islander peoples now and into the future.

The journey of the NAEC and its approach to the development of Indigenous education policy in Australia can provide important lessons to our current and future leaders, educators and governments — specifically, in its approach to engaging Aboriginal and Torres Strait Islander voices nationally and influencing a co-ordinated policy approach to achieve positive educational outcomes. This book provides educators and leaders with access to important historical and political contexts to inform future practice and relationships. The experiences and insights of Aboriginal and Torres Strait Islander scholars and leaders provide an awareness of past successes and challenges in the education of Aboriginal and Torres

Strait Islander peoples across all levels of Western education. The voices of these Aboriginal and Torres Strait Islander leaders record a journey that provides mentorship and knowledges to future generations, inspiring the continuation of the enhancement and development of self-determination individually and as a community through education for Aboriginal and Torres Strait Islander peoples.

This book is a celebration of the leadership and the legacy that these amazing Aboriginal and Torres Strait Islander scholars have passed along to our future generations.

Terminology

In this book, I use the word 'Aboriginal', and occasionally the word 'Indigenous', to include all Aboriginal and Torres Strait Islander peoples and nations throughout Australia. I use 'Aboriginal' when discussing a specific Aboriginal person or nation, and where it is part of an official name or title. The use of language changes over time, but because this book looks back to the mid-1900s, I retain, in quotes, the use of language that is no longer considered appropriate. It is not my intention to disregard the recognition of differences in cultures and knowledge systems among Aboriginal and Torres Strait Islander peoples.

CHAPTER 1

The dawning of a national approach to Aboriginal and Torres Strait Islander education

> Two hundred years of nothing — forty years of something really good.
> (Stephen Albert, interview, 2012)

Since colonisation, government policies and practices, as well as the attitudes of the broader society, have resulted in exclusion, discrimination and the oppression of Aboriginal and Torres Strait Islander peoples in Australia. For many years, Aboriginal and Torres Strait Islander peoples received little or no formal education.

Throughout history, government policies have created intergenerational disadvantage, which has manifested in the long-term institutional inequality of educational outcomes between Indigenous and non-Indigenous people that are evident today. Policies for Aboriginal and Torres Strait Islander peoples developed without an Aboriginal or Torres Strait Islander voice have, time and time again, proven unsuccessful because most non-Indigenous people lack an understanding of the culture and historical contexts and experiences that influence our lives.

It was not until the late 1960s that the Australian Government realised that Aboriginal and Torres Strait Islander education was in crisis. A very different approach was needed if any positive outcomes were going to be achieved. Census data from 1971, which was cited in a Schools Commission (1975) report, highlighted this crisis (Table 1.1).

Table 1.1. School participation rates for Aborigines and Torres Strait Islander and total population, Australia, 1971 (Schools Commission 1975, p. 4).

AGE	ABORIGINES AND TORRES STRAIT ISLANDER	ALL AUSTRALIANS
Years	%	%
15	59.64	81.5
16	28.16	53.7
17	7.96	28.8
18	2.51	7.6
19	0.61	1.3

The 1973 *Schools in Australia* report

After a resounding federal election victory, Gough Whitlam's Labor government took office in December 1972. After twenty-three years of Liberal–Country Party government, the Labor government brought with it strong principles of equality and access, and its actions were to mark historic changes for Aboriginal and Torres Strait Islander peoples. One of the greatest achievements attributed to the Whitlam government is the transformation of education in Australia, which began with the establishment in 1973 of the Schools Commission as a policy-making agency. Kim Beazley (Snr), Minister for Education from 1972 to 1975, was a strong advocate and was proactive in initiating a better future for Aboriginal and Torres Strait Islander peoples through education.

In December 1972, the Interim Committee for the Australian Schools Commission was established to undertake a review of the distribution of funding to government and non-government schools. The review would also recommend the necessary resourcing required and a means for evaluation. Chaired by Professor Peter Karmel, the committee was instructed to submit a report within a very limited timeframe. Although outside the scope of the review, the *Schools in Australia* report (Karmel 1973) provided significant observations to highlight the environment of education for Aboriginal and Torres Strait Islander children. Case studies in the report demonstrated the inconsistencies in school conditions, observing that schools with large enrolments of Aboriginal and Torres Strait Islander children had the worst conditions (Karmel 1973, p. 46). The conditions experienced at one of these communities and schools led a visiting committee member to comment, 'We have nothing but admiration for the staff of this school, not only for their professional and dedicated service, but for remaining and teaching under such adverse physical conditions' (Karmel 1973, p. 46).

Given the poor conditions, the report claimed that for Aboriginal and Torres Strait Islander children, 'schooling should offer a means of redress for the economic and political disadvantages of their background rather than a compounding of them' (Karmel 1973, p. 48). Notably, the report further claimed that 'the problems of prejudice may exacerbate those of poverty' (Karmel 1973, p. 92).

The *Schools in Australia* report was a significant review in the history of education in Australia and its recommendations would direct the development of national education policy, including for Aboriginal and Torres Strait Islander education, over the next twenty years (Schwab 1995). The report concluded that Aboriginal and Torres Strait Islander children were among the most educationally disadvantaged groups in Australia. Given its scope and limited timeframe, the Interim Committee for the Australian Schools Commission could not deliver a comprehensive insight into the education of Aboriginal and Torres Strait Islander children. Instead, it recommended to the Schools Commission that it undertake a special study to explore opportunities to identify a 'co-ordinated policy' for Aboriginal and Torres Strait Islander education (Karmel 1973, p. 92).

Gaining a voice: the Aboriginal Consultative Group

From 1973 to 1977, the political environment and attitudes towards the needs of Aboriginal and Torres Strait Islander peoples were in a process of change. It had become obvious to the government that if Aboriginal and Torres Strait Islander education was going to progress, Aboriginal and Torres Strait Islander peoples needed to determine how that should happen. Aboriginal and Torres Strait Islander voices were to become the key strategy for setting the agenda for the future.

Following the advice of the *Schools in Australia* report (Karmel 1973), the Interim Committee for the Australian Schools Commission directed that when the Schools Commission was fully functional, a committee with a full membership of Aboriginal and Torres Strait Islander people should be established to provide advice on Aboriginal and Torres Strait Islander education. As a result, in December 1974, the national Aboriginal Consultative Group (ACG) was established to engage an Aboriginal and Torres Strait Islander voice towards the advancement of Aboriginal and Torres Strait Islander education. This was the first time that Aboriginal and Torres Strait Islander voices were heard in the education arena on a national level.

The appointment of the ACG was the first step in the evolution of Indigenous participation in Indigenous education policy. A full Aboriginal and Torres Strait Islander committee, to provide advice to the Schools Commission from an Aboriginal and Torres Strait Islander perspective, presented an opportunity for Aboriginal and Torres Strait Islander peoples to resurrect their traditional educational practices, which had been interrupted by past Aboriginal affairs policies. The new direction also provided an opportunity to access a Western education, which Aboriginal and Torres Strait Islander peoples had been excluded from until now.

Largely based on the recommendation in the *Schools in Australia* report to undertake a separate study on Aboriginal and Torres Strait Islander education and the need for a co-ordinated policy (Karmel 1973, p. 92), the Schools Commission authorised the ACG to undertake a special inquiry. Margaret Valadian, who was the first female Aboriginal university graduate, gaining an undergraduate degree in Australia, was the chairperson of the special inquiry committee.

This was a long-awaited achievement. Prior to this, in 1963, the Aboriginal Education Consultative Committee had been established by non-Indigenous people to consult with Aboriginal and Torres Strait Islander peoples on how to increase educational outcomes. The committee was made up of non-Indigenous volunteers and received limited funding, primarily from donations (Williams 2013). Although it was the first recognition of the need for Indigenous communities and families to

Figure 1.1. Members of the Aboriginal Consultative Group: David Anderson, National Aboriginal Committee (NAC), Vic.; Jill Churnside, preschool teacher, WA; Roslyn Ella, teacher, NSW; Walter Fejo, NAC, NT; Rex Granites, teaching assistant, NT; Eric Hayward, community worker, WA; Nita Koolmatrie, teacher, SA; Verna Langdon, community worker, Tas.; Ted Loban, NAC, Torres Strait Islands; Bruce McGuiness, NAC, Vic.; Natascha McNamara, lecturer, SA; Michael Miller, teacher, Queensland; George Mye, NAC, Torres Strait Islands; Wiyendji Nunggula, house-father, NT; May O'Brien, teacher, WA; James Stewart, teacher, SA; and Margaret Valadian, social worker, NSW. Special advisors: John Moriarty, Department of Aboriginal Affairs, and Eric Willmot, Department of Education (ACG, 1975, p. 1).

have a voice in their own educational future, Indigenous people did not lead this voice; non-Indigenous people were still acting as intermediaries. It would take another ten years for the need for Aboriginal and Torres Strait Islander voices in their own decision-making to be realised through the birth of the ACG. Colin Bourke, an inaugural member of the NAEC, recalls this social movement:

> Whitlam got elected and Kim Beazley Snr became the Minister for Education. One of the first things they did was look at the total situation and tried to overcome some of the disadvantages. They started the Disadvantaged Schools Program and then eventually they got Ken McKinnon, ex New Guinea [previously superintendent of schools in Papua New Guinea], to set up the . . . Schools Commission. It was that commission that decided to get the opinion of Aboriginal people when they set up the Aboriginal Consultative Group to the Schools Commission in 1974. (Colin Bourke, interview, 2013)

Inaugural NAEC member May O'Brien recalls the phone call from Kim Beazley Snr requesting a meeting:

> He called me, and I went and saw him. I said to him, 'You're Minister for Education, what are you doing for the Aboriginal people?' He responded, 'What do you want?' and I said, 'Better education! All our kids are there, they haven't got government teachers and they should be included!' He sort of looked at me and said, 'I'm doing this and this and that'. I said, 'Have you asked us?' I told him there's a group of Aboriginal people, you can pick any Aboriginal people who are around here and who are speaking out and form a committee. So that's what he did. He got a committee going called the Aboriginal Consultative Group. With that I had made a friend in a person who could change things. (May O'Brien, interview, 2014)

As a result of her early interactions and recommendations to Beazley, May was an obvious appointment to the ACG.

May O'Brien (nee Miller) was described by Stephen Albert (2012) as being the 'matriarch of the NAEC'.

MAY O'BRIEN

May was born in the goldfields of Western Australia in 1933 and, with a passion for education, became the first Aboriginal teacher in Western Australia and later the first Aboriginal person to be a superintendent with the Department of Education in Western Australia. Her upbringing was both full of challenges and opportunities:

I was born in the bush because, at that time, there were a group of non-Aboriginal people who were saying that a good Aboriginal person is a dead one. Because I was in that era, when they were picking up all the part-Aboriginal kids like me and taking them off their parents. I was little when I was taken to the mission; I was about five. But all the time I was with my uncle. He was a young man and he was made a man [initiated through ceremony], so he could make decisions. So he looked after my mum, who was a teenager. The government made a ruling that all the part-Aboriginal kids, they would be sending us to homes . . . bad places, which were terrible. But I stayed at Mount Margaret [mission]. My uncle made sure he fought them. We were allowed to come into town, till lunchtime, and lunchtime they wanted us to be out . . . the police officers used to come on their horseback and, if we were not out of town, we would be whipped out of town. Or whipped and taken. They would pick you up, saying to the Aboriginal mother and families, 'We're taking your kids away'. That's how a number of kids came down here to the homes here, like New Norcia and all of those places. If we went to a government settlement, we would never see our people again. I went to high school when there was a change in government here in Australia. It was the white women that were concerned about the education and welfare of Aboriginal people. They hammered the government that was in power at the time, and said all of these kids, Aboriginal black or not, or half or quarter caste, they all have to be educated. So, it was the white women that fought and fought for us. So, if it wasn't for the white women, I wouldn't be

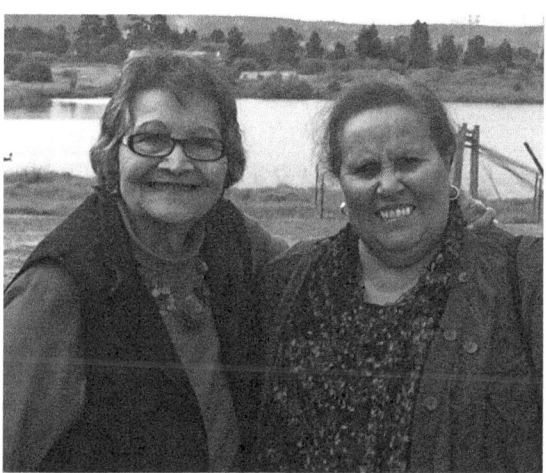

Figure 1.2. May O'Brien and Carol Garlett, 2014 (photo: Leanne Holt).

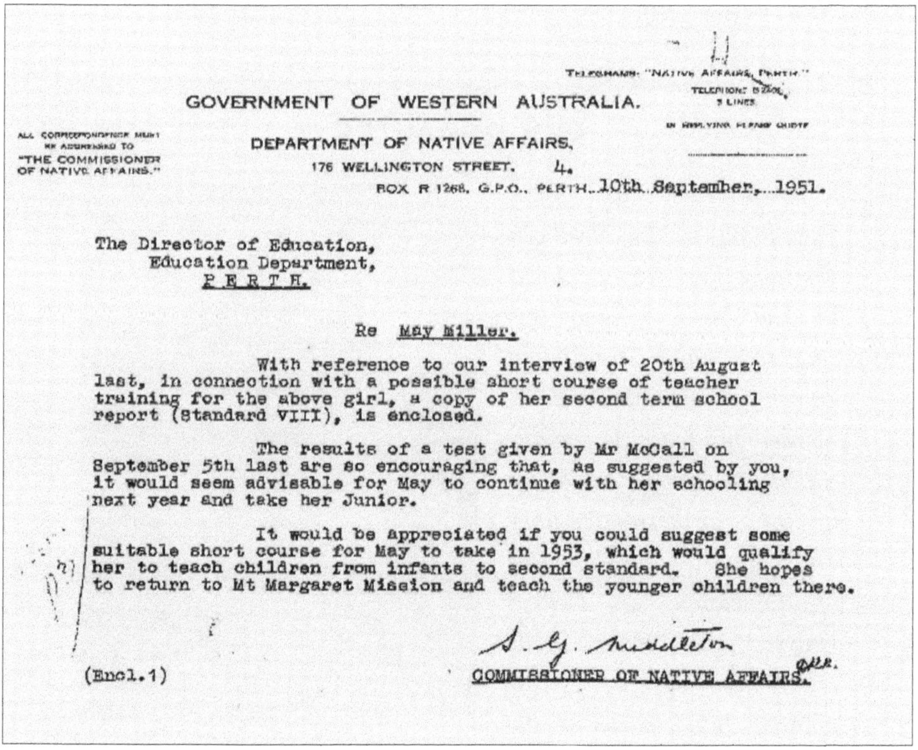

TELEGRAMS: "NATIVE AFFAIRS, PERTH."
3 LINES.

GOVERNMENT OF WESTERN AUSTRALIA.

ALL CORRESPONDENCE MUST BE ADDRESSED TO "THE COMMISSIONER OF NATIVE AFFAIRS."

DEPARTMENT OF NATIVE AFFAIRS,
176 WELLINGTON STREET. 4.
BOX R 1268, G.P.O., PERTH. 10th September, 1951.

The Director of Education,
Education Department,
P E R T H.

Re May Miller.

With reference to our interview of 20th August last, in connection with a possible short course of teacher training for the above girl, a copy of her second term school report (Standard VIII), is enclosed.

The results of a test given by Mr McCall on September 5th last are so encouraging that, as suggested by you, it would seem advisable for May to continue with her schooling next year and take her Junior.

It would be appreciated if you could suggest some suitable short course for May to take in 1953, which would qualify her to teach children from infants to second standard. She hopes to return to Mt Margaret Mission and teach the younger children there.

S. G. Middleton
COMMISSIONER OF NATIVE AFFAIRS.

(Encl.1)

Figure 1.3. Letter from the Western Australian Department of Native Affairs to the Director of Education, 10 September 1951 (courtesy May O'Brien).

where I am today, because they fought hard. Everybody else would say . . . 'a good nigger is a dead one'. That was their attitude. (May O'Brien, interview, 2014)

May's teachers supported her ambition to become a teacher. Because she was a state ward and in line with assimilation legislation, negotiations between the Department of Education and the Western Australian Department of Native Affairs enabled her to pursue teacher training. Figure 1.3 shows one letter from the departmental correspondence regarding May between 1950 and 1953.

Rex Granites was also appointed to the ACG, as he was a teaching assistant in the Northern Territory (NT) and, like May, later transitioned from the ACG to the NAEC.

REX GRANITES

A Warlpiri man from Yuendumu in the Northern Territory, Rex was appointed on the basis of both his education and traditional knowledge. He had commenced his teaching qualifications at Kormilda College in the Northern Territory and completed his Bachelor of Education at Deakin University in Victoria. His experiences on the NAEC allowed him to share the knowledge he had obtained from his learnings and

Figure 1.4. Japanangka Rex Granites, 2014 (photo: Leanne Holt).

> *experiences. He reflects on the contribution he was making to the NAEC:*
>
> I was still a teacher, no matter what, not trained, but also trained, but I was still a teacher and who got me there is my own people, listening and understanding and connecting with the Country. They were my teachers. Then I had to do it in the white way, I had to go to university and teachers college . . . But I already knew what was going on because I had it, my knowledge and understanding. I had the experience and understanding from where I was from, to give that knowledge to others who did not. I think we did a very good job, both listening from each other and me sharing my traditional background . . . they were mostly from a city life, city people. I was out from the bush giving them all the knowledge I had. When I'm doing that, it's with my cultural behaviours in and out of the communities — which is how it should be. What I listen to is my spirit and my spirit is the only way I can do things. (Rex Granites, interview, 2014)

The ACG met regularly from 1974 and explored all aspects of Aboriginal and Torres Strait Islander education. It aimed to provide opportunities that bridged the gap resulting from past policies, providing development opportunities and access programs that would contribute to increasing the confidence of Aboriginal and Torres Strait Islander people to embark on further education after previously being excluded (ACG 1975).

The 1975 *Education for Aborigines* report

A June 1975 report, *Education for Aborigines: Report to the Schools Commission* (ACG 1975), marked a significant milestone for the future of Aboriginal and Torres Strait Islander education. The most significant conclusion that the ACG highlighted was that 'Aboriginal people should be involved in their own education at all levels, and that they should be responsible for and have some realistic control of this process' (ACG 1975, p. ii). The report stated:

> We see education as the most important strategy for achieving realistic self-determination for the Aboriginal people of Australia. We do not see education as a method of producing an anglicised Aborigine but rather as an instrument for creating an informed community with intellectual and technological skills, in harmony with our own cultural values and identity. We wish to be Aboriginal citizens in a changing Australia. (ACG 1975, p. 3)

The ACG, unlike any previous committee, had embarked on strong consultation with and input from Aboriginal and Torres Strait Islander peoples and communities in relation to their study. The significance the *Education for Aborigines* (ACG 1975) report held for the ACG, in setting the foundation for a new beginning, including the rebuilding of lives, cultures, communities and survival, was reflected in a poem that prefaces the report:

> A NEW DAWNING
> We began with a dawning — Djuwani
> We were always here
> This place is our dreaming
> We neither changed it nor harmed it
> But the world changed around us
> Now we must start again
> (ACG 1975, p. i)

The vision of the ACG was to:

> . . . see education as the most important strategy for achieving realistic self-determination for the Aboriginal people of Australia . . . Education should be a constructive process, building on what a child is and developing his or her natural potential, not destroying and denying his birthright. (ACG 1975, p. 3)

This vision acknowledged the post-colonial journey of Aboriginal and Torres Strait Islander peoples while emphasising their inherent rights to culture and identity. The ACG further emphasised the importance of maintaining cultural knowledges as part of the education process:

> Every child has a right to be brought up as a member of his own culture. This does not mean that he must be prevented from learning about (and learning from) other cultures . . . The child should nevertheless be educated in a way that he is able to function successfully in both his own culture and the wider Australian society if he so desires. (ACG 1975, p. 5)

The ACG emphasised that Aboriginal and Torres Strait Islander peoples have unique cultural values and perspectives that unite and identify them separately to non-Indigenous people. Therefore, Aboriginal and Torres Strait Islander identity should be respected and fostered throughout educational experiences.

The birth of the National Aboriginal Education Committee

The first recommendation of the *Education for Aborigines* report was to provide a foundation for the future of Aboriginal and Torres Strait Islander education and policy development. Recommendation 1 concluded: 'We recommend to the Australian Government that it establish a separate statutory funding body called the National Aboriginal Education Commission' (ACG 1975, p. 9).

The report highlighted four aspirations to guide the NAEC in its early stages: increase Aboriginal and Torres Strait Islander teachers, embed Aboriginal and Torres Strait Islander cultural awareness, foster community inclusion and focus on improvements for all levels of education. A major strategy of the NAEC was to increase the number of Aboriginal and Torres Strait Islander teachers and other professional positions, including the development and upgrading of Aboriginal and Torres Strait Islander teacher aides.

The second major priority for the NAEC was to overcome the lack of awareness and understanding of Aboriginal and Torres Strait Islander culture across Australian society. The inclusion of Aboriginal and Torres

Strait Islander studies in the school curriculum was seen as a positive step towards education on the many aspects of Aboriginal and Torres Strait Islander culture, and it was envisioned that this would result in a more informed society. The provision of suitable resources and texts to provide an unbiased and accurate historical account would also be seen to complement the delivery of Aboriginal studies.

In addition to the focus on school education, continued investigation into the poor delivery of programs by Technical and Further Education (TAFE) training institutions, tertiary institutions and early childhood education would also become a mandate of the NAEC. But the ACG was not satisfied with the brief attention to the needs of Aboriginal and Torres Strait Islander peoples accessing TAFE, and delivered a comprehensive report to the Schools Commission on *Aboriginal Access to and Use of Technical and Further Education* (ACG 1976). The ACG was particularly interested in identifying TAFE as a crucial link to overcoming some of the major challenges, including the need to develop employment skills and increase technical and managerial qualifications: 'Developing a wide range of marketable skills that can be utilized for self-management and community development programs by members of Aboriginal communities is absolutely essential and should be given high priority' (ACG 1976, p. 1).

The foundational work of the ACG significantly influenced Aboriginal and Torres Strait Islander educational priorities nationally. Despite the 1975 change in government from the Labor Whitlam government to the Liberal Fraser government, the work of the ACG had bipartisan support and, in 1976, Senator JL Carrick, Minister for Education, sought Cabinet approval for the establishment of a national committee on Aboriginal and Torres Strait Islander education, as recommended by the ACG. A press release by Senator Carrick immediately after the Cabinet decision stated that the membership would be attracted through nominations from a wide variety of sources:

> The time is now ripe for consultation procedures to be developed on a formal basis. There is room for much more Aboriginal involvement and participation in the development, planning and assessment of activities

across all educational levels. I am sure they will give us valuable guidance. (Department of Education 1976)

The 1970s were a progressive time for the education of Aboriginal and Torres Strait Islander peoples within a Eurocentric environment. Through the recommendations of the *Education for Aborigines* (ACG 1975) report and the *Aboriginal Access to and Use of Technical and Further Education* (ACG 1976) report, Aboriginal and Torres Strait Islander peoples began to have a voice in determining the future directions for Aboriginal and Torres Strait Islander education. The ACG had opened up the doors for Aboriginal and Torres Strait Islander peoples to both engage in education and have a strong voice in decision-making related to policies and programs to advance Aboriginal and Torres Strait Islander education. It had provided the conceptual framework and foundations to move Aboriginal and Torres Strait Islander education policy forward. Through its own recommendation, the ACG was superseded by the NAEC, which would provide a full-time presence in the Department of Education.

Margaret Valadian, Natascha McNamara, May O'Brien and Rex Granites, members of the ACG, all went on to be members of the NAEC. This provided a level of consistency in relating the discussions and outcomes of the ACG to the NAEC. The advancement of Aboriginal and Torres Strait Islander education was to be a primary focus of governments. The long-awaited new dawn had arrived.

CHAPTER 2

A voice in education: the first term of the NAEC, 1977–80

> In the past, white people had been making all our decisions, but now we were making our own. It became about playing their game and being able to beat them at it. We believed in education and a lot had to be done. So, it was our first time when we were actually in white politics, putting forward our views. Sometimes people thought we were radical. (May O'Brien, interview, 2014)

The ACG recommendation for a national body was based on the premise that Aboriginal and Torres Strait Islander peoples should have a voice in Aboriginal and Torres Strait Islander education and be able to influence decision making. The first term of the NAEC, from 1977 to 1980, commenced with the appointment and formation of the NAEC. This term saw the implementation of a community-driven structure that would empower Aboriginal and Torres Strait Islander peoples nationally, giving rise to their voices being integral to the future of Aboriginal and Torres Strait Islander education and driving the campaign for the appointment of Aboriginal and Torres Strait Islander teachers. The foundations laid in the first term were crucial to determining the success of the NAEC into the 1980s.

The appointment and formation of the NAEC

In March 1977, the NAEC was appointed by the Liberal Fraser government. It comprised nineteen members, with a full-time chairperson and eighteen part-time representatives. It was envisaged that the NAEC would have a holistic educational focus on preschool education, school education, TAFE and higher education. In a media release on 17 March 1977, the Minister for Education, Senator Carrick, announced the establishment of the NAEC:

> It is now almost ten years since the 1967 Referendum widened the Commonwealth Government's responsibility for Aboriginal and Torres Strait Islander people. This period has seen the growth of more interest and activity in Aboriginal education than ever before with Commonwealth funds developing programs and helping education authorities throughout the country to make special efforts for Aboriginal people at all levels of education ... The [National Aboriginal Education] Committee will be responsible for providing my Department and me with informed Aboriginal views on the educational needs of Aboriginal people and appropriate methods of meeting these needs. Its advice will be available also to the Minister and Department of Aboriginal Affairs and other authorities concerned with education of Aboriginal people ... The establishment of the Committee places significant responsibilities in the hands of Aboriginal people. I trust it will contribute to policy initiatives which will serve to redress the educational imbalance which Aboriginal people experience and which will recognize the cultural plural nature of Australian society. (Carrick 1977, pp. 3–4)

Crucial to the composition of the NAEC was the appointment of a chairperson who would provide leadership in consolidating a future vision for the NAEC and establish its credibility in the eyes of the Aboriginal and Torres Strait Islander community and the government.

Stephen Albert was appointed as the inaugural chairperson. Interest for the position was sought through an advertisement and Stephen was identified and nominated by his peers as the best man for the job:

I didn't even know about chairing, even getting the job. I was a student in Adelaide at the Institute of Technology doing sociology and community development, and a bit of psychology. We used to come together for a meeting for the national congress [of tertiary students]. This one was at Monash [University] and, after the meeting, there were a few Indigenous people starting tertiary study, so we set up a students' union called the National Aboriginal Torres Strait Islander Students Union — NATSISU. It sounded a bit Japanese but that didn't worry me 'cause my old man was a Jap [Japanese] anyway. Gino Silvani [Aboriginal student, later held leadership roles in Aboriginal health] was the chair, Gary Foley [Aboriginal student, activist, writer, actor, academic] was the [public relations] person and I was the treasurer — everyone trusted me with the money because I was a Catholic. When the newspaper came out, Gary said, 'There's a job there with the education department. I don't think I'll go for it, ASIO [Australian Security Intelligence Organisation] already has my photo.' Bruce McGuiness [Aboriginal student, activist, held leadership roles in health and education] said, 'Yeah me too', and some others agreed ... then they all looked at me and said, 'They haven't got your photo, black fella from the bush, we'll put your name in' — so they nominated me for the job. I was still studying and these two blokes from Canberra took me out for dinner and that was the interview. Went back to studying and about three months later the message came across, you got the job! I was the youngest senior public servant in town; I was 27. (Stephen Albert, interview, 2012)

STEPHEN ALBERT

Stephen, a descendant of the Bardi people in the north of Western Australia, was born in Broome in what he describes as the 'back hospital' (the 'front hospital' was for whites only). He was brought up on the shores of Roebuck Bay at Morgan's Camp and, later, at Kennedy Hill. Stephen came from a Catholic family and attended a Catholic school. His passion was always music. After starting as a diesel mechanic, his interest in education and the welfare of his people first became apparent when he was playing in his band, the Broome Beats. In an interview (Ohlsson 1977), Stephen elaborates on this period when he observed the poor treatment of Aboriginal people in the communities in which the band played. He was passionate about ensuring social justice for his people and, on his commencement as chairperson, he said, 'If there is going to be harmony between our two societies then it will have to be through education. When white people have a better awareness of Aboriginals then maybe our kids will have a better time' (Ohlsson 1977, p. 2).

Figure 2.1. Stephen Albert (NAEC 1985b, p. 1).

Post NAEC, Stephen continued to be a strong ambassador for education as an Elder, teacher, musician, actor and highly respected mentor for both Indigenous and non-Indigenous communities.

Soon after Stephen's appointment as chairperson, Senator Carrick, in announcing the establishment of the NAEC, provided a summary of the breadth of Stephen's qualifications and experience:

> Mr Albert has lectured to school students and trainee teachers. He has been a member of the Regional Council for Social Development in Alice Springs and was a member of the Aboriginal Legal Rights Movement in Adelaide. He is a qualified tradesman and is currently undertaking studies at the South Australian Institute of Technology. He lectures in the Community Learning Unit at the Aboriginal Community College. His experience of traditional Aboriginal education and contemporary Australian education will be of great benefit to the Committee. (Carrick 1977, p. 5)

The period of Stephen's chairmanship was a time of new insights, new voices and a new page in Aboriginal and Torres Strait Islander education. Stephen's leadership provided an excellent start for the foundation committee. Colin Bourke, an inaugural member of the NAEC, believed Stephen was a strong and fair leader:

> He was a good chairman in that he was equitable, even-handed and willing to listen. He didn't have a pre-set agenda . . . Stephen didn't have that baggage . . . Probably couldn't have got a better person to be chair, to be honest, because he had the traditional background in Broome and in his experience in the rest of Australia, plus his open-mindedness. We all had our troubles of course, we were all human beings, but as a group I would have thought it was a very good group to work with and that we all got on the one page fairly easily in relation to what we wanted to do . . . So it was a good working atmosphere. Plus I think the feeling of adventure, if you like, because it was all new ground. We were going where no one had gone before. So I thought the first couple of years were very prolific. (Colin Bourke, interview, 2013)

Patsy Cameron, another inaugural NAEC member, also commends Stephen on his leadership style:

> He had a very eloquent style, very intelligent man, young. All of us were young in those days and we all didn't know each other. So, it was just an interesting time to not only wonder and look at our first direction, which would have been setting the future agenda, no doubt, for the first few meetings, but it was also just getting to know each other. He was very strong — he was spearheading our committee — and all the others that stood by us. (Patsy Cameron, interview, 2013)

Stephen was the first senior Aboriginal appointment in the Department of Education. Charles Perkins had previously been appointed to a senior role within the Department of Aboriginal Affairs (the first Aboriginal person to be appointed to a senior public service role) and had been providing leadership on Aboriginal and Torres Strait Islander matters across all areas of government. Stephen tells the story about his negotiations with Charles Perkins shortly after he was appointed as chairperson. They discussed how they were going to work together, given there was some crossover, with the NAEC providing educational advice to the Department of Aboriginal Affairs. Stephen's story is a good example of how Aboriginal people use humour when negotiating what could otherwise be seen as difficult situations and is also an example of his character:

> [I said to Charlie,] 'Hey bro, you stick with Aboriginal Affairs and leave education to me.' Then we had a deal and that was it. So I got to tell you, next thing he asked us [the Committee] for lunch: 'Let's go to the Hermitage.' That was the best restaurant in town [Sydney] and, of course, everything is $30 to $40 and so, you know, all my members, they all went for the expensive meals: 'I want crayfish mornay' or something like that. He was like, 'Where you black fellas come from?', 'cause he's got to pay out, you see. We said to him, 'It isn't every day we have lunch with Charlie Perkins.' He looked at us and gave us a big grin, after that he said, 'Hey Baamba [Stephen Albert], I'm not bringing you mob to me again.' I said, 'Don't worry, we'll shout you next time.' But I think the best part is learning the politics within the politics, within the Aboriginal organisations, and getting support. (Stephen Albert, interview, 2012)

The chairperson position was an appointment as a senior public servant in the Commonwealth Department of Education, reporting directly to the departmental secretary. The seniority of the position provided the opportunity for direct access to both the secretary and the minister. The position was aligned with other heads of departments in the Schools Commission, including the Education, Research and Development Committee and migrant education.

With the exception of the chairperson, the inaugural members of the NAEC were recruited as part-time appointments. They represented all levels of education and traditional/community perspectives, and were from all states and territories and the Torres Strait Islands (Carrick 1977). Eric Willmot, Commonwealth schools officer, was instrumental in attracting people from across Australia to nominate for positions. Willmot worked with Ken Jones, Secretary of the Department of Education, to do this (Colin Bourke, interview, 2013). The composition of the NAEC was crucial to its success:

> The key thing was that every Aboriginal person on that committee was all melded together. There was no one saying, 'No, I don't want that.' They all said, 'Better education.' We have some aims that we wanted for our kids and for our adults. Some of the non-Aboriginal people in government were saying [that we] wouldn't know how to choose people and that, 'We didn't know much about education so how can we make a good choice?' Well, I think we made the best choices. (May O'Brien, interview, 2014)

Later, representatives from each state and territory Aboriginal Education Consultative Group were nominated (see Chapter 3). In addition to these members, specialist representatives were also selected through application with a nomination. The NAEC chairperson, part-time deputy chairperson and its secretariat formed an Aboriginal and Torres Strait Islander presence in the Department of Education. This provided opportunities for important networking and collaboration in key educational areas, such as with the Schools Commission and the Curriculum Development Centre (CDC), which was responsible for all curriculum content in Australian schools, including the new area of Indigenous studies.

An executive officer in the NAEC led the administrative team, playing a vital role in ensuring effective communications with all relevant stakeholders, and assisted with the development of media releases, co-ordination of the NAEC and other administrative duties.

Lillian Holt was the first executive officer for the NAEC (1978–80) and was a member in the later years of the NAEC. She was appointed for her expertise in tertiary education. Lillian applied for the position of executive officer for the NAEC and was offered the job in Canberra:

> That first week I arrived in Canberra, I flew up to Alice Springs [NT] to run things and here I was the executive officer. I wasn't too sure what was happening, but I knew that I had to make sure that the minutes got done and all this type of thing. I remember when I was appointed, my salary was $16,000 a year and I thought I was in clover. (Lillian Holt, interview, 2013)

Although Lillian enjoyed working with the NAEC and making connections with the other members, she found the bureaucracy difficult to deal with, particularly as the executive officer:

> I've never been a bureaucracy person. I've always been a bit of a heretic and a rebel, so I just hated the way everything was kind of like the spirit was squeezed out of it and you had to adhere to it. It was all about the quantitative ticking off process . . . But I could just feel my whole spirit being squashed. I'm not good at structure and bureaucracy. I'm more of a big picture person and an ideas person. I felt fairly discontented and disconcerted by the whole process of working in bureaucracy. On the other side, there were some really good times. We used to socialise after work, letting off steam. You had to in those days. We had about three or four meetings a year, the full committee. We met in different places, met with different people, different communities and things. I remember leaving Canberra to go to Darwin for an NAEC meeting. It was about five degrees in the morning and I think it was August or something. I got to Darwin that afternoon and it was absolutely boiling, something like 32 degrees. I was in my winter clothes and my luggage hadn't come through. I was just absolutely sweating in these cold winter clothes [laughs]. But I'm glad I spent this time. You know, every journey begins with the first step and it was leading on to different things . . . I can still see the office where we worked in Canberra, where the NAEC was situated. I think it was on the twelfth floor because I used to walk up these twelve flights and down. In those days I was so slim. I was so young and slim. You know, to walk up and down, that was just part of my exercise. (Lillian Holt, interview, 2013)

LILLIAN HOLT

Lillian was born on Cherbourg Aboriginal Reserve in Queensland. She describes her childhood experiences and growing interest in education:

My mum, she was only educated to fourth grade because of the policies of the day. My father was one of those so-called stockmen.

It didn't mean he was dumb, it just meant he didn't have qualifications and wasn't schooled, as was my grandfather. My grandfather was put on Cherbourg, which was supposedly set up for difficult and disadvantaged Aboriginal people. I don't think he would have seen himself as difficult nor disadvantaged but those were labels. If anything, he probably would have been difficult, because he stuck up for his rights. That's how I came to be born on Cherbourg and, because my dad didn't have an education, he always said, 'I want you kids to get educated. Don't be like me, you know, I can't read and write.' So, Mum and Dad, they were also products of assimilation. Their exemption certificates, they were like the glittering prize that a lot of Aboriginal people aspired to in those days, understandably, because it meant freedom. They could leave the Mission and go out and marry who they wanted to. They could freely associate with whoever they want[ed] and they didn't have to report to anybody. (Lillian Holt, interview, 2013)

Lillian started working in 1962; at the age of seventeen, she was the first Aboriginal person employed by the Australian Broadcasting Commission in Brisbane. She commenced a social work degree in the late 1960s at The University of Queensland but later withdrew. In 1974, she recommenced studies and describes her experiences of working in tertiary education:

In those days, there was no mature age entry or special entry and so I'd actually studied in the '60s to get my matriculation. I completed a BA [Bachelor of Arts] in English and journalism. My first job after that was in Armidale [NSW] at the College of Advanced Education, a tutor in the multicultural studies unit; they had an Aboriginal element in it under the umbrella of multicultural studies. There were these final-year teacher trainees and there was much resistance to it, which I've encountered subsequently, about these things where they have to do a unit or two in terms of Aboriginal issues. I just hated it because, having been a tutor, you could smell the hostility of some of them and the attitudes, it was draining. (Lillian Holt, interview, 2013)

After serving as the executive officer for two years, Lillian received an overseas study award to study in Colorado, where she completed a Master of Arts. On returning, she worked at the College of Aboriginal Education in Adelaide, now known as Tauondi. During her work there, from 1980 to 1996, she was appointed the first Aboriginal principal of the college. After a short stint at the University of Southern Queensland in 1997, she was employed as the director, Centre for Indigenous Education, at The University of Melbourne in 1998 and remained there until she retired in 2005.

Setting the national agenda

Shortly after Stephen Albert was appointed as chairperson, the press approached him and asked him what he was going to do. Drawing on an Aboriginal analogy, he recalls responding in the following way:

> I'm the spearhead and the woomera. Like the spear thrower is the committee and there was a black hand and the hand was the people throwing us, giving us direction where to go. That's how I described myself... I thought it was just natural, and so I kept that and in our letterhead there was the spear, a woomera and a black hand throwing it. John Budby was the little turtle [second chair] and Paul Hughes [third chair] was dingo footprints going on a hunt. We all had our things. (Stephen Albert, interview, 2012)

Three weeks after Stephen commenced his appointment, he organised the first meeting, which was held in Canberra, April 1977, and provided an opportunity for members to get to know each other and exchange initial views:

> For me, in the first year, my biggest challenge was bringing a group of these people and having them in the one room because they came from all areas and walks of life. You know, all different sizes, shapes, different colours, all that, it didn't matter; but having in my mind how to get them all together, help each other and synchronise the way we were heading. But my first thoughts were, wow, I have all these people I've got to deal

Figure 2.2. The NAEC logo was designed by Kaye Price and featured on a badge worn by NAEC members (photo: Alicia O'Bryan).

with and work with, and realising that they probably were the best in the country. And then, after working with them, I knew I had the best in the country because [of] all the knowledge they brought with them. I think one of the first things I said at the meeting was, 'I hope you have left your paddles outside the room.' But then everybody looked at me and laughed and said, 'Yes, no one's rowing their own canoe here.' But I had to get that straight, that if they had an agenda they had to leave it outside. We had our agenda. I think that was the toughest thing I had to say, but I had to say it at the beginning. I let everybody have their say but not to over-power anybody else . . . In the end they all felt good about being together and working on the same thing. (Stephen Albert, interview, 2012)

The outcomes of the first meeting were published in a press release (NAEC 1977) that emphasised the importance of the government's commitment and funding support, which reflected an appropriate investment in advancing Aboriginal and Torres Strait Islander education. The press release also included the resolution of the first meeting: 'It is the opinion of this committee, that any committee, meeting to decide on any issues involving Aboriginal Education be composed of at least 50% Aboriginal membership' (Ohlsson 1977, p. 2). The resolution had been made due to concerns about recent events in the Northern Territory, where Aboriginal and Torres Strait Islander views were not considered and decisions were constantly being made without consulting Aboriginal and Torres Strait Islander peoples. Members of the NAEC believed that Aboriginal and Torres Strait Islander views and knowledges were not being appropriately represented in decision-making in relation to Aboriginal and Torres Strait Islander education right across the country.

The second meeting was again held in Canberra, early in June 1977. The NAEC wasted no time in setting priorities and calling for action. It called for a survey into early childhood education; agreed to undertaking an investigation into the Black Community School in Townsville, Queensland (see Chapter 4); and to complete a review of current curriculum development, with a vision to examining all the resources currently used in Aboriginal and Torres Strait Islander studies. In relation to curriculum development, the NAEC nominated members to the Curriculum Development Centre in the Department of Education to assist with relevant projects. It was further determined that the NAEC should focus on the training of Aboriginal and Torres Strait Islander teachers to work in schools with Aboriginal and Torres Strait Islander populations so that non-Indigenous teachers and students could develop a greater awareness and understanding of Aboriginal and Torres Strait Islander culture. The NAEC sought to expand bilingual education programs and ensure that, in the process of improving the Western educational outcomes of Aboriginal and Torres Strait Islander children, these children did not become disconnected from their own people and culture (Albert 1977).

Taking NAEC meetings to communities

After the initial two meetings in Canberra, the NAEC decided that if it was serious about connecting with Aboriginal and Torres Strait Islander communities, it needed to be seen in communities outside Canberra.

> Really early . . . we decided that we wanted to get out into communities. We wanted to go out — not sit in Canberra and have meetings there in this big, flash place. We wanted to get out into communities, go out, meet

the people and talk to people about their education experiences and aspirations, to get feedback from them first-hand . . . the first one was to Tasmania. We went to Alice Springs, Darwin and all over the country. (Patsy Cameron, interview, 2013)

Didimain Uibo, a Northern Territory member of the NAEC from 1980 to 1984, believed there was reciprocal benefits to taking NAEC meetings to communities:

We spread across different areas and we met at different places around the Territory and around Australia, which [was] good. We met with local people who came and talked to us and welcomed us to their Country. So, it was good meeting and sharing from our point of view on education and what it's like in the community. It's not a rosy posy sometimes in the community because there's a lot of other business going on and they don't always concentrate much on the education. (Didimain Uibo, interview, 2014)

The strategy to move outside the confines of Canberra to meet with communities and state education departments was focused on empowering communities to give them a voice in national educational affairs. It was also about ensuring accountability and transparency. This was a first for communities. Prior to this, all committees focused on Aboriginal and Torres Strait Islander education policy had operated out of Canberra and, when required, brought relevant expertise to Canberra.

The Department of Education funded travel for NAEC members, with sitting fees paid for the days spent at meetings. A lot of members had not travelled far from their communities and definitely not from one side of the country to the other. The opportunity to travel to communities nationally was as much an educational experience for members as it was a benefit to the communities. Kaye Price, a Tasmanian NAEC member and executive officer, discusses the influence of these visits on her:

We used to meet all over the country — we rarely had our committee meetings in Canberra. We had them at places like Yuendumu, Flinders Island, Thursday Island or Cunnamulla. So we actually were able to get out and meet people. For me, in particular, it just opened up a whole new world. I could tell you anything about the education in Tasmania — but when we went to those places and saw how people lived and the hardships that people endured, it was just a whole educative process for most of us on that committee. That's why the NAEC was started, to meet the educational needs of all Aboriginal and Torres Strait Islander peoples. (Kaye Price, interview, 2013)

Given the controversy in Tasmania relating to the myth that Aboriginal people were extinct (Cameron & Miller 2011, p. 32), Stephen Albert decided that the third meeting, in August 1977, would be held in Tasmania. The meeting was an excellent opportunity for NAEC members to understand the Aboriginal education challenges in Tasmania. Also, it sent a message to the Tasmanian Department of Education and the broader community that a space needed to be opened up to create educational opportunities for Tasmanian Aboriginal people. The meeting in Tasmania would have a positive impact:

> I took the committee to Tasmania to make a statement. Coming from a national committee, I think that was the first time that the Tasmanian Kooris were recognised, because we had one of our members [Patsy Cameron] from there, and I promised her we'd go to Tasmania. As the chair, I would go to all the state ministers, state deputy generals, and talk to them and say where we were coming from. So, it was a good thing to go to Tasmania. (Stephen Albert, interview, 2012)

For Patsy Cameron, coming together and bonding over unique experiences was important for the collegiality of the NAEC in supporting and understanding the challenges experienced in Aboriginal and Torres Strait Islander education in different areas. Patsy tells a story of sharing part of her own culture with the NAEC in its early stages:

> I'm going to tell you something funny. I think, apart from all of the work that we did with the committee and subcommittees, I think the most memorable things were those things that made us join together and bond as a very significant group of people with that purpose. One of my most memorable moments is when I took mutton birds to Canberra for a big feed of mutton birds — I think it might have been the second meeting before we came to Hobart. We were having the meeting in the

government offices, the same place where they were cooking them. The smell of mutton birds was sort of permeating through all of these buildings. I remember Stephen saying, 'Patsy, what are those birds?' I'd say, 'They're mutton birds, Stephen. They're mutton birds.' He said, 'Do you mean they're birds that go baaaaa?' 'No.' Of course, mutton birds have a distinct smell. They've got a very strong, oily, fishy smell. A few people declined the incredible experience of tasting a mutton bird for the first time. Although, I think having those experiences . . . bonded us together as a group of people with wide experiences, from different geographic locations, [and] added to a very strong committee. They were the good things. Coming to Tasmania for the first time and having our meeting . . . would probably be the most incredible experience for me. To have the group say, 'Yes, we've got to go down there and support Patsy. That is the first thing on our agenda outside of Canberra.' What an amazing thing that was and an amazing response to me when I was saying, 'Well, we're forgotten.' It was just amazing, it was a real response. It was action rather than just words or reaction. (Patsy Cameron, interview, 2013)

PATSY CAMERON

Patsy was a community worker on Flinders Island in Tasmania when she was appointed to the NAEC. She continues to contribute to education, culture and heritage on her traditional community of Cape Barren Island (off the north-east coast of Tasmania) and in the wider Australian communities. She tells of her own educational background:

Figure 2.3. Patsy Cameron and the author at Patsy's home, Tasmania, 2013 (photo: Leanne Holt).

My education level was I'd completed grade nine. I

never did go on. Then it was immediately into raising a family. So my level of education was very restricted to a very basic secondary schooling. I certainly had a lot to learn. My learning was in terms of experiencing the cultural diversity across Australia . . . I think I probably was the greenhorn amongst all of them with the least worldview. Mine was very much a Tasmanian experience up until then. Of course, my knowledge of my own community, of our experiences, of our educational levels and standards at that time were certainly known. (Patsy Cameron, interview, 2013)

Patsy was born in 1947 and grew up on Flinders Island. Patsy has traced her family back on her mother's side from Flinders and Cape Barren islands for four generations, and her father's connections to the Coastal Plains nation on the east coast of the state. Prior to her appointment to the NAEC, Patsy had been very involved in local politics, following in her father's footsteps, not just in her local community, but across the state. She had been a member of the National Museum of Australia Advisory Committee and the World Heritage Committee in Tasmania. When Patsy attended her first NAEC meeting, the other members met her with surprise. She recalls this meeting in Canberra:

The first thing I was challenged with was one of the members who commented to me, 'Oh, I thought you were extinct. I thought all of you in Tasmania were extinct.' Of course, the worst thing that can happen to a Tasmanian is to be challenged, especially with other black fellas. In the midst of all this, I found myself explaining me, myself and my heritage. The person who challenged my Aboriginality, in a warm sense I must say, not the usual way, but still challenged it, probably incited me then to say, 'Well, it seems to me that Australia knows about what goes on amongst Aboriginal Australians, especially the Top End. Tasmania has been missed off the map.' I remember talking about the fact that Tasmania had been neglected, that we were the invisible people; we seem to be the forgotten people. (Patsy Cameron, interview, 2013)

> *Patsy was an inaugural member of the NAEC and founder of the TASAECG. After her term on the NAEC, Patsy maintained membership on the TASAECG and became very involved in the development of the Centre for Aboriginal Research and Education/Riawunna at the University of Tasmania. She was appointed in the role of Aboriginal employment strategy co-ordinator and, before retiring, she was deputy head of the centre and was responsible for the introduction of the Aboriginal studies major. Patsy continues her work in providing cultural knowledges and education to school students and visitors to Cape Barren Island.*

The belief of the majority of NAEC members was that the social connectivity was just as important as the professional aspects. Whether it was letting off steam, relaxing with friends or getting to know each other in an informal setting, these were integral to the productivity and culture of the NAEC:

> Probably at the end of every day, we would have a party practically. Stephen would sing and play his guitar and he was magic and we all relaxed together. We'd eat together, have a few drinks together, maybe more than a few sometimes — sing, and it was just a good feeling and the friendships were very good. We all did something, we were all together. We didn't have any splinter groups. It was the whole group. Everyone worked very well together and contributed. Some contributed more than others, there's no doubt about that, but that happens in any committee. Some had more experience than others but then everybody contributed in the end and put in what they thought. (Colin Bourke, interview, 2013)

The meeting in Tasmania was a success, based on the hype created by the presence of the NAEC and from the meetings with the Tasmanian Department of Education. The media promotion related to the meeting sent a strong but positive message. The flow-on effect was that the NAEC supported the development of a Tasmanian Aboriginal Education Consultative Group (see Chapter 3).

The NAEC had three to four general meetings per year, with the strategy of holding the majority of meetings outside Canberra to visit communities viewed as essential. Stephen discussed the meeting strategy with the Minister for Education, Senator Carrick. Although the minister was happy to support the strategy, the travel arrangements for the NAEC still needed to be negotiated, because it was government policy for senior public servants at the level of chairperson to fly first class. Stephen wanted to ensure that all members felt they were equally valued and there was no privilege for one member over the others:

> I said to the minister, 'I can't fly first [or business] class if my committee is flying economy. I might as well book my tickets economy.' And he said, 'No, you can't do that, otherwise all the heads of government will have to go economy' . . . He said, 'I will tell you what, you fly your members first [or business] class.' So everybody got to fly first class. (Stephen Albert, interview, 2012)

As well as ensuring there was no perceived hierarchy, the other significant advantage to all members flying first or business class was that they were able to interact with ministers, as well as other key senior government staff, while travelling. This was particularly useful when everyone was travelling to the same event or meeting, allowing positions and priorities to be discussed informally prior to the event. Bob Morgan (interview, 2015), a New South Wales member from 1979 to 1989, explained that this ensured open exchange and created opportunities for positive discussions.

Developing relationships with non-Indigenous people was an important initiative because it would have been impossible for the NAEC to achieve its goals without their support and collaboration. It was also vital that the NAEC worked to change the negative attitudes towards Aboriginal and Torres Strait Islander peoples. The NAEC actively engaged with non-Indigenous people across government departments and community organisations:

> We were soon making networks with all the non-Indigenous people around the country and some of them could see the turning point. They wanted to be in that journey, so there was a whole heap of white people

around the place that ended up giving us a hand. There's a few I could name, but there was a whole lot of them ... every time we see each other now, we're all like, 'Hello, how you going?' And I must say the non-Indigenous staff we had were very dedicated, including Ian Hason [and] Anne Sipalene. (Stephen Albert, interview, 2012)

Although travelling to different places was extremely valuable for consultation and two-way communication with communities and wider networks, it was a big commitment for the members, who needed to balance their local and state commitments, family commitments and national commitments, and at times it was quite stressful. Patsy describes the effect of the travel on her private life:

> We would travel one day, for a three-day meeting. It was like every month I was packing my bag for a week ... I was forever travelling. I remember one time I had a dear, old uncle. He'd turn up at my house, getting me to play [American musician] Charley Pride and doing things. This was just as I'm packing to go on the plane, trying to organise my children and everything else. Dear old uncle would turn up. I remember arriving in Brisbane once with a pair of desert boots on. I had no other shoes and it was 35 degrees up there. Anyway, it was a lot of travel. It was a lot of commitment. Sometimes I just wonder now in hindsight how on earth I managed to do it all. We did. All of us did. It was not just for me but for the other members that were from all over. (Patsy Cameron, interview, 2013)

Some community responsibilities overlapped and priorities had to be considered or negotiated. At these times, it was sometimes difficult for members to navigate local expectations with national ones:

> I came under some criticism. At the time, I was a member of the Tasmanian Aboriginal Centre [TAC]; they had nominated my membership for the NAEC. There would be some times when I might have to go to the NAEC when it meant I couldn't go to a TAC meeting. That's why I would be criticised, 'Oh, you can go to a meeting up there, but you can't come here to this meeting.' I said, 'Well, make up your mind, you either want me to do this or you don't. Tasmania's got a voice on this committee, so what do you want?' At the end of the day, I always felt that

Figure 2.4. Phil Stewart, Patsy Cameron, Colin Bourke and Stephen Albert meeting in Tasmania, August 1977 (*Mercury* newspaper, courtesy Patsy Cameron).

members of the community were on side because of the very nature of the way that we'd conduct the meetings. I've actually got a photograph of Eddie Mabo [at the time, principal of the Black Community School] on my desk, where we were sitting at Cape Barren Island — we went there as a community of people and people appreciated the fact that you did that. (Kaye Price, interview, 2013)

There were also times when visits to communities exposed challenges, such as racism and negative social attitudes. Colin Bourke provides a telling illustration of encountering racism during his NAEC work:

> We went down to Tasmania and it was quite interesting because we met in the Commonwealth offices down there, and at lunch we went down to the cafeteria . . . As we walked in, Stephen was in front and then George Passi [inaugural Torres Strait Islander member of the NAEC] and a few others followed. The whole conversation in the place stopped. Just like if someone said, 'Be quiet!' They just looked at us like they'd never seen eighteen Aboriginal people before. One old lady, we called her old, I don't know, she was probably in her fifties, she sat there with her mouth open. She was at the next table to George Passi and she just looked at him and looked at him and looked at him. She said to the person next to her, 'Isn't he black?' It was quite strange. So that was an interesting thing that happened. It was a big place, probably a couple of hundred people, and they stopped, absolutely stopped. (Colin Bourke, interview, 2013)

Experiences like these were not confined to Tasmania. Eleanor Bourke, a Victorian member, reflects on visiting a community in the north of Western Australia for a meeting:

> We were in a place where we were staying at this accommodation, which was pretty basic, but it had a separate bar for Aboriginal people. Well, when all the eastern seaboard people saw that, they were just absolutely horrified. We said, 'Well, why are we staying in a place like this, where there's a separate bar?' Those sorts of things, they pull you up. Here we were talking about high-level policy and arguing things, finer points of curriculum and the rest of it, and here, this was still with us, you know? Those sorts of things really were challenges and how you handled them were challenges. (Eleanor Bourke, interview, 2013)

However, visiting communities was overall a good opportunity for the NAEC members to witness the breadth of educational disadvantage for Aboriginal and Torres Strait Islander peoples across regional, rural and urban Australia. Few members had travelled outside their communities or regions and to get this exposure was extremely valuable. It was also a good opportunity for the NAEC members to get to know each other and spend time together in a more casual setting. Kaye Price recalls some of the humour as they shared new experiences:

> I remember on Thursday Island [in the Torres Strait] Pearl Duncan saying to Bob [Morgan], 'Oh, Bob, you're incorrigible,' and he said, 'No, I'm not, I'm Church of England.' And Hazel [McKellar], when we had a dinner in Cairns [in Queensland]. There was a menu. It had after-dinner mints and Hazel said to me, 'Why do we have our mince after dinner?' Got to love her. She's like me, naive — never seen after dinner mints before. She thought it was that meat mince. (Kaye Price, interview, 2013)

There was real respect for and value given to the mentorship and collegiality shared among the members. This filtered through to each term as different members came and went, bringing with them different experiences and backgrounds:

> I remember the very first meeting that I attended, and this probably opened up my eyes, too, to a lot of other stuff. That meeting was up in the Torres Strait, we first of all started off in Cairns. That was the meeting where I first met Eric Willmot and Paul [Hughes] and a lot of other members — May O'Brien and others, who've since become legends in Aboriginal education . . . I was the baby in arms. We had all these people in this room and Eric Willmot gave a presentation about the 1000 teachers model [1000 Aboriginal teachers by 1990, see Chapter 4]. I was completely blown away, because this was a black guy and he was articulating so many great things. As we were growing up, you always were made to feel inferior and that the real bastions of knowledge existed in the white world. But all I remember at that time is that all this great mystique and intellect . . . was emerging . . . That was the first time that I guess, intuitively, I always believed that we had the capacity, that we could be as gifted and talented as any race of people . . . But it was important for us to claim our space and not just try to do what it was that white fellas were doing, but doing it in an Aboriginal way. We were creating spaces and knowledge that was authentically Indigenous, authentically Aboriginal. Basically, it was about the principles of self-determination in social and restorative justice, reciprocity and accountability to community, and all that type of stuff. That is perhaps the initial thing that impressed me beyond anything else. The NAEC provided the vehicle to exercise and apply that knowledge and that power and that responsibility. (Bob Morgan, interview, 2015)

BOB MORGAN

Bob Morgan, a Gamilaraay man who was born and raised in Walgett, New South Wales, was the longest-serving member of the NAEC, from his appointment in 1979 through to its abolition in 1989. He served under every chairperson.

Bob was raised by his mother and spent his early years living in a shanty on the banks of the Namoi River in Walgett. His mother was part of the generations who were denied access to white schools, so she never learned how to read or write. However, she reinforced for Bob the importance of education, which resulted in a lifelong passion. In the late 1960s, he left Walgett, catching a train to Sydney to attend the Sydney Technical College. After undertaking further studies in Armidale, he returned to Sydney to take up a position as a youth officer at the now defunct Foundation for Aboriginal Affairs. In 1980, he was appointed as a commissioner on the NSW Education Commission and served as a member of the NSW Anti-Discrimination Board.

Even after leaving Walgett, Bob maintained a strong connection back to his community, providing mentorship and leadership, and helping to negotiate funding to implement community-driven projects. After retiring from the position of president of the NSWAECG in 1988, Bob spent a year with the NSW Ministry of Education before taking up

Figure 2.5. Bob Morgan (National Aboriginal and Torres Strait Islander Higher Education Conference Program, 1992).

the position of director, Jumbunna Indigenous House of Learning at the University of Technology Sydney, which he held until 2000 when he semi-retired.

While Bob was studying at the University of New England in Armidale, New South Wales, he shared a flat with Lillian Holt, who was the first executive officer of the NAEC. A few years later, when Bob was working for the Aboriginal Medical Service in Sydney, he reconnected with Lillian at a conference and she encouraged him to apply for a position on the NAEC: 'I remember her giving me a form, so I filled it out and never thought anything about it after that' (Bob Morgan, interview, 2015). It was a very competitive process to get a position on the NAEC and Bob explained how he was not the first choice:

I always tell my mates in the NAEC that I was second choice. Because they made the offer firstly to a mate of mine who's now passed — Jacko [Jack] Walker [at the time, an Aboriginal welfare officer with the Department of Corrective Services]. Jacko couldn't get approval from his employer, so he declined. So, I was the next person on the ladder and that's how I became a member of the NAEC. (Bob Morgan, interview, 2015)

The Aboriginal Medical Service, where Bob was working at the time, also refused to provide him with leave to attend meetings. So he resigned and started his membership of the NAEC.

Bob recalls how young he was at the time of his appointment and how overwhelmed he was at first:

> I was a little bit overawed by the intellect that was around the table. I was tremendously impressed with blokes like Eric Willmot, whom I believe had the greatest impact . . . and Hughsie [Paul Hughes], [John] Budby and Colin [Bourke], all the blokes I spent many, many years as a colleague and friend with . . . all those people had a profound impact on my thinking. (Bob Morgan, interview, 2015)

In addition to holding the general meetings, workshops were held with the communities. NAEC members saw the programs that were currently being delivered, which provided them with a national viewpoint and ensured they were well informed. This first-hand experience motivated them to continue to fight for better educational conditions:

> I became more outspoken and a real fighter for Aboriginal education, gaining an understanding of the disadvantage of Aboriginal people across the whole of Australia. It was wonderful going to those communities. Everybody seemed to have great enthusiasm. (Pearl Duncan, interview, 2015)

The drought was over. Aboriginal and Torres Strait Islander peoples were regaining a voice in the education of their people. Freshwater flowed strongly down the mountains, bringing life to the river once more.

CHAPTER 3

Community collaboration: the Aboriginal Education Consultative Groups

> My most memorable moment is that through the NAEC, the [Northern] Territory has a Territory Indigenous education committee. So Indigenous and non-Indigenous people can talk about education and what's [the] problem, what is good and what's not good and [the] need for more of this going on [Aboriginal voices leading to action]. (Didimain Uibo, interview, 2014)

The *Education for Aborigines* report by the ACG to the Schools Commission recommended that one role of the NAEC was to 'Establish close involvement and responsiveness to the ideas and aspirations of local community groups and regional associations for educational purposes' (ACG 1975, p. 5). The strategy to underpin this recommendation was the establishment of state and territory Aboriginal Education Consultative Groups (AECGs), which would ensure a continuum of relevant input into the NAEC and provide a conduit between national and state education initiatives and discussions. This strengthened the NAEC and provided communities with a long-awaited voice in determining their own futures.

Responding to the ACG's recommendation, in one of his first public presentations as chairperson of the NAEC, Stephen Albert announced:

> Consultation with Aboriginal people at all levels is one of the major roles of the NAEC. In order to carry out this role, the NAEC has requested that state Aboriginal education advisory groups be set up to advise the state departments of education. This would ensure that consultation within the state with Aborigines can be achieved and the outcome expressed.
>
> Between the NAEC and the state AECGs, a national network could evolve which would include Aboriginal communities, Aboriginal organisations, Aboriginal teachers, teacher assistants, teacher aides, individuals and most important ... Aboriginal parents. When this network is achieved and becomes a working component, it is then up to the government to respond positively. (Albert 1977, interview, p. 3)

Development of the state and territory education groups

By the time the NAEC was operational in 1977, Victoria and Queensland already had state education consultative groups. On advice from the NAEC, the Schools Commission provided funding to the NAEC to establish consultative groups across all states and territories for the purpose of providing advice to state government, as well as contributing to the agendas and priorities of the NAEC (West 1988). Over the next three years, this was achieved, with the exception of Western Australia, which did not set up a consultative committee until 1984. West (1988, p. 22) highlights the importance of these committees: 'Through continued negotiation and liaison with Aboriginal communities, governmental departments and relevant ministers, the NAEC has established a network in which "grass roots" opinions can be co-ordinated to maintain the Government's commitment to self-management and self-determination.'

The link with the state and territory consultative groups was a major strength of the NAEC. The NAEC was only involved in national programs and advice — it was the state consultative committees that were responsible for consulting and advising the state government departments on issues such as state policy and funding. The outcomes of state relationships were communicated to the NAEC by the state representatives:

> What they said at the state level, we [the NAEC] were saying in that room, that was how the network worked. We always had somebody from the state consultative group on the committee [the NAEC], like Bob [Morgan] from NSW. So, when somebody came on the national committee, we would encourage the state committee to get them on their committee, so that there was continuity and there wasn't any sort of you can have that, you can't have that . . . we were all part of forming as one group and that's the way it was. (Stephen Albert, interview, 2012)

The AECGs played a vital role in bringing Aboriginal and Torres Strait Islander communities together and collaborating with the NAEC to ensure all states and territories had a voice in developing a national agenda. It was an exciting time for the communities; at last they had a role in determining their own futures and that of future generations. This state and national collaborative model entrenched the principles of community accountability and provided the NAEC with Aboriginal and Torres

Figure 3.1. The NAEC members, 1980 (NAEC archives).

Strait Islander voices that stretched across all states and territories, and at a regional level.

The NAEC provided advice on new and existing programs, and reviewed and evaluated outcomes against the needs of people and communities. Although there were similarities and common goals, there were also differences between the NAEC and the AECGs, which had their own politics, histories, geography and cultural perspectives. The following brief overview of the development of AECGs across Australia provides evidence of the varied nature by which the AECGs were introduced.

Queensland

In 1976, the Queensland Aboriginal and Torres Strait Islander Consultative Committee, which reported to the Director General of the Queensland Department of Education, was the first state consultative committee established by their state education department. In 1975, the acting supervisor, Aboriginal Education Branch, was an Aboriginal person and had initiated a number of actions and strategies reflective of the recommendations made in the ACG's report to the Schools Commission (ACG 1975). However, in 1976, the recruitment of a new acting supervisor resulted in a non-Indigenous appointment. The department decided that this created the need for a consultative structure that would provide a link between the Queensland Department of Education and the Aboriginal and Torres Strait Islander community resulting in the establishment of the Queensland AECG (Beaton 1978).

Victoria

Victoria introduced the Victorian Aboriginal Consultative Committee in 1976. The process adopted by the Victorian Department of Education was to set up an interim steering group to provide recommendations on the composition and guidelines for the introduction of the state AECG and, additionally, to seek funding through a submission to the Schools Commission. In 1976, the funding proposal resulted in funding for the establishment of the Victorian AECG, and also proposed the delivery of a seminar series across the state for local Aboriginal communities to promote education opportunities and receive input regarding the communities' expectations and aspirations.

New South Wales

The NSW Aboriginal Education Advisory Group was established as a state committee in 1977, becoming the NSW Aboriginal Education Consultative Group (NSWAECG) in 1979. The NSW Government took over the funding of the NSWAECG in 1980 when Australian Government funding was no longer available. John Lester, an NAEC member from 1980 to 1983, was working in the Department of Education at the time and worked closely with the AECG:

> In the early '80s, the AECG was starting to pick up momentum and it was a pretty halcyon period of time in New South Wales itself. The AECG was being established, as were AECGs all around the country. New South Wales had an AECG since about '77, but it was a departmental-run show. The original chair of the AECG was Bobby Merritt; he had no educational background but had written *The Cake Man*.[1] He was there for a while and then John Heath got the role. Bob [Morgan] took over after John Heath, when we reconstituted the AECG and we went about making it more community-based and community-driven. (John Lester, interview, 2015)

In recognition of the quality of advice being provided to the state government, the NSW Minister for Education, Paul Lander, formally recognised the NSWAECG in 1981 as the principal advisory body to the state in relation to Aboriginal education. Following this, in 1982, the NSWAECG formed local consultative groups to provide localised advice and decision-making.

---

1 A play about life on Erambie Mission, Cowra, NSW. Published by Currency Press, Woollahra, NSW, 1978.

We probably became the first group that was truly autonomous and that weren't appointed by the state. In New South Wales, the AECG used to be an appointed committee. Its members were appointed by the department. The person who was driving it all was the then assistant director of Special Programs from the Department of Education, Bill Rose. I became a member of the NAEC before I became president of the AECG, because when I became an NAEC member, I was then invited to attend one of the meetings of the AECG. I still remember the meeting. It was in the Aboriginal Hostel's building . . . I remember going to that meeting and they asked if I wanted to be a member of the AECG. I said, 'No, I disagree with the structure.' I said I don't believe that someone like Bill Rose — who became one of our best allies and our best supporters actually — he shouldn't have the power that he had — and he did have a lot of power at that time in deciding who would sit on the AECG. I disagreed with the way in which the members were selected and appointed.

So they gave me a challenge and said, 'Well, what should it be like?' That's when I worked with John Lester and Chubby [Keith] Hall [executive member of NSWAECG]. We came up with a model. I wrote it up and then took it back to them at the next meeting of the AECG. I recommended that we should have a structure in New South Wales that was community-based and the community should elect who we want to represent our interests. To my amazement, all of the then-members of the AECG agreed. They said, 'Yeah, this is how it should be.' Because of my membership on the NAEC, I was then able to negotiate funding to allow for us to go out into our communities and set up local AECGs which then nominated their representative to the regional AECGs and which then formed the state committee. They never let me forget it, but I never did any of that. I had an accident at Parliament House. I was working with [Aboriginal activist] Pat O'Shane on land rights stuff and I fell down the stairs and busted my back and ended up in hospital. So Chubby and Johnny had to go all around the state and set up all those committees. They had a ball.

That was a really heady period of our evolution as a community-based organisation as well. I'm proud of the fact that it still exists and that we had some role in deciding how that should operate. So that relationship between the AECG and the NAEC was important for us

> because, from the New South Wales point of view, we [came] strictly from a community perspective, and all the stuff that I argued and advocated for at the national level, that came from the AECG. I had my own ideas about some stuff, but I gave an undertaking to our committee that I would only push for stuff that was endorsed and came from the state committee. There were other things that I did, spoke about and advocated for that was outside of this but primarily that's what the source of the motivation and accountability was. (Bob Morgan, interview, 2015)

In 1981, Bob commenced as full-time president of the NSWAECG. After his first term on the NAEC, subsequent appointments were on the basis of his representation of the NSWAECG.

> Apart from meeting a lot of those individuals that I mentioned — that was a highlight of course and they've all become valued friends and colleagues. We didn't always agree on things and I guess I became recognised as a person that always questioned. I thought that it was what we should be doing. I owed it to the people that entrusted me to ask questions. I didn't want to just go along because I was a member of the boys' club. I took my role as president of the AECG and as a New South Wales representative very seriously. I believed in community accountability and I still do. (Bob Morgan, interview, 2015)

In 1982, the NSWAECG was heavily involved in the introduction of the first Aboriginal Education Policy for the New South Wales Department of Education (NSWAECG 2015). In 1983, the NSWAECG became an incorporated body and is still operational today. Its work is a testament to the men and women who overcame the challenges to its success:

> New South Wales has always had the problem of being so large and having people right across the state. It was slow to get the AECG going, but once it got going, it was powerful, absolutely powerful, including their work with the teachers union. The education union did some terrific work for them, really pushed national policy as well. But it always had a problem in terms of the size and the local groups, having the tyranny of distance problem. (Eleanor Bourke, interview, 2013)

South Australia

The South Australian AECG (SAAECG) was established in 1977 through a grant from the Schools Commission and continued to be funded through the South Australian Department of Education. The SAAECG was formed as a link between community and the government to undertake research, collect and disseminate information, and provide advice and involvement in policy and planning.

The SAAECG determined that the establishment of state principles and philosophies needed to form its foundation. This was similar to a document simultaneously being worked on by the NAEC from a national perspective:

> Establishment of philosophies and purposes for Aboriginal education are a necessary foundation for Aboriginal social and community development, these philosophies and purposes can best be established by regular consultation and review by Aboriginal people, communities and professionals. (SAAECG 1983, p. 22)

In 1983, the SAAECG released an article titled 'Rationale, aims and objectives for Aboriginal education in South Australia' (SAAECG 1983). The rationale behind the document was to respond to the past failures of the education system for Aboriginal people. This included the provision of an educational environment that acknowledged Aboriginal heritage, culture and identity, emphasising that the methodology and pedagogy used with Western education is not solely appropriate for Aboriginal students. Deficit model thinking was also called into question and the document stated that education decision makers needed to look beyond blaming Aboriginal people for educational limitations and towards producing proactive educational programs that responded to Aboriginal values and perspectives to bring about positive outcomes. Finally, the rationale defined the rights of every Aboriginal person: a right to an education that recognises Aboriginal identity while achieving academic success (SAAECG 1983, p. 22). Although the content of this document had similarities to and alignment with the later NAEC *Philosophy, Aims and Policy Guidelines for Aboriginal and Torres Strait Islander Education* (1985b), the

South Australian document reflected the specific principles, aims and philosophies of the South Australian Aboriginal communities, experiences and cultures.

Northern Territory

The Northern Territory AECG (NTAECG) was established in 1978 through funding from the Northern Territory Department of Education to provide an Aboriginal viewpoint on education to the Minister for Education. Shortly after its inception, the NTAECG believed it should have an Aboriginal name from the local language; it became known as Feppi, which is an Aboriginal word from the Murrinh-Patha language, meaning 'rock' or 'foundation' (West 1988). The NTAECG had representation from all regional areas of the Northern Territory, as well as specialist appointments. A full-time secretariat was employed by the Department of Education, inclusive of the chairperson, two deputy chairpersons and a policy analyst, project co-ordinator, field officer and general administration officer.

West (1988, p. 24) identified the strengths of Feppi in an article he wrote as chairperson of the NAEC:

> Feppi is the voice of Aboriginal people in the NT. It provides the NT Education Department and the NT Government with Aboriginal views on education and can ensure that those views highlight such things as the needs and aspirations of the various groups of Aborigines in the NT; and the influences and values which must be considered when educational issues arise.

The departmental control, however, was and continues to be contested, with Feppi arguing for community control similar to the NSWAECG model. This was reiterated by Wendy Ludwig, a member of the NAEC during 1983 and 1986:

> For a long time, there was a very conservative government in the Northern Territory — the Country Liberal Party. Despite all of the hard work that individual people did inside Feppi, for those of us that were

outside of that set of arrangements, and certainly from my point of view, I saw it as a very conservative group. They had good intentions, strong views and good vision about where things should be going but [were] totally hamstrung by NT Government. (Wendy Ludwig, interview, 2016)

The social, professional, emotional and cultural connections were all important to individuals and Feppi as a community of Aboriginal educators:

I think maybe the whole three years [involved in Feppi and NAEC] was a really memorable and important time both in my development as an Aboriginal person being involved in the education game and being able to see how . . . all the efforts of people in communities all around the country could be brought to national conferences where targets and priorities were agreed upon. From there [I saw] how that was fed up and used to influence national policy direction and funding through the likes of Paul [Hughes] and Errol [West] and Peter [Buckskin] and various other people that were in Canberra. It was just a really good learning experience and exposure. For somebody that came from the other end of the country [Northern Territory], not only physically were we removed, but politically and mentally removed from a whole range of different ways of thinking and looking at the world. That is a really important part of the conferences as well, just to be with other like-minded people. Unlike now, you were only one or might be only three or four black people in a whole institution and every day is a fight and you're battling, pushing all of these intrusions away. So, to be somewhere where you're safe with a whole group of other people that you can relate to about those struggles and all of those kinds of things and just get your power back to go back out into really isolated kind of environments and do the stuff that we needed to do was very important. That whole three years of experiences was a memorable one that obviously sticks with me. (Wendy Ludwig, interview, 2016)

Feppi provided a model for national and state education information to be shared across communities:

Numbulwar was my home, so I had to send in information [about] what the school was doing. So, I put a report to [Feppi for the NAEC] . . . and also because we met at different locations around Australia, we had to have one or two meeting[s] outside of Canberra and one was here in Darwin. (Didimain Uibo, interview, 2014)

Tasmania

The Tasmanian AECG (TASAECG) was established in 1979 through the negotiations of Patsy Cameron, an NAEC member, and the Tasmanian Department of Education. Like the NSWAECG, the members were elected from regions across Tasmania by the local Aboriginal communities. The purpose of the TASAECG was to provide the Department of Education with advice to increase the participation of Aboriginal people in education, and to provide input into the national agenda through the NAEC.

In her negotiations for the development of the TASAECG, Patsy called on the NAEC to provide support:

> I needed the NAEC to rally behind that and to help me then pursue the aim of establishing [the] Aboriginal Education Consultative [Group] in Tasmania. The first step towards that was flying to Victoria to go to the Victorian . . . meetings and to take part in the Victorian discussion. From that, some of the Victorians came into Tasmania and assisted me in developing our consultative committee here. That's how we first started the Tasmanian Aboriginal Education Consultative [Group]. Since then, it's metamorphosed into different committees. Now it's an incorporated body and still very much with community people. It was important having state consultative committees where Aboriginal people could ensure that the aims, objectives and the aspirations of Aboriginal communities, families and school bodies could develop programs that would meet the needs of Aboriginal people and kids. (Patsy Cameron, interview, 2013)

Australian Capital Territory

The Australian Capital Territory AECG (ACTAECG) was established in 1980 with representatives from the Schools Department, Canberra College of Advanced Education, Australian National University and the Teachers Federation. The ACTAECG was appointed by the ACT Government and was recognised as the principal advisor on Aboriginal and Torres Strait Islander education in the ACT (West 1988).

Western Australia

Western Australia was the last state to implement a consultative committee, eventually introducing the Western Australian AECG (WAAECG) in June 1984. May O'Brien was ultimately responsible for the development of the subgroups that led to the establishment of the WAAECG. She had left the NAEC and was working as a superintendent for the Western Australian Department of Education.

> They made me a superintendent in the education department. I hated the job because I was marking people who were at teachers college with me. I said, 'I don't want this job in the education department because I have to mark teachers who were at teachers college with me.' Then they said, 'Well, go and do your own thing then.' I said, 'My own thing? Why, thank you.' I did my own thing in the education department. I set up all the Aboriginal committees on education in all the areas in Western Australia. Every area, we had an Aboriginal education committee, funded by my funds that they gave me for what I was doing. So that's how it all started up. So, I set up all these committees. Let them go and helped them with whatever they needed. This is how the WAAECG came about. (May O'Brien, interview, 2014)

Collaborative workshops

The collaborative efforts of the NAEC and AECGs ensured that they were presenting a consolidated viewpoint, which held more weight in the negotiation of strategies that called for long-term commitments. To ensure that wider consultations happened between the NAEC and AECGs, workshops were held to discuss joint priorities. The first workshop was held in Canberra in February 1979, with a second workshop held in November 1979. The workshops clarified the independent roles of the AECGs; provided the NAEC with guidance in relation to setting priorities; established closer links; and encouraged AECGs to establish and support local and regional Aboriginal and Torres Strait Islander education committees (NAEC 1980a).

In March 1980, the NAEC held a three-day collaborative workshop in Tasmania with representatives from each AECG, resulting in a briefing document that outlined the outcomes and recommendations of the workshop for the purpose of a meeting with state superintendents the following day. The briefing document emphasised major areas for discussion, including the importance of formal consultation processes with Aboriginal and Torres Strait Islander peoples, commitment to the organisation of AECGs; the development of Aboriginal and Torres Strait Islander professional staff; and attention to the development of Aboriginal and Torres Strait Islander curriculum and Aboriginal and Torres Strait Islander studies (NAEC 1980a).

The three-day workshop was extremely important:

Figure 3.2. Margaret Valadian, Kaye Price, Stephen Albert and Natascha McNamara at the Department of Aboriginal Affairs state superintendents meeting, Hobart, 1980 (*Mercury* newspaper, courtesy Kaye Price).

> You were talking directly to superintendents who had the policy and program responsibilities for Aboriginal education in state and territory jurisdictions. That was really important for the leadership of the NAEC, bringing together the players in the room and having really decent conversations, but also putting the money on the table because the Department of Aboriginal Affairs in those days used to have Aboriginal funding. (Peter Buckskin, interview, 2015)

Empowering connections

The NAEC was a national network of Aboriginal people sharing and connecting with others from diverse cultural and experiential backgrounds. These connections continued beyond the NAEC. Its members view the period when the NAEC operated as an empowering time for the movement of Aboriginal and Torres Strait Islander peoples in education:

> Well, the network and friendships ... where else would you get to meet people from all around Australia? We were with people that were in so-called traditional communities, people with totally different upbringings. I was lucky to work in a national setting as well, but it was complemented by being able to visit communities through the NAEC and make those friendships. Those networks were invaluable ... Always meant you had a contact somewhere you could talk to if you were looking for some information. You could use the network, and that's just priceless really. I think that's what's probably most missed is that network, because it was cyclical, it kept churning people in and out and you couldn't go to the airport without meeting people that were on the national circuit in those days. That was an unbelievable opportunity ... It was just tremendous, so that was the value of the conferences, of the meeting in different places and getting a look at what other people did and how they did it in different places. (Eleanor Bourke, interview, 2013)

NAEC members felt the connections and relationships were empowering in an otherwise bureaucratic environment that was quite sterile. The intellect that was brought to the table from the group was exceptional and although there may have been some criticism by non-Indigenous people, the NAEC met the challenge with a united strength:

> I think the memorable part for me is that we were all together with one voice ... We had disagreements, not arguments, but disagreements. But in the end, we all had to say whether we were in agreement with what was passed, or somebody would pass a motion so that at the end we'd all shake hands [laughs]. So that's good. But we wouldn't pass anything if there was a lot of disagreement. Everybody had a chance to give their opinion. People were willing to change their little bits or big bits of it. We had fun doing it ... [laughs]. Good fun. Our biggest challenge was that someone in the education system or the government was willing to let us have a go. Because some of the politicians would think, 'Oh, well, you let them have a go for a few months and then they're going to become a big flop.' We had news for them: we weren't going to die. We wanted to fight, and fight we did, with our mouths, vocally. Yeah, it was good. (May O'Brien, interview, 2014)

The rich and diverse cultural and community strength that members presented was vital for the success of the NAEC:

> All of us ... in that committee were so into it and we were so strong in looking at our communities, so this is an opportunity we have — now speak out so that they can listen what's good in those areas. All of us members were there with one voice and one talk ... we were on one page. Well, I had that experience and understanding [of] where I was. To be young, to get on the board, I was filled with that. Just for me to give that knowledge to others who did not [have it]. But I think we did a very good job, both listening [to] each other, and me, from my traditional background, giving it to those who were all from a city life, city people. I was out from the bush, giving them all the knowledge that I had. (Rex Granites, interview, 2014)

Reaching out into communities and establishing the AECGs were major strategies for the widening of Aboriginal and Torres Strait Islander perspectives and voices with the inclusion of individuals and communities across Australia. The need for this gave rise to a regular argument:

> At a meeting I was at one day, we wanted the systems and sectors to report on how they were implementing school community partnerships, which was part of the national Aboriginal education plan. [Someone from one] of the sectors got up and said how they'd implemented fifteen school community partnerships. The question was asked, 'Who negotiated these on behalf of the Aboriginal communities?' The response was that it was a white fella that had done this. He worked with the school and the community. We were saying, 'Well, how can he do that, because we actually needed somebody independent of the schools to do that?' The response then was, 'Oh, this person has been working with Aboriginal people for so long [as] he's almost one of them, an Aboriginal.' One of the members just said, 'A mouse born in a biscuit tin is still a mouse. It isn't a biscuit, it's still a mouse.' (May O'Brien, interview, 2014)

Having state and territory AECG representation on the NAEC provided a strong framework for drawing on diverse Aboriginal and Torres Strait Islander values and perspectives, and contributed strongly towards education policy development.

Aboriginal and Torres Strait Islander peoples' preference regarding the structure of the state committees was for committees that were autonomous from the state and Commonwealth education departments and that empowered their own voices, self-management and control without dominant influences. It was a model that moved further away from what Bob Morgan coined the 'guest paradigm' for Aboriginal and Torres Strait Islander peoples in systems of education. Equally important were the connections to the communities, whose input was deemed integral in understanding the diverse aspects of Aboriginal and Torres Strait Islander education across regional, rural, remote and urban communities.

CHAPTER 4

Redefining access to education

> I enjoyed [it] when we visited the communities and look[ed] at their projects. For me it was . . . a great triumph to see Aboriginal people standing up for themselves and wanting things, demanding their rights and demanding to be educated. (Pearl Duncan, interview, 2015)

The NAEC provided Aboriginal and Torres Strait Islander peoples an opportunity to engage in their own educational futures, and those of their children, for the first time since the arrival of the colonisers. This marked a move for the inclusion of the whole nation towards the advancement of Aboriginal and Torres Strait Islander education. The first term of the NAEC, from 1977 to 1980, saw the redefining of access to education, with key achievements in involvement and leadership in National Aboriginal Education Conferences, community-driven schooling, and the training and employment of Aboriginal and Torres Strait Islander teachers.

Taking over the space: National Aboriginal Education Conferences

The first National Aboriginal Education Conference was held in 1976 in Adelaide (before the NAEC was appointed in March 1977) and was initiated by the South Australian Institute of Teachers (Paul Hughes, interview, 2013). The second and third conferences were in Perth and Darwin respectively. These first three conferences had little input from Aboriginal and Torres Strait Islander peoples. However, at the fourth conference, which was held in Brisbane in 1979 and was titled 'Education in the 80s: Role of Aboriginal and Torres Strait Islanders', the NAEC was invited to co-manage the conference:

> The fourth National Aboriginal Education Conference was hosted by Queensland University. There was a non-Indigenous woman named Betty Watts, who was a great supporter of Aboriginal education and, through Queensland University, produced the *Aboriginal Child at School* journal . . . The NAEC had decided that the conferences were something that Aboriginal people — educators — should be doing and that it should be our conference. Then to Betty's credit . . . and . . . the other people that had been involved in running the conferences, they agreed. They said, 'Yeah, we should be supporting them and not running them.' So the NAEC took them over. (Bob Morgan, interview, 2015)

Prior to 1979, the presentations and discussions at the National Aboriginal Education Conferences had been led mainly by non-Indigenous teachers and academics. The time had come for Aboriginal and Torres Strait Islander voices to dominate the space. McConnochie (1982, p. 36) describes the 'unprecedented' change in the space of Aboriginal and Torres Strait Islander education:

> The National Aboriginal Education Conference at Brisbane in 1979 was a unique and stirring event: planned and organised by the NAEC and several Aboriginal consultants, with Aborigines giving all the keynote addresses and taking most leadership roles, with more Aborigines than non-Aborigines in attendance, and with preference being given to Aboriginal input, the conference had an unprecedented Aboriginal character . . . Gone are the days of 'the same old white faces, year after year'.

The NAEC aligned these conferences with their current priorities, inviting AECG members as well as other Aboriginal and Torres Strait Islander and non-Indigenous stakeholders. The conferences were funded by the Schools Commission and were co-ordinated by the NAEC and the AECGs. At times the conferences attracted attendances of more than two hundred people.

The conference agendas focused on all aspects of education, including early childhood, primary, secondary, TAFE, tertiary, traditional and non-traditional education. The conference outcomes formed the basis of wider consultation, debate and discussion for the provision of advice to the Australian Government:

> They were the foundation of the way we got information in from community, broad scoping sort of advice about where we were going. So NAEC was well substantiated by community direction. Workshops that were held at these national conferences were outstanding. There was a clause in the Commonwealth Study Grants in those days, where you could hold conferences and they would pay for them. That's how we funded it. We were funding the AECG and we were funding these national conferences. They were called activities and there was a subset in the policy where we could do that. So it gave us the opportunity to bring these people together, which was fairly unique. Eventually it stopped when they tightened up on money. (John Lester, interview, 2015)

The conferences ran for five days, concluding with recommendations and outcomes:

> We had a national conference that lasted a week, five days of concentrating on all the things currently going on. Nowadays, if a national conference lasts a couple of days, it's a big conference. So getting into depth about things was a lot more the case in those days . . . We spent a lot more time looking at information coming forward but nobody had done a whole lot of particular research about the best way to teach Aboriginal studies or the best way to teach Aboriginal kids, the best way to deal with racism. All those sorts of things were in their infancy in terms of anybody else making comment about them or researching them in various sorts of ways. (Paul Hughes, interview, 2013)

The conferences were consultative and included workshops, discussions and debates, with sessions where a person could present a paper with a five-minute question time at the conclusion of the presentation. The NAEC chairperson, supported by NAEC members, provided leadership to ensure the conversations and discussions at the workshops resulted in productive recommendations and policy advice. Initially, the last day of the conferences provided the opportunity for individual recommendations to be heard; however, as the conferences grew, this process was reviewed. The new process only allowed for recommendations to be made that evolved from the discussions and themes of the conference, which achieved more productive results for the outcomes of the conferences (Paul Hughes, interview, 2013).

Like the fourth conference, the fifth conference, 'An Aboriginal Perspective on Creating Positive Learning Environments', aimed to reinforce the imperative of an Aboriginal and Torres Strait Islander voice in education. It was held in 1980 at Medlow Bath, Katoomba, New South Wales, and was co-ordinated by the NSWAECG in collaboration with the NAEC. The conference focused on heightening the voices of students and parents (NAEC 1981). Aboriginal Year 12 students were invited to participate and engage in workshops. They were then invited to deliver a presentation defining their perspectives and to present a list of recommendations for consideration by the NAEC and wider conference audience. The students also outlined what they saw as the responsibilities in the future for Aboriginal and Torres Strait Islander education such as more Aboriginal and Torres Strait Islander teachers in schools. Aboriginal parents also presented their views and ideas on education. The two primary areas of concern raised at this conference were about changing teacher attitudes and increasing Aboriginal and Torres Strait Islander involvement in program development (NAEC 1981).

The conferences provided a forum for a collective community voice in the development of state and national policies and programs. They instilled a sharing of information between the states and territories, providing the NAEC with wider community perspectives to inform decision-making. Additionally, they provided Aboriginal and Torres Strait Islander teachers, who were usually minorities in their school environments, an empowering

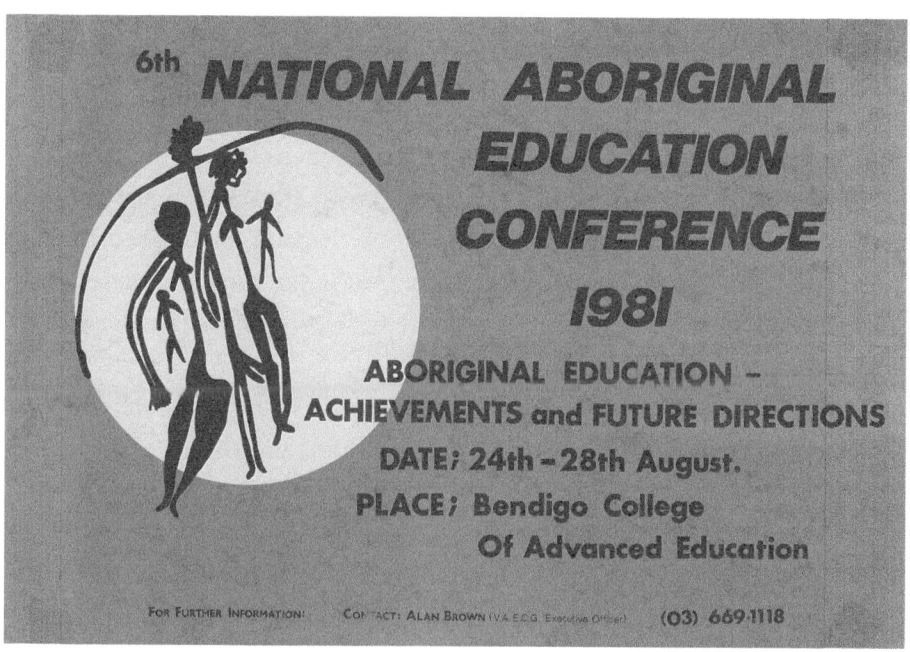

Figure 4.1. Logo of the 6th National Aboriginal Education Conference, 1981 (courtesy AIATSIS Collections).

space to discuss and debate Aboriginal and Torres Strait Islander education and a means of forming professional relationships:

> It was about sharing knowledge and getting Indigenous voices into the education systems where there were very little voices because there weren't a lot of Aboriginal teachers. There wasn't a lot of Aboriginal leadership. (Peter Buckskin, interview, 2015)

In the evenings during the conferences, activities were organised to bring everyone together in an informal setting to continue building connections and relationships. These activities included games, dancing, singing, skits or just getting together. This time was seen as just as important as the formal conference because it allowed people to unwind and strengthen bonds. Activity nights became a regular part of the conference agendas, allowing the blending of serious work with important social interaction.

At the fifth conference in Katoomba, the Commonwealth Minister for Education, Wallace Fife, addressed the conference and detailed the progress of Aboriginal and Torres Strait Islander peoples in having a voice in the directions and priorities of Aboriginal and Torres Strait Islander education. He stated that in 1971, at a similar conference, there were only four Aboriginal and Torres Strait Islander participants, or 10 per cent of conference participants, which was in contrast to the current conference, which had at least 75 per cent Aboriginal and Torres Strait Islander participation (Fife 1980b).

The sixth and seventh conferences focused on the development of policy and actions within the initial rationale, aims and objectives (NAEC 1985b). In 1981, the sixth NAEC conference, 'Aboriginal Education — Achievements and Future Directions', was held in Bendigo, Victoria, followed in 1982 by the seventh conference, 'Words into Actions: Priority Programmes in Aboriginal Education', in Goulburn, New South Wales.

Community-driven schooling: a study into the Townsville Black Community School

The Black Community School in Townsville had been opened as a result of the concerns of a group of Aboriginal and Torres Strait Islander parents who felt that the public schools were not providing an appropriate education for their children (Reynolds 1981). At the first meeting of the NAEC, in April 1977, the Department of Education raised concerns about the Black Community School, as detailed in the following correspondence:

> The situation at this moment is that the school faces closure at the end of first term, i.e. in May, if the Department of Aboriginal Affairs [DAA] withdraws its financial support, as it is thinking of doing.
>
> DAA is concerned about the low student attendance and apparent lack of interest by the parents. While DAA considers it to be an important educational facility, they take the view that they should avoid funding projects which they consider important but which the community does not.

> Before making a decision about withdrawal of funding, they have asked for the advice of this department. Our response has been to request DAA to postpone a final decision until the National Aboriginal Education Committee has had the chance to decide whether it would wish to be involved in the matter. DAA has agreed to this.
>
> From the department's point of view, NAEC involvement would be highly desirable. Much of the issue turns on the question of community support, and Aboriginal community feeling about such an intensively Aboriginal project as the Black Community School and its future is something which the NAEC is, we believe, particularly qualified to investigate. (NAEC 1977, p. 2)

During the second meeting of the NAEC, a resolution was passed:

> The National Aboriginal Education Committee wishes to evaluate the school and requests that the funding continue to the end of the 1977 school year and include provisions of transport for students. The Committee considers that an evaluation cannot be carried out unless teachers and students are secure and operating under normal conditions. (NAEC 1977, p. 3)

The Black Community School had been under a lot of scrutiny since its inception. Due to their concerns that their children were not engaged or succeeding in the public school system, Aboriginal and Torres Strait Islander parents, together with community members, formed a committee and opened their independent school in 1973. The Black Community School immediately attracted attention from the Queensland Minister for Education and the Department of Education, which opposed the opening of the school because it thought the school was segregationist (Reynolds 1981). This was a hypocritical stance given the past policies of Queensland and other Australian state governments that had long excluded Aboriginal and Torres Strait Islander children from attending school (Reynolds 1981). The Queensland Department of Education initially rejected the application for the school, stating that it was against the *Queensland Education Act 1964–1970*. In the initial stages of attempting to register the school, the Minister for Education announced, 'It is most unlikely I would approve of a school based on such provocative and emotional principles. I certainly do not approve of such a move' (Reynolds 1981, p. 64).

The parents and community sought legal advice, which concluded that there were no grounds to reject the application to open the school. Despite continued criticism, the school commenced with an enrolment of ten primary school students and two teachers who undertook to teach at half pay as they believed in the school's aims. Up until independent assessments were undertaken in 1976 and 1978, all of the speculations of failure made by the department and other parties were unfounded and without evidence. In fact, the Schools Commission report in 1977 stated, 'Most school syllabuses, value systems and operational patterns both fail to reinforce the group identity of black students or to utilise the experiences and traditions students bring' (Reynolds 1981, p. 65).

The parents involved in establishing the Black Community School had sought to provide an alternative educational environment that was respectful of the values, beliefs and experiences of their children. They believed that their children were not being provided with a positive school environment in the public school system due to racism and discrimination, and teachers' lack of awareness of the environments and cultures of Aboriginal and Torres Strait Islander children. The Black Community School aimed to harness the involvement of parents and community in the learning experience; inspire aspiration and hope in children; appoint teachers with the same visions as the community; and create further educational opportunities post-school (NAEC 1977). The principal of the school, Edward Koiki (Eddie) Mabo, a Meriam man from Mer (Murray Island) in the Torres Strait, and whose name has become synonymous with the Mabo Case, had a philosophy that reflected that:

> All children should be taught in their own school by their own people. He sees this school as the first in attaining this ideal where children learn from [the] base of their own culture and identity moving gradually into the learning needed for life in European society. This is what the normal European school does from the European base. (NAEC 1977, p. 3)

The NAEC conducted an intensive week-long study of the school in August 1977. The study was conducted by a subcommittee of the NAEC (Stephen Albert, Paul Hughes, John Budby, Patsy Cameron, Colin Bourke and George Passi) and investigated Aboriginal and Torres Strait Islander community perceptions and the school's effectiveness in contributing to educational outcomes. In December 1977, the NAEC tabled the evaluation report:

> There was quite a lot of discussion about who was using the school, what the purposes of the school was and whether funding should be continued. The ... Schools Commission was contributing to their funding at the time. So the NAEC was asked to go and do a study of the Black Community School. I remember Colin, Paul and I [were] involved, Stephen and, of course, our executive. Stephen and I did the community consultations. We went out talking to all the families around Townsville which included Torres Strait Islander families and Aboriginal families. Paul and Colin were doing a lot of the gathering of data. So we'd meet each evening. We were probably a week up there really doing intensive data collection and interviews with community and bringing it all together in order to come up with recommendations to the ... Schools Commission about whether funding should continue. (Patsy Cameron, interview, 2013)

The report tabled findings regarding concerns about the school governance, administration and leadership, as well as the lack of support by government agencies. Due to the financial restrictions, Eddie Mabo's position as the director/principal and chairperson of the school council was unpaid. Additionally, the school appointed one trained teacher and three teacher aides, with one of these being unpaid. The major concern was that even though the director/principal was passionate and fully committed to the school, he lacked governance, finance and management experience and qualifications. This was having a detrimental effect on the day-to-day running of the school, the quality of education offered and opportunities for future funding. Added to this was the director/principal's need to balance running the school with seeking other employment to attract an income to survive. The lack of involvement from the Queensland Department of Education and the Department of Aboriginal Affairs was also noted in the report. The response from both departments during the investigation was that the director/principal was not forthcoming in asking for their involvement or assistance (NAEC 1977).

The NAEC (1977) report also found, from a more positive viewpoint, that the children were very happy in the school environment and that this created a high level of motivation towards their studies and a willingness to learn. Parents and the wider Aboriginal and Torres Strait Islander community involved in the school spoke highly of having an alternative option for their children.

The NAEC made eleven recommendations, primarily relating to professional training and development of staff and management, as well as encouraging a high level of support and assistance from relevant departments. The NAEC concluded by stating:

> The NAEC feels that the school lacks so many support services that we consider it almost impossible to evaluate its success or otherwise. It certainly needs a number of conditions applying to it and to other agencies to enable it to function well. It cannot be considered a failure at this stage ... At this point in time the people who use its services do not see anything wrong with the school. The NAEC supports them in their views that their children are learning in a happy school environment which gives them the opportunity to develop personally and socially within their own cultural milieu, free of the pressures and potential damage involved in attending other schools. The students have a security and confidence which may assist them to cope better with secondary education than in other primary schools.
>
> We therefore recommend that the Department of Aboriginal Affairs funding continue, at least to the end of the 1979 school year provided that the recommendations the NAEC has made are implemented or are in motion by the end of this financial year. (NAEC 1977, p. 26)

Following the NAEC's study on the Black Community School, the NAEC was asked to review the outcomes of the study by the Commonwealth Department of Education to ascertain whether the recommendations had been implemented. Three NAEC members, including the chairperson, visited the school in early August 1979 and discussed progress with the DAA and Eddie Mabo. At the conclusion of this meeting, the DAA and Schools Commission agreed to support the future of the Black Community School.

Peter Buckskin recalled working with Eddie Mabo and being part of the NAEC's support for the Black Community School:

> Then you got to meet people like Eddie Mabo and hear his story about his island home and I never met Torres Strait Islander people before, until I got into the NAEC. Then with Eddie's big fight for the Townsville Aboriginal Community School, and us supporting that. It was an NAEC movement. (Peter Buckskin, interview, 2015)

John Heath also reflected on working with Eddie Mabo and not fully understanding at the time the significance of his fight for native title:

> When I think back on Eddie Mabo's time there, and he was a [NAEC] member when I was a member. What I distinctly remember the most about him was when he didn't turn up to meetings. I remember the conversation about Eddie that he can't come because he's full on with this native title thing on Murray Island. At that stage, I certainly didn't know the significance of that. (John Heath, interview, 2016)

The school was seen as highly innovative and, although it had low enrolment numbers, it had provided significant evidence of the values of an alternative educational environment based on principles of self-determination. The recommendations of the NAEC (1977) report aimed to build on foundations that were laid under challenging political circumstances. Unfortunately, the Black Community School closed in 1985 due to insufficient funding. However, it provided a model of success that could be duplicated in the future for the education of Aboriginal and Torres Strait Islander children. Today, similar models across Australia extend from preschool to high school. These schools are built on the values and principles that were the foundation of the Townsville Black Community School.

Alternative schooling for Aboriginal and Torres Strait Islander students was being explored by many communities at this time. However, changing attitudes of Commonwealth, state and territory ministers in their relationships with communities proved, at times, challenging. Communities and AECGs appealed to the NAEC to assist in negotiations with ministers and senior government officials. An example of this was when senior members of the community in Alice Springs asked the NAEC to negotiate with the Territory government for registration of their proposed community-driven and managed school. They were constantly being blocked by the attitudes of the government:

> One of the tough cats we had was Marshall Perron, Cabinet Member for Education and Planning in the Northern Territory. The Arrernte Council of Elders wanted to register the Yipirinya Aboriginal School. There were fringe dwellers that had their own camp and they wanted to put a school on it because the kids weren't attending the normal school. They had come to the [Northern Territory] department with their registrations the same as other schools but they wanted to also teach in language and they were continually being knocked back. I went to Alice Springs with Errol West and we took Mr Perron out to the casino the night we arrived. The next day, we met at the proposed school and in the end we got the registration. (Stephen Albert, interview, 2012)

At the NAEC conference in Brisbane in 1979, a resolution was passed to support the Yipirinya School Council in its objectives to operate an Aboriginal school in Alice Springs. At the 1980 conference in Katoomba, a further supportive resolution was made to continue the school's operations (Budby 1980a).

The 1979 *Education and Employment of Aboriginal and Torres Strait Islander Teachers* report

In 1979, the NAEC undertook research to develop a submission for the National Inquiry into Teacher Education (NITE) (Auchmuty 1980). To prepare the submission, the NAEC undertook substantial research that responded to the needs of Aboriginal and Torres Strait Islander peoples from their own perspectives. This contrasted with previous research that focused on existing challenges and often resulted in a deficit view (Hughes & Willmot 1979). The final paper for the submission was the *Report to the NAEC: The Education and Employment of Aboriginal and Torres Strait Islander Teachers* (EEATSIT) (Hughes & Willmot 1979). The outcomes of this paper and its submission to NITE resulted in strong future directives, including the development of the NAEC's 1000 Aboriginal teachers by 1990 initiative.

The study for the EEATSIT paper was undertaken between April and September 1979. The NAEC put together a steering committee of NAEC members and a research team drawn from government appointments, including a consultant from the Commonwealth Department of Education.

The NITE terms of reference were established to examine and assess the quality of pre-service teacher education programs in Colleges of Advanced Education (CAEs) and other educational institutions. The NAEC study investigated the appropriateness of programs for Aboriginal and Torres Strait Islander students; the levels of student outcomes; the contributions to students' personal and social development; the recruitment of and access for Aboriginal students to undertake education programs; and the employment of Aboriginal and Torres Strait Islander teachers. The NAEC steering committee had provided clear guidance that the study was to be investigative rather than evaluative and should identify future opportunities for a national approach to Aboriginal and Torres Strait Islander teacher training and employment.

The NAEC research team developed a societal framework for the EEATSIT paper using social, economic and geographic data from the national census to ensure recognition of diverse cultural groups across Australia. The framework guided a greater understanding of the differences between Aboriginal and Torres Strait Islander peoples from different geographic areas:

> Eric [Willmot] and Paul [Hughes] are pretty smart guys and, having been involved for a long time now, they could see that things were different for Aboriginal and Torres Strait kids in urban, rural, remote and very remote areas and that while some things might be the same, we at

times needed to do things differently, define them into categories. (Kaye Price, interview, 2013)

As a part of the wider consultation undertaken for the report in September 1979, the NAEC held a national workshop in Sydney for Aboriginal and Torres Strait Islander teachers and teacher aides. The workshop highlighted that, in 1977, more than 600 Aboriginal and Torres Strait Islander teacher aides were employed across the states and the Northern Territory, but only 72 qualified Aboriginal and Torres Strait Islander teachers taught in schools (Albert 1979).

The EEATSIT report (Hughes & Willmot 1979, p. 25) concluded that the employment of Aboriginal and Torres Strait Islander teachers provided a means for Aboriginal and Torres Strait Islander peoples to achieve social and economic equality. It identified that although there was great potential to increase participation in teacher education, the current environment did not provide a self-sustainable foundation. The challenge related to sustainability focused on the longitudinal commitment of the government to continue support for special Aboriginal and Torres Strait Islander teacher education programs and a further commitment to employing more Aboriginal and Torres Strait Islander teachers. An increase in the employment of Aboriginal and Torres Strait Islander teachers and the numbers of teaching students in pre-service teaching programs was becoming evident. A number of Indigenous-targeted programs had also recently been introduced and had the potential to attract increased enrolments in initial teacher education. However, further attention to increasing participation in teacher education was needed if an impact was to be achieved.

The report also found that at the current rate, there would be approximately 400 Aboriginal and Torres Strait Islander teacher graduates in the next decade, instead of the 5000 required by 1990 to achieve parity with non-Indigenous teachers on a representative population basis:

> When they did the report, we had seventy-two identified Aboriginal people as teachers. What they did was look at the number of Aboriginal students in the country and they said if we've got this number of students, we should have this number of teachers. That was the rationale behind the figure of

> 1000 Aboriginal teachers in classrooms, and people always leave off the bit about 1000 Aboriginal teachers in classrooms [not just employed outside the classroom] . . . Because we had people like me and Paul [Hughes], a growing number of people, working in government departments, we wanted to see the teachers in the classroom. (Kaye Price, interview, 2013)
>
> The figure of 1000 gave the committee a goal to work towards. It was also a goal that the Australian Government could adopt as a positive promise in their overall approach to Indigenous affairs. (Victor Forrest, interview, 2016)

The EEATSIT report recommended two major areas of action: first, to graduate 1000 Aboriginal and Torres Strait Islander teachers by 1990 (Hughes & Willmot 1979). This strategy would be vital to produce enough Aboriginal and Torres Strait Islander teachers to have a broad positive impact on the outcomes of children in the classroom and communities more generally:

> A next generation of economists, engineers, doctors, politicians, journalists and public servants of the future. In one generation Aboriginal society will have produced its managerial and political head, and more importantly, an intellectual arm that will be able to contribute to the shaping of Australia's destiny. (Hughes & Willmot 1982, p. 22)

Training and graduating teachers, however, was the priority:

> We recognised the importance of training professionals in all facets of life. But we all thought teachers were more important than anybody because we were trying to influence education. Not architectural designs or even health, though we recognised health was very important too. (Colin Bourke, 2013)

The report also noted the urgency in attracting Aboriginal and Torres Strait Islander teachers from remote and traditional communities because, at this stage, no qualified teachers or teaching students were from traditional communities.

Second, the report recommended that Aboriginal and Torres Strait Islander teachers were to be properly prepared to teach both Indigenous and non-Indigenous students and contribute to both societies (Hughes & Willmot 1979, p. 25). From an Aboriginal and Torres Strait Islander community perspective, preparing teachers relevant to the particular geographic categories (based on where they intended to work) was integral to developing successful relationships with communities that would result in better educational outcomes. If education about Aboriginal and Torres Strait Islander societies and perspectives was not incorporated into teaching programs, there was a risk of the continued privilege of Western knowledges in schools, which would be detrimental to Aboriginal and Torres Strait Islander communities:

> It will be a most important role for indigenous people to ensure that the philosophies and ideologies on which these future programs are based do create a new part of native Australian society, and does not simply take part of it away and lose it forever. (Hughes & Willmot 1979, p. 148)

Victor Forrest commented on the concerns NAEC members had about this issue:

> Although, one of the things that myself, Maurie Ryan [NT NAEC member] and Stephen Albert were quite concerned about was the education levels and the way education was being presented to traditional kids. As I always argued, and I guess I still do ... you teach an Aboriginal kid who comes from a traditional background whose first language is not English — English might be the second, third or fourth language to them — you teach Western education in English only and the understanding is quite ridiculous, and they're bound to fail. It was one of the issues that we kept on bringing up at meetings of NAEC. (Victor Forrest, interview, 2016)

There was also an emphasis on upskilling Aboriginal and Torres Strait Islander teacher aides to allow them more influence in children's learning. It was noted that the appointment of Aboriginal and Torres Strait Islander teacher aides had made a significant difference to the educational outcomes of Aboriginal and Torres Strait Islander children. However, as time progressed, the use of teacher aides became problematic because it meant that Aboriginal and Torres Strait Islander peoples remained as guests in the classroom instead of being trained teachers (Hughes & Willmot 1979, p. 23):

> I went to Sydney during my first round teaching. It was green pastures in a sense because there was a national inquiry into teacher education at the same time and so people like Deirdre Jordan, she was a consultant and she met us Aboriginal teachers — well, there wasn't too many, but Aboriginal education workers and Aboriginal teachers. Myself and Coral [Fong] were the only two registered teachers that were teaching in the Kimberley [WA]. So, we were quite novel in the eyes of the community because they saw teacher aides and assistants working for us in the classroom. The fact that we had influence — well, we didn't think we had too much influence, but they saw us having great power and having the same responsibilities as other teachers, and teachers paying us a respect that they probably didn't to teacher's aides. I thought they were treating everyone the same, but the education workers thought we were quite privileged in terms of the teachers that negotiated with us, unlike how they negotiated with them in terms of their role in the school. (Peter Buckskin, interview, 2015)

The excellence of the study was recognised by the Minister for Education, Wallace Fife, who stated in a press release that the NAEC submission to NITE had been 'a thorough and thoughtful piece of work, based on careful research promoted and controlled by the NAEC itself' (Fife 1980a, p. 3).

The *Report of the National Inquiry into Teacher Education* (Auchmuty 1980, p. 26) sent a strong message on the importance of education for the future of Aboriginal and Torres Strait Islander peoples:

> The [Auchmuty] Committee [led the National Inquiry into Teacher Education] believes that the schooling system has failed to meet the needs of the Aboriginal people. Education is the key to development and self-management of Aboriginals as of any other people: to fulfil this role, the education system must both reflect and meet the needs and aspirations of Aboriginal people.

In response to the NAEC submission, the NITE report (Auchmuty 1980, p. 196) made a number of recommendations related to teacher education, including endorsing the target of 1000 Aboriginal and Torres Strait Islander teachers by 1990:

> The Aboriginal community desires that many of its people who are both willing and able should gain entry to various professions. Teaching is one of these professions. The committee endorses the initial target of one thousand trained teachers set by the National Aboriginal Education Committee in its submission. If this target is to be attained from the base number of 72 trained teachers in 1979, a significant number of Aboriginal people must gain entry to the teacher education institutions.

NITE also recommended that the NAEC undertake an evaluation of the three enclaves that existed at the time in tertiary institutions, which included special entry programs and support services, to identify effective models to attract and retain Aboriginal and Torres Strait Islander students (Auchmuty 1980, p. 196).

A time for evolution

The NAEC submission to NITE would have a significant impact on the NAEC's priorities and future directions. In 1979, Stephen Albert had suggested that the evolution of Aboriginal and Torres Strait Islander education should move from consultation to involvement to responsibility. This first term of the NAEC marked the beginning of this evolution, providing a means of real consultation in directing the policy and operations of Aboriginal and Torres Strait Islander education. Responsibility would become a reality when Aboriginal and Torres Strait Islander peoples overcame their status as guests within the Western system.

CHAPTER 5

Taking our place in education: the second term of the NAEC, 1980–83

> The NAEC wishes to make it very clear that Aboriginal and Torres Strait Islander education is for Aboriginal and Torres Strait Islander people. The time has come for us to take the major responsibility for its development. Our people's futures are at stake. We cannot be a part of this country unless we ensure that education allows us to take our place as Aboriginal and Torres Strait Islander Australians with pride in our own identity and with confidence that we can play our part in Australian society. (NAEC 1980b, p. 5)

Throughout the second term of the NAEC, under the chairmanship of John Budby, work largely consisted of the consolidation of policy to provide direction across all levels of Aboriginal and Torres Strait Islander education for both Indigenous and non-Indigenous educators. In this term, NAEC membership began to be decided by Aboriginal and Torres Strait Islander peoples rather than the Commonwealth Department of Education, which was a major step towards self-determination. It also saw the development of specialist positions that would allow the NAEC to be more highly informed and able to target studies into relevant issues.

The second chairperson and members

The position of NAEC chairperson was a three-year appointment. Following Stephen Albert's term, John Budby was appointed as the second chairperson by the Minister for Education, Wallace Fife, on 9 April 1980. John introduced a strong emphasis on curriculum development and Aboriginal and Torres Strait Islander studies (Fife 1980a). He had previously worked in Papua New Guinea and drew on this experience to move these priorities forward for Aboriginal and Torres Strait Islander peoples.

John had completed his schooling in Mackay, Queensland, in 1964. He completed a teacher training course through the Australian School of Pacific Administration. The training aimed to prepare educators to teach in either the Northern Territory or Papua New Guinea and, once he completed his teacher training, John took up a teaching appointment in Papua New Guinea. He remained there for the next seven years, returning to Australia in 1975. Shortly after his return, he was appointed as an advisory teacher for the Queensland Department of Education, and this included the role of executive officer to the newly established Queensland Aboriginal and Torres Strait Islander Consultative Committee (Budby 1980b).

> Educationally, Budby was really strong, being a secondary teacher . . . When he came, it [the NAEC] was right into really focusing on education policy and, to some extent, debate about theory, in particular Aboriginal studies. (Eleanor Bourke, interview, 2013)

Laurie Padmore, a Tasmanian member, 1981–84, shares some fond memories of John:

> I tell you, one of the funniest incidents I ever seen. When we used to go to meetings in the MLC tower and John Budby . . . was the chair, and Vic [Victor Forrest] — he'd always be there. He'd be the comedian always. Anyhow, I was sitting down and we were really serious — we're going through these papers . . . and old John is explaining something to us. John had a way — he was a hands man — he always used to use his hands, waving them around the place. He . . . was talking about a level — about two or three levels — and as he said it, he would move

his arms up and down — level one, level two, level that and this. We're sitting down there and Vic's looking too, but Vic just went over and said to him . . . 'John, our brother, you're going to take off if you keep doing that — you'll start flying.' What could you do? Everyone just busted out laughing. What could you do? John's looking at him and he's laughing, too. Oh geez, it was so funny, but it was serious — it was really serious — very intense conversation that we were in, and then Vic comes up and he goes and breaks it like that. I suppose [he] took the tension out of it. (Laurie Padmore, interview, 2013)

Immediately after John's appointment as chairperson, he published an article in the *Aboriginal Child at School* journal that focused on his insights into the past, present and future position of Aboriginal and Torres Strait Islander education (Budby 1980b). In the article, he drew on his experiences in the 1970s of working in education in Papua New Guinea. An understudy program in Papua New Guinea trained local people by having them shadow the expatriates who were working in the education system. With this shadowing being accompanied by other training and the simultaneous acquisition of teaching qualifications, local people were able to take over the positions in the longer term. This was a model John believed needed to be adopted in Australia if it was going to encourage the 600 Aboriginal and Torres Strait Islander peoples who were working as teacher's aides to become qualified teachers:

> If we are going to look at people already in the field, such as the teacher aides/teacher assistants, we need then to negotiate not only with colleges of teacher education to encourage them to make some allowance for the practical experience of our present teacher aide force and provide some sort of bridging enrichment courses to assist them to become teachers, but also improve financial assistance to such people. (Budby 1980b, p. 9)

Another area that John identified as integral to the improvement of Aboriginal and Torres Strait Islander education was parent and community involvement in schools. He suggested that this would contribute to greater parent involvement in children's education inside and outside the classroom; parent and community contribution to curriculum development; teacher awareness of community culture and perspectives; and an increased student interest in schooling.

John discussed the model adopted by the Queensland Department of Education, which had two types of local advisory groups that included parents. The first model was attached to school principals. The second was a regional structure with representatives from each high school who were responsible to the regional director. John explained that the groups were responsible for identifying appropriate selections of Aboriginal and Torres Strait Islander student counsellors to work with students on academic development and goal setting and to provide individual assistance with their education. Student counsellors were also an important link between the school, advisory committees and parents, and were therefore expected to have strong engagement with these groups (Budby 1980b).

From John's perspective, the most significant developments over the previous decade related to the increased involvement of Aboriginal and Torres Strait Islander peoples in decision-making around policy and to the increase in the number of students remaining in school to complete Years 11 and 12:

> In the past, statistics had indicated that Aboriginal children tend to leave school either at Year 10 or at age 15, whichever comes first, but in the last five years at least there has been a greater number of Aboriginal children attending school beyond Year 10, and this has been a very important factor which needs to be followed through in the next few years. (Budby 1980b, p. 7)

Budby (1980b) proposed that the contributing factors for the increase in senior school enrolment were the involvement of parents, greater awareness of the educational systems and a growing perception in Aboriginal and Torres Strait Islander communities of the value of education. Initiatives established by the state education departments to support Aboriginal and Torres Strait Islander education included the appointment of positions that focused on the needs and aspirations of students. The Aboriginal Secondary Grants Scheme had also assisted in overcoming some of the financial challenges of remaining at school for the individual and the family (Budby 1980b). John believed, however, that the grants scheme placed students under a great deal of pressure because of assumptions by teachers that the grants were equivalent to scholarships and were based on the same expectations:

> In my experience as an advisory teacher, in which I travelled around most of Queensland and talked to many secondary teachers, some of them seemed to believe falsely that because you get paid to come to school you should be able to learn. (Budby 1980b, p. 10)

The Aboriginal Secondary Grants Scheme was not a scholarship and, therefore, there was no logic to this reasoning. It highlighted the need for more education for non-Indigenous teachers who were teaching Aboriginal and Torres Strait Islander students.

In a February 1980 meeting in Adelaide, the NAEC had decided on new criteria for future members and developed a nomination form. The nomination form put a greater emphasis on community involvement.

This was also the first term in which state representatives had been included through nominations and endorsement from the AECGs or equivalent community groups. This marked a distinct shift in self-determination: NAEC members were no longer selected by the Australian Government. Instead, representation was decided by Aboriginal and Torres Strait Islander peoples. The AECGs endorsed or ratified the representative appointments, which ensured accountability back to the community. Given this selection process, there was no opposition to who was selected to sit on the NAEC and, in a lot of cases, the representative was the chairperson of the state or territory committee. These people were in a good position to disseminate information in and out of their AECGs. Bob Morgan explains the significance of this shift towards self-determination:

> The AECG had to be in a power position where we'd endorse or ratified all the appointments because our position was that if you don't have accountability to the community, then all you are is an appointee to a government organisation or committee like [the] NAEC, without being accountable to the community. So, all of our members on the NAEC

would be required to come to AECG committees and report. (Bob Morgan, interview, 2015)

Peter Buckskin was another nominated appointment during this term. He was a trained primary teacher in the Kimberley, Western Australia, when he was appointed and had a number of people watching his progress:

> I was one of the very first intakes of the Aboriginal teacher educational program at Mount Lawley Teachers College and May O'Brien was a superintendent in the education department responsible for Aboriginal education. Part of her job was to advise us on the course and the program, but also . . . to find us jobs at the end of the three or four years' training . . . so she kept a close eye on us and helped us work out which part of the state we would want to go to. (Peter Buckskin, interview, 2015)

PETER BUCKSKIN

A Narungga man from the Yorke Peninsula in South Australia, Peter was the youngest appointment to the NAEC (1981–88).

While Peter was at school in South Australia, he stayed in an Aboriginal hostel with children who had come to school in Adelaide from the Kimberley. Peter became interested in teaching in the Kimberley, where he had completed some of the practical components of his degree at Nulungu Catholic College in Broome. Although he was offered a position with a public school, he decided to go back to the Catholic system and acquired a full-time role at Nulungu:

Figure 5.1. Peter Buckskin, 2016 (photo: Leanne Holt).

Part of my study was to do majors in remedial maths and teaching English as a second language, because I knew I wanted to go into a bush school and work with kids who probably would have issues in terms of their competencies around English and skills with maths. I participated in the community and indeed the Catholic community of Broome. Then I met a bloke called Stevie Albert. He had just become chairman of the NAEC. (Peter Buckskin, interview, 2015)

As May O'Brien and Stephen Albert watched Peter's career progression, they started to encourage him to consider membership of the NAEC. On an invitation from May, Peter became involved in a project in Sydney, where he had the opportunity to meet other Aboriginal and Torres Strait Islander teachers and education workers:

I went to a conference on the east coast in Sydney, meeting Margaret Valadian and Natascha McNamara . . . running a conference around Aboriginal leadership and promoting Aboriginal teachers in a sense. That's where I met Kaye Price . . . and later I got to meet Linda Burney; she was then an Aboriginal teacher, now politician, and that network kind of grew. (Peter Buckskin, interview, 2015)

A short time later, Peter returned home to Adelaide, as his grandfather was quite ill: 'He was like my first parent in a sense, so I wanted to go home and give something back to the family' (Peter Buckskin, 2015). Once back in Adelaide, Peter worked at the newly established Alternative School for Aboriginal secondary students and became involved in the SAAECG. Through this group, he reconnected with Paul Hughes, whom he had initially met at Mount Lawley Teachers College. Encouraged by Paul, he successfully applied for a position with the South Australian Department of Education and commenced a part-time position on the SAAECG:

There were few Aboriginal teachers in the space, so people were looking for leadership. People wanted to engage Aboriginal voices, and so they approached people like me to sit on the consultative committee . . . I continually learnt about the NAEC through Paul and the other state member, a wonderful old fella called George Tongerie, who is now passed. Uncle George wanted to retire because he was an old fella. He said, 'Hey, get the young fella to go on — Paul, you know, that young teacher at the school you met the other day. That dark-skinned bloke, you know.' (Peter Buckskin, interview, 2015)

Peter was elected as the SAAECG chairperson in 1983 at the age of twenty-three. At the time, the position was a part-time role. Peter then applied for a position on the NAEC and was successful:

In a sense, I was projected up in a leadership role probably far too early in my life I think now. We were doing some pretty heavy lifting with very little resources, but the NAEC members, people like Uncle George [Tongerie] who were experienced and came from a community welfare type portfolio, so were truly outside the education system ... [they were] bringing that community perspective into how you support kids from community welfare in the education system ... Around the table was this amazing group of people, who decided to take me under their wing. (Peter Buckskin, interview, 2015)

While on the NAEC, Peter continued working as an education officer in the South Australian Department of Education. Like other members of the NAEC, he was balancing working in the department, being chairperson of the AECG and being on the executive of the NAEC.

The chairperson position on the SAAECG then became a full-time role, which Peter filled. After his term as chairperson, he was appointed superintendent of schools for Aboriginal and Torres Strait Islander education in South Australia. Post-NAEC, Peter transferred to Canberra to work for the Aboriginal and Torres Strait Islander Commission (ATSIC) before being appointed assistant secretary and group manager in the Commonwealth Department of Education, Employment and Training in 1995. Peter remained in this position for eight years, working on reviews and with committees, and influencing policy development at the highest level. Over Peter's career, he also held senior positions responsible for broader Aboriginal and

Torres Strait Islander affairs. Peter continues to contribute strongly to education locally, nationally and internationally.

During this term, the Commonwealth Minister for Education, Senator Susan Ryan, had just been appointed and she was determined to develop strong relationships with all the members of the NAEC. She wanted to understand how she could support the committee on advancing Aboriginal and Torres Strait Islander higher education and took advantage of any opportunity to meet with members:

> When the minister would come into the state, it was Susan Ryan's practice to catch up with the NAEC people. So I'd be a very junior education officer, class one, and the minister would come in and everyone would know the minister is on the floor. Then I'd probably get half an hour with her in an office, in a very hierarchical Department of Education, where even in the tearoom, people had their seats and their particular cup. (Peter Buckskin, interview, 2015)

LAURIE PADMORE

A Dulguburra Yidinji man, Laurie was the third Tasmanian representative on the NAEC from 1982 to 1985 and was nominated through the TASAECG. Although living in Tasmania, he came from Queensland:

I was doing factory work then, and I was glad that I was able to do something for the people around Tasmania. I was just getting to know the different cultural aspects associated with Aboriginal people down here and I really admired them. I still really admire them for the tenacity, and for people like Patsy [Cameron] . . . and Kaye Price . . . I'm a mainlander; however, they told me at the time, they chose me in some respects because I was more or less a grassroots person. I thought that was an advantage but also a disadvantage because I had no idea about education. (Laurie Padmore, interview, 2013)

Just before joining the NAEC, Laurie commenced working with the Tasmanian Department of Education as a home school liaison officer, the second to be appointed in the state. He knew no communities or families in the area, so he joined the Tasmanian Aboriginal Centre to get a better understanding of the local communities. Here he met Roy Maynard, who was the legal aid officer at the centre at the time. Laurie later teamed up with Roy at the Aboriginal Education Unit and found his mentorship and cultural teachings as invaluable for his local knowledge. He worked closely with the TASAECG and adopted many educational programs and initiatives.

Laurie attributes his achievements, as well as the knowledge and confidence he gained, to the contacts and networks he built while on the NAEC. With the TASAECG and Patsy Cameron, he was active in negotiating funding for the first Aboriginal counsellor at the University of Tasmania. He was also responsible for developing mentoring and cultural programs with school students, as well as homework centres across the state. He actively encouraged parent involvement in education. Laurie remained in education for the rest of his career and had a real passion for working with youth and communities to achieve better educational outcomes.

Laurie was nervous about his first NAEC meeting because he had not previously been involved in education and did not have a good understanding of the related political aspects. Paul Hughes chaired the meeting, and Laurie recalls other members, such as Peter Buckskin, Victor Forrest and Maurie Ryan, making him feel comfortable:

> They're legends, those guys. I went there and they said, 'Look, mate, don't worry, you learn off us.' I was really amazed the way it all worked, the way Paul chaired. I really enjoyed it because they taught me so much. It really educated me politically and, when I came back, it gave me ideas. (Laurie Padmore, interview, 2013)

Figure 5.2. John Budby (NAEC 1985b, p. 2).

Specialist appointments

After the first term of the NAEC, five specialist positions were appointed through nominations by the Department of Education. In each NAEC term, different people with specific expertise contributed up-to-date knowledge related to modes of education or other relevant specialisations. The specialist positions were also responsible for leading relevant subgroups or studies aimed at advising the NAEC to allow informed discussion and decision-making. Specific studies were normally funded through the Education, Research and Development Committee in the Commonwealth Department of Education. An example of this was the investigation into bilingual education:

> We had two bilingual programs we were looking into to get a sense of how they worked, so we had to rely on Rex Granites' expertise, as one was at Yuendumu [Rex's country] and another program [was] in Maningrida. (Stephen Albert, interview, 2012)

Figure 5.3. Peter Buckskin, Laurie Padmore, Victor Forrest, Pat (Julia) Williamson, Mary Atkinson and Ted (Eric) Hampton at an NAEC meeting, 1981 (photo: NAEC archives).

The importance of the expert positions grew as the NAEC became more established and was responsible for providing advice on a wide range of operational and strategic educational matters to the Department of Education and the Department of Aboriginal Affairs. All specialist positions were not necessarily filled for each term of the NAEC; it was dependent on the accessibility of experts and the particular needs of the NAEC at the time of selection.

Pearl Duncan was a specialist appointment from 1981 to 1983. Pearl was a schoolteacher in Queensland and applied to become a member of the NAEC in its second term. She missed out to a person from Moree, New South Wales, who attended two meetings before resigning; Pearl was next in line. Pearl felt she had a lot to contribute to the NAEC: 'I was the first qualified Aboriginal schoolteacher in Australia to have graduated at a tertiary institution' (Pearl Duncan, interview, 2015). Additionally, she felt the NAEC could contribute a lot to her own knowledge and experience.

PEARL DUNCAN

Pearl, a Gamilaraay woman, grew up and went to school in a small town called Bundarra, New South Wales, where racism was rife. Pearl says she was very lucky growing up and she talks about the postmaster's wife taking an interest in her education:

I was always known at the school to be a bright girl. The teacher told my mother I was clever when I was in the kindergarten class. The postmaster's wife took an interest in me and encouraged my education. My mother knew everybody because she used to do everybody's housework. She was a single mother and she scrubbed floors and did the washing. In those days they didn't have washing machines or vacuum cleaners. So, everyone took an interest in me. But my mother would always say to me, 'Education is a right, not a privilege.' (Pearl Duncan, interview, 2015)

Pearl started her post-school education when she was seventeen through funding provided by the Australian Anglican Board of Missions. She attended Sydney Teachers College. Nearly twenty years later, Pearl completed a Bachelor of Letters in Anthropology (with Honours) at the Australian National University before completing a Master of Education at the University of Canberra in 1992. While studying in Canberra, she worked for the Department of Aboriginal Affairs and the Australian Institute of Aboriginal and Torres Strait Islander Studies as a research officer. Pearl commenced her teaching career in Yarrabah Aboriginal Community School in North Queensland and then, after two years, moved to a Torres Strait Islander community school, also in North Queensland: 'I worked in the Torres Strait. I loved the Torres Strait people and had a lovely time there. My nickname was Pearl of the Pacific' (Pearl Duncan, interview, 2015). *She later taught in Sydney metropolitan schools and did a stint teaching in Auckland, New Zealand:*

The only time I taught Aboriginal and Torres Strait Islander children was the two years at Yarrabah when I taught there, and the three years when I was in the Torres Strait. After that, it was just thirty years in public schools, mainly in Sydney. I taught mainly white children. So, I was removed from Aboriginal stuff at the time. I had no idea about how ill-educated Aboriginal people were. See, my mother had a good education and her aunties all had good education. They all were integrated, sort of. They knew their rights. I had no idea about these separate schools and things that they had, and how the schools were ill-equipped and some of the teachers weren't even properly qualified. I had no idea that was going on until I joined the NAEC — so it was good for me. (Pearl Duncan, interview, 2015)

Pearl had a seven-year appointment at Northern Rivers CAE (now Southern Cross University) and was head of the Aboriginal and Torres Strait Islander unit at Queensland University of Technology for four years. Pearl was a visiting scholar at prestigious international universities, such as The University of British Columbia in Canada. On her retirement, Pearl completed a doctorate at The University of Queensland. Her thesis was titled 'The role of Aboriginal humour in cultural survival and resistance' (Duncan 2014).

John Lester was also appointed as a specialist, with expertise in primary teaching. John, a Wonnarua man, was a member of the NAEC from 1980 to 1982. John's membership of the NAEC was encouraged by Bob Morgan, who, at that stage, was an acquaintance: 'I was asked if I was prepared to be nominated as a specialist representative in New South Wales . . . Bob [Morgan] . . . was representing New South Wales in his own right . . . I was to be appointed representing primary school teachers' (John Lester, interview, 2015). Just after John's appointment to the NAEC, he took up an acting position with the NSW Department of Education as the Aboriginal liaison officer. Later he was appointed to the upgraded role of senior education officer. The position also incorporated the role of executive officer of the NSWAECG, so it was vital to ensure these responsibilities blended into each other. However, with the further addition of the NAEC membership, it became a balancing act between the three responsibilities, which, although they complemented each other nicely, were all significant roles to undertake.

When the position for chairperson came up, John threw his hat in the ring, but he knew that Paul Hughes had also applied for the position:

> Paul was very cemented in Comm-Ed [Commonwealth education]; he was very well respected. He was doing a lot of work at that stage and he was most dominant. I used it [applying for chair] as a learning tool and to understand the politics. (John Lester, interview, 2015)

Although John was unsuccessful in his application for the chair position, Paul invited him to act as deputy chair for six months. John agreed to the position, which was located in Canberra. He recalls how difficult it was leaving his family in Sydney and how this experience influenced his future priorities:

> I remember I used to come home most weekends if I could. At the time, my son would have been about three . . . He was really upset one night and my wife said you better go in and see him. So, I went in, and he's crying and wouldn't go to sleep. I said, 'Well, what's up mate?' He looked me in the eye and he said, 'I don't want to go to sleep because I know when I go to sleep, you won't be here in the morning' . . . it just [tore] at my heart. I could have chased other things at a national level, but I chose [after the six months deputy chair appointment] to concentrate on New South Wales, which I had a genuine commitment to. (John Lester, interview, 2015)

JOHN LESTER

When John was appointed to the NAEC, he was a teacher at Darlington Primary School in inner-suburban Sydney. He had completed a Diploma of Teaching at the College of Advanced Education, Armidale (now University of New England), and had commenced his teaching career as the first Aboriginal teacher at Redfern Primary School before moving to Darlington, again as the first Aboriginal teacher:

After spending three years at Redfern, I transferred to Darlington because there were more Aboriginal kids there. There was a large percentage at Redfern Primary but most of the kids from 'The Block' [Aboriginal housing complex located in Redfern] went to Darlington . . . and that's the school I attended when I was a kid, so I wanted to go back there. (John Lester, interview, 2015)

Figure 5.4. John Lester, University of Newcastle, 2017 (photo: courtesy of University of Newcastle).

In 1983, after his NAEC membership, John became the first head of an Aboriginal unit at TAFE NSW, followed by other appointments in New South Wales. He was the first Aboriginal principal of a TAFE college at Griffith and then, through winning a promotion, he was appointed to another TAFE principal position at Grafton College before acting as assistant director at the Coffs Harbour Education Campus. He went on to assume senior roles in state Aboriginal education and Indigenous higher education.

When the call for applications for NAEC membership came out, Batchelor College in the Northern Territory nominated Didimain Uibo and encouraged her to apply:

> Someone from the college said we've nominated you, go along and just see if you like it or not . . . There was three representatives from the Northern Territory. There was Maurie Ryan, myself and, for a while, Rex Granites. (Didimain Uibo, interview, 2014)

At the time of her appointment to the NAEC, Didimain Uibo was living and studying at Batchelor College, south of Darwin (now Batchelor Institute of Indigenous Tertiary Education).

DIDIMAIN UIBO

Didimain had a strong focus on bicultural teaching and preparing Aboriginal students for positions in Aboriginal communities, such as teachers, teacher aides or police, or running their own businesses. She put a large emphasis on parent involvement to overcome the perception of school as a foreign environment, especially for Aboriginal students. She recalls her own school experience:

When ten o'clock came, the bell would go and I thought that meant home time. I used to go down to the beach. My brother said, 'Why did you run away from school?' I thought it was home time; the bell would ring, you would have morning tea and go home. So, next time, I stayed and then the second bell would go, I would have my lunch and go home. My brother would find me sitting on the beach playing. Slowly, my brother had to hold my hand and walk me back up until I knew when it was the right time to go home. (Didimain Uibo, interview, 2014)

Didimain went back to her community in 2000 to work as a teacher. While in the role, she was asked to act as the principal at Numbulwar School, which incorporated preschool, primary school, high school and post-secondary students. She acted in the principal role for twelve months before successfully applying for the position and staying on. Didimain was the principal of Numbulwar School for many years until, due to her health, she returned to Darwin and commenced employment with the Northern Territory Department of Education as a senior adviser in cross-cultural awareness for remote and urban teachers. She attended schools to promote Indigenous studies and provide Aboriginal educational advice.

CHAPTER 6

From consultation to involvement: raising our voices

> You've got to get people in the system — and the systems of running things. That was a big push from us because, as a member group, we knew how limited our long-term influence was. You were meeting five times or six times a year, for three days, various places; you needed to know that once you'd leave that there'd be someone behind you carrying on the message. (Colin Bourke, interview, 2013)

During its second term, the NAEC carried on the momentum of the previous term by enacting identified agendas. The NAEC was developing relationships with government based on respect and accountability. Its members were seen as experts in the advancement of Aboriginal and Torres Strait Islander education.

The primary focus of John Budby's term as chairperson was on expanding the initial *Rationale, Aims and Objectives in Aboriginal Education* (NAEC 1980b) document to include guidelines to ensure the visions of Aboriginal and Torres Strait Islander peoples could be actioned to result in increased educational outcomes at all levels. The document provided a comprehensive and co-ordinated policy position across all levels of Aboriginal and Torres Strait Islander education that ensured a shared vision and resulted in the first consolidated national policy for Aboriginal and Torres Strait Islander education.

Additionally, during this phase, there was much discussion on 'Aboriginalisation' — employing Aboriginal and Torres Strait Islander people across all government departments and appointing them to senior positions in the Department of Education and the Department of Aboriginal Affairs.

Fostering strong government relationships

The education portfolio within the Department of Education was extensive. It was responsible for universities and colleges of advanced education; schools' policy; Commonwealth involvement with TAFE; the Australian Capital Territory education system; the Schools Commission and the Tertiary Education Commission; Aboriginal and Torres Strait Islander education; and international education. To ensure Aboriginal and Torres Strait Islander education was a priority within the breadth of the education portfolio, it was crucial to have a strong and positive relationship with the ministers responsible for education.

The focus of Aboriginal and Torres Strait Islander education fitted well with the Australian Government's broader policies and presented a positive profile. The focus suited the government's current philosophy and the government was able to commit funding to ensure that actions were achieved to meet the priorities. This created a good starting position and a positive environment for the second term of the NAEC. There had been a time in the first couple of years of the NAEC's existence when government departments were reluctant to accept NAEC advice. However, after the NAEC registered a protest in 1978 to Senator John Carrick, the Minister for Education, and Mr Viner, the Minister for Aboriginal Affairs, the departments were instructed to be more responsive to the advice of the NAEC (Budby 1980a).

Achieving bipartisan government support for Aboriginal and Torres Strait Islander education was also vital to ensuring that longer-term policy and strategies were maintained, as a change of government could bring undone years of positive work:

> It's a very interesting area of social policy because it does demonstrate how long it takes to get this kind of policy reform embedded. You can get a key and energetic minister who says, we'll do it. The next person who comes in may not have that same view. Then the government, after a long time, changes and it goes back to, no, we're not going to do that. So, you make a bit of progress and then you're back again. For example, it is quite extraordinary in the year 2016 that we don't have totally embedded Aboriginal experience in its broader sense across all of our curricula. (Susan Ryan, interview, 2016)

The implementation of the AECGs had been successful and the AECG chairpersons had all developed strong connections with their state and territory ministers. Most of the chairpersons were also represented on the NAEC, which allowed a consistency in communications between state/territory and national perspectives. Although the relationships were productive, some jurisdictions found it harder than others to achieve a natural, progressive flow of outcomes. This was particularly the case in Queensland and the Northern Territory, which both had conservative governments at the time:

> The most difficult thing was the inequities between states, which we really didn't have any control over. The West [Western Australia] and the Territory, even Queensland, were always very hard because they had conservative governments and it was very hard to break through . . . I can remember, under John Budby's chairmanship, we were to visit the Torres Strait and . . . the trip was planned for us to fly in and land at Horn Island, before going to Thursday Island, then you had to get a boat across. The initial feedback was that the Queensland Government wouldn't approve people going, and that's hard to believe in this day and age. It was approved partly because John Budby was a Queenslander and he was critical — because Queensland was pretty archaic then, as was the Territory, and parts of the West. So, in the initial organising, there was talk about us not being able to go, but eventually it happened. It would have been too embarrassing. I mean, this is the '80s, for heaven's sake! It wasn't uncommon to happen in Queensland, because they were so accustomed to controlling people's movement. (Eleanor Bourke, interview, 2013)

Although the AECG chairpersons were a constant voice to the state departments of education, the NAEC would additionally meet with all the education ministers and superintendents of each jurisdiction, along with the Department of Aboriginal Affairs, at least twice a year. The Department of Aboriginal Affairs also had responsibility for funding educational programs, so the relationships needed to span both departments. Discussions were related to the key focus of the NAEC at any given time and reinforced the position of the AECGs to complement the national agenda. The NAEC supported what the states and territories were doing in terms of community consultation and involvement, community employment, and community bilingual or bicultural education. It demonstrated to all levels of government the strength and consistency of consolidated Aboriginal and Torres Strait Islander voices nationally. In addition to the community voices being established outside of government, the NAEC also saw the need for stronger Aboriginal and Torres Strait Islander voices from within government departments.

The strategy of Aboriginalisation

The NAEC identified the need for the Department of Education to employ Aboriginal and Torres Strait Islander peoples in positions across all areas of the department. It termed this strategy 'Aboriginalisation' (Stephen Albert, interview, 2012). The NAEC determined that Aboriginal and Torres Strait Islander peoples must move from a role of consultation to a position of involvement, including holding positions of inclusion and internal influence in decision-making.

The Commonwealth Department of Education responded positively to the recommended idea of Aboriginalisation and it was subsequently extended to the Department of Aboriginal Affairs. It did not take long for the idea to spread across Canberra and it was adopted by all government departments. Aboriginalisation was also the basis for one of the NAEC's primary initiatives: the appointment of 1000 Aboriginal teachers by 1990. However, Aboriginalisation would, to some extent, become detrimental to the initiative:

> Stephen [Albert] came up with the whole idea of 'Aboriginalising' . . . then the public service decided that's a good idea and started having schemes to try to get Aboriginal people working in the public service. These teachers that were graduating were going straight into public services; they were never in the classroom. That was something that we hadn't counted on, that we didn't get our teachers in the schools. (Pearl Duncan, interview, 2015)

Over time, Aboriginal and Torres Strait Islander peoples were successfully moving into senior positions across all areas of government. This not only had a positive effect on the provision of an Indigenous voice in the departments but also created pride in Aboriginal and Torres Strait Islander communities:

> I think all the Aboriginal education units were headed by non-Indigenous superintendents or directors. So, when I met people like Penny Tripcony, who was the first director of Aboriginal Education in the Victorian education system, I was real privileged to see Penny and her contribution. Because we thought she was quite special, in being this lone Aboriginal woman from Queensland but married into a big Victorian family, and then getting promoted to be a superintendent in the Victorian education system. (Peter Buckskin, interview, 2015)

The NAEC saw this as a necessity for the successful future of Aboriginal education:

> I thought that the next step for us is to start to win those jobs, to be the Aboriginal director versus the administration secretary, to be the directors of the units inside the Commonwealth education department. At the end of the day, I became Assistant Secretary and then Group Manager for a number of years in the Commonwealth, so I was well known for being the Aboriginal voice in that department. (Peter Buckskin, interview, 2015)

Members of the NAEC developed enough confidence to apply for senior government positions and were 'headhunted' for them. The mentorship and exposure to increasing Aboriginal and Torres Strait Islander leadership inspired the career aspirations of NAEC members and other Aboriginal and Torres Strait Islander peoples:

> We say you can't be what you can't see. I was lucky enough to be exposed from an early age, even undergraduate, to meet people like May O'Brien and Paul Hughes, Natascha McNamara, people like Margaret Valadian. (Peter Buckskin, interview, 2015)

Throughout the 1980s, employment of Aboriginal and Torres Strait Islander peoples in the public service increased substantially (Larkin 2013). Networking across the different departments was crucial to a holistic approach to Aboriginal and Torres Strait Islander advancement. However, although the number of Aboriginal and Torres Strait Islander public servants had increased, Aboriginal and Torres Strait Islander people were still very much a minority, and so continued social connections and professional mentorship to other Aboriginal and Torres Strait Islander people across government departments remained of high importance to their ongoing wellbeing:

> Being able to play guitar and entertain people, I think that was really good because, on the weekends, I'd bring the guitar and get everybody together, because in Canberra, they were now working in hostels, Department of Aboriginal Affairs, and they'd just started working in social security services. (Stephen Albert, interview, 2012)

The inclusion of clearer policy directives that resulted in employment targets being set and employment strategies being developed created a momentum for Aboriginal and Torres Strait Islander people to be employed in the public sector, including, and importantly, in roles of policy influence.

The first consolidated national policy for Aboriginal and Torres Strait Islander education

The second term of the NAEC placed a particularly strong focus on consultation for and development of a document that would advance aims, objectives and guidelines for Aboriginal and Torres Strait Islander education from an Aboriginal and Torres Strait Islander perspective. It would be the first holistic policy document developed by Aboriginal and Torres Strait Islander people in Australia that looked to advancing Aboriginal and Torres Strait Islander education in a Western system. It aimed to provide the foundations for future programs and policies, as well as to consolidate a vision for the NAEC and the Department of Education. The broad agendas of the NAEC created initial challenges and emphasised the importance of producing a document that specified a direction:

> We had the whole scope of education for Indigenous Australians and, at the time, there's basically nothing there. That's a huge challenge. Then how do you get it all together, how do you actually get it down as to what you want? Once we got our aims and objectives in place, I thought that straightened us up quite a lot. If we hadn't had them, we would have probably gone a bit hither and thither. (Colin Bourke, interview, 2013)

At the first meeting of the NAEC, a paper titled 'Aims in Aboriginal education', developed by the Departmental Advisory Group on Aboriginal Education (NAEC 1980b), had been tabled. Soon after, the NAEC resolved that it needed to develop a comprehensive paper to provide rationales, aims and objectives from an Aboriginal and Torres Strait Islander viewpoint. Between 1978 and 1979, consultation with more than 1000 Aboriginal and Torres Strait Islander communities occurred regarding the contents and expectations of such a document. In February 1980, at an NAEC meeting in Adelaide, the first draft of *Rationale, Aims and Objectives in Aboriginal Education* (NAEC 1980b) was received and passed. The first draft reinforced the need for a significant change in education for Aboriginal and Torres Strait Islander peoples:

> Since 1788, the Aborigines of Australia have been subjected in varying degrees to an education system which has aimed to rationalise their dispossession from the land, deprecate their culture and, in general, endeavour to make the indigenous people of this country lose their own rich cultural background and think, act and hold the same values as middle-class Europeans. (NAEC 1980b, p. 1)

The NAEC concluded that further consultation with Aboriginal and Torres Strait Islander peoples and education providers was still needed. The first draft document was used as a discussion paper and distributed to education groups and Aboriginal and Torres Strait Islander organisations and committees across all states and territories for consultation and input. Additionally, forums and summits were held to ensure sufficient opportunities were provided for Aboriginal and Torres Strait Islander voices to be heard. The further consultation aimed to expand on the first draft document by developing a plan of action linked to the aims and objectives. This became one of the priorities of the NAEC from 1980 through to 1985, when the final document was tabled (NAEC 1985b).

Colin Bourke played a significant role in the drafting of the first draft of the NAEC document.

COLIN BOURKE

Colin, a Gamilaraay man who grew up in Yarrawonga, Victoria, was an inaugural member of the NAEC and, at the time of his appointment, was the director of the Centre for Research into Aboriginal Affairs at Monash University. Colin was one of the first Aboriginal people to hold a senior position in a university, which was an outstanding achievement, considering the challenges he faced in attaining university qualifications:

Things have changed. I went to teachers college in 1955. At that time, I applied to go to Melbourne University. There was one university in Victoria... there was no commerce... there was only the arts stream or the science stream. To do science, you had to have two maths, pure calculus and pure maths, plus two sciences, physics and chemistry. To get into arts, you had to have a language and, in most cases in Australia, that was French. If you didn't have them, you couldn't go to university. There were no special entries that I know of. I couldn't go to Melbourne University because I didn't have French in Form 6. I didn't have any languages. So, things have changed there.

I went to the Geelong Teachers' College. It was good. I became a teacher, taught for twenty years before I became supervisor for Aboriginal education. I was the head teacher in 1957 in a little school and then I was principal of Lakeside — Whittlesea Primary School in '70, '72, and Lakeside Primary School '74 . . . and then I went to become a supervisor for Aboriginal education in '75. I started my degree in 1968. I couldn't get into commerce. I was teaching at Bacchus Marsh and I used to drive down two nights a week after school to Melbourne Uni. I had to redo my matric before I got in because it wasn't good enough. Twenty years teaching and I had to redo my matric because I didn't have any honours on my matric. Education was for the privileged and Aboriginal people weren't part of the privileged. See, when I was at school, if you got your merit, which was Year 8, you could leave school at fourteen and you were educated. That was in Yarrawonga, where I grew up. A Year 8 merit was it. There was no high school in Yarrawonga, so there was no provision for Aboriginal people to go to university until about '68. It was '68 when Aboriginal study grants had started. (Colin Bourke, interview, 2013)

Colin was a member of the NAEC for five years over two separate appointments. He later went on to complete a master's degree in education at the Canberra College of Advanced Education. He had been

Figure 6.1. Colin Bourke (second from left) with staff of Monash University where he was Director of the Centre for Research into Aboriginal Affairs from 1977–1981 (courtesy: Monash University).

> *employed as the general manager of the Aboriginal Development Commission and soon after acquired the role of Assistant Secretary for the Department of Aboriginal Affairs. Later he became deputy principal of the Australian Institute of Aboriginal and Torres Strait Islander Studies, before relocating to South Australia, where he led the Aboriginal task force at the South Australian Institute of Technology. When the institute merged with the University of South Australia, the task force became the School of Aboriginal and Islander Administration and, with Colin's leadership, evolved to become the faculty of Aboriginal and Torres Strait Islander studies, the first in any university in Australia. Colin retired from the University of South Australia in 1998 and at the time was acting deputy vice-chancellor. The same year, Colin was conferred the title of Emeritus Professor by the University of South Australia. Colin was the first Aboriginal principal in Victoria, the first Aboriginal Assistant Secretary, the first Aboriginal deputy vice-chancellor and the first chairperson of the Victorian AECG, of which he was also one of the founders.*

Bob Morgan highlights the contributions that Colin made to the NAEC and wider Aboriginal and Torres Strait Islander education agendas:

> Colin was quiet, unassuming, a really deep thinker . . . he's one of those unsung heroes and doesn't get enough of the recognition that I believe he deserves for his role in Aboriginal education, and he's a gun of a man. (Bob Morgan, interview, 2015)

The first draft document (NAEC 1980b) provided the foundation for policy discussion and workshops. After more than three years of consultation and research, the final document, *Philosophy, Aims and Policy Guidelines for Aboriginal and Torres Strait Islander Education*, was published in 1985 (NAEC 1985b). The final document included a philosophical viewpoint to inform the aims for the future of Aboriginal and Torres Strait Islander education from early childhood through to vocational and higher education.

At the core of this philosophical viewpoint were the following principles: education was the key to an ongoing existence for Aboriginal and Torres Strait Islander peoples; educational practices must consider Aboriginal and Torres Strait Islander epistemologies; the need for the acquisition of academic and technological skills should occur in conjunction with cultural identity and values; knowledge and understanding were needed by all Australians of the history and perspectives of Aboriginal and Torres Strait Islander peoples as traditional custodians of the land; cross-cultural programs were needed to promote the value of cultural diversity and the uniqueness of Aboriginal and Torres Strait Islander culture, enabling respectful and productive relationships between Indigenous and non-Indigenous people; involvement of Aboriginal and Torres Strait Islander people was necessary in policy development and decision-making; and the employment of Aboriginal and Torres Strait Islander people should occur across professions and service delivery (NAEC 1980b).

The aims that flowed on, reflective of these principles, were:

- That Aboriginal and Torres Strait Islander education be a process that builds on our cultural heritage and world view.
- That educational programs be developed using Aboriginal learning styles accompanied by an appropriate pedagogy.
- That Aboriginal and Torres Strait Islander education lead to personal development and the acquisition of the skills and learning needed for Australia today.
- That Australia as a whole become aware of its Aboriginal and Torres Strait Islander heritage and history.
- That Aboriginal and Torres Strait Islander Studies be the core of further cross-cultural studies for multicultural Australia.
- That Aboriginal and Torres Strait Islander peoples be given the responsibility for planning and implementing policies on Aboriginal education.
- That Aboriginal and Torres Strait Islander people be trained for and employed in education service delivery. (NAEC 1985b, p. 5)

The *Philosophy, Aims and Policy Guidelines for Aboriginal and Torres Strait Islander Education* (NAEC 1985b) provided guidelines in relation to each area of education, including: education for our community; curriculum; early childhood education; primary education; secondary education; bicultural bilingual education; tertiary education; Aboriginal and Torres Strait Islander studies; independent Aboriginal and Torres Strait Islander schools; research; and administration of Aboriginal and Torres Strait Islander education.

The NAEC (1985b) called for an Aboriginal and Torres Strait Islander education commission, as a statutory body, to be developed to include a wider membership than the existing NAEC and increased staffing. The NAEC determined that this would strengthen the outcomes conducive to the government priorities of consultation and self-determination. The commission would have overall responsibility for administering and evaluating Aboriginal and Torres Strait Islander education programs at all levels; training and employment of Aboriginal and Torres Strait Islander people in education; educational research; delivery of Commonwealth Aboriginal and Torres Strait Islander support programs, such as ABSTUDY; provision of expertise to education providers; monitoring educational outcomes; and the development and implementation of relevant policies.

The then minister for Education, Susan Ryan, recalls the controversy related to the establishment of another commission — the NAEC — when there was already a Schools Commission and a Tertiary Education Commission:

> I appointed Paul [Hughes] onto the Schools Commission. The possibility of an Aboriginal education commission had many strengths, but I imagine one of the reasons why it didn't progress was that there was a mood in the Cabinet I was a part of against commissions like the Schools Commission and the Tertiary Education Commission. There was resentment of them. My Cabinet colleagues took the view that the commissions go and they put in these reports about resource needs, expectations are raised and, of course, we were dealing with very tight budgeting. So, there was a feeling that they caused the government trouble because they raised hopes. I didn't share that concern because my view was that you want to have it all set up where they could provide advice, like, we can't do all that, but we can do this or this. But they were becoming unpopular.

> When I lost the education portfolio after the 1987 election, John Dawkins [Minister for Employment, Education and Training, 1987–91] was my replacement and he abolished the commissions. (Susan Ryan, interview, 2016)

Susan Ryan tabled the *Philosophy, Aims and Policy Guidelines for Aboriginal and Torres Strait Islander Education* (NAEC 1985b) document in parliament in 1985. In her parliamentary address, she stated:

> The NAEC is the government's principal adviser in the field of Aboriginal education. I value that advice very highly. In this report as in all its work, the NAEC has taken pains to ensure that its approach reflects Aboriginal community views, that its conclusions have been reached only after extensive consultation, and that its recommendations are directly related to the resolution of some of the practical, day-to-day problems facing Aboriginals. All honourable senators will appreciate the difficulties entailed in formulating a coherent and comprehensive set of aims and guidelines for all Aboriginal and Torres Strait Islander communities. We need to start, as the NAEC has started, by recognising the importance of diversity, of flexibility, of incremental progress and of continuing consultations with all the communities involved.
>
> Our policies in the field of Aboriginal education are developed in full cooperation with the states and the Northern Territory. We would also welcome cooperation from the Opposition and the Australian Democrats. The stakes are too high for any partisan squabbling or divisions. We all need to work together to make progress in the important areas the NAEC has outlined, since achievement of those aims will benefit and develop all Australians. (NAEC 1985a)

The document received bipartisan support and resulted in the first consolidated national policy for Aboriginal and Torres Strait Islander education. It was time for the government to respond effectively to the NAEC's policy directives — there would only be a sustainable future where the salt water and fresh water met.

CHAPTER 7

Introducing Aboriginal and Torres Strait Islander studies: a change in education

> We see the need for change in education for both Aboriginal and non-Aboriginal people, teachers and their children: to create an Australia where the values and cultures of both people thrive. (ACG 1975, p. 3)

Another primary focus of the second term of the NAEC was the appropriate application of Aboriginal studies[2] across the curriculum at all levels of education and teacher training. Against a background of ignorance, ethnocentrism and racism, a Commonwealth Aboriginal Studies Working Group (CASWG) was established to oversee the introduction of Aboriginal studies content in schools. This group met with varying levels of success; however, it represented an important change in Aboriginal and Torres Strait Islander education.

Eleanor Bourke recalls the discussions and debates regarding the meaning of Aboriginal studies:

---

[2] Documents and initiatives used the term Aboriginal Studies however related to Aboriginal and Torres Strait Islander histories and kowledges.

> We were right into debating what Aboriginal studies meant and the distinction between Aboriginal studies meaning teaching other Australians about things Aboriginal and then the need for something different for Aboriginal people in terms of knowing certain things about culture, but not necessarily wanting to have the same curriculum as non-Aboriginal people had. So that entire sort of debate was going on. (Eleanor Bourke, interview, 2013)

Offering Aboriginal and Torres Strait Islander studies to all students was seen as generating knowledge of the values, practices and histories of Aboriginal and Torres Strait Islander peoples and developing a better understanding of the culture clash that challenged Aboriginal and Torres Strait Islander peoples. On the other hand, the education of Aboriginal and Torres Strait Islander students demonstrated consideration for their culture and identity as well as the values and experiences they brought from their communities. The work of the ACG had provided a foundation for this study; it had argued that the education of Aboriginal and Torres Strait Islander students should equally value an Aboriginal and Western viewpoint:

> Aboriginal and Torres Strait Islander culture should be retained and ... Aboriginal identity should be actively developed through education. It is accepted that some parts of Aboriginal culture and folklore associated with survival in pre-European times should now be replaced with those skills which will allow the Aboriginal people to participate equally in the trade and professional areas of the Australian economy ... We are not prepared, however, to sacrifice social values such as responsibility for the well-being of others, sharing and non-destructive competition. These are a fundamental part of our identity. (ACG 1975, p. 4)

Throughout the 1980s, numerous national and state-led conferences and workshops, and research, focused on the implementation of Aboriginal studies in the education curriculum. In July 1980, the Australian Education Council, responsible for school curriculum, requested the establishment of the Commonwealth Aboriginal Studies Working Group. The terms of reference for the group were to 'Ascertain the extent and nature of

Aboriginal studies programs in the States and Territories' and to 'Identify areas of need' (CASWG 1982, p. 1).

The CASWG (1982) reported that its establishment was recommended as a result of an NAEC discussion paper, 'Teaching about Aboriginals and Torres Strait Islanders'. The NAEC paper was developed from views expressed at the 1978 National Aboriginal Studies Seminar in Alice Springs. The CASWG was set up in October 1980, chaired by John Budby, the then chairperson of the NAEC.

The NAEC and CASWG developed a draft statement on Aboriginal studies in 1981. This was informed by workshops and seminars that had been held in 1978 and 1979 (CASWG 1982) as a response to a report from the Select Committee on Aborigines and Torres Strait Islanders, chaired by Neville Bonner, who at the time was a Liberal Party senator, and the first Indigenous person in Australian parliament. In 1976, he had argued that the importance of Aboriginal studies for all Australians should be recognised (Bonner 1976). Aboriginal studies was high on the NAEC's agenda as a strategy for contributing to moving Australian society towards a true and accurate knowledge of Aboriginal and Torres Strait Islander peoples and communities, as Kaye Price explains:

> The whole need to have Aboriginal studies, of whatever version or style, was a big one. You can look back at the recommendations and look at the ones that were taken up and implemented, and maybe the kinds of things we said weren't new. But if you go back to Neville Bonner's first inquiry that he chaired, and his report, his committee recommended that there should be Aboriginal studies in every school curriculum. So, it wasn't new, but we were actually able to get in and do it as a group of people . . . I must admit I knew nothing about curriculum at that stage. I just taught what was in the Tasmanian curriculum. I didn't know anything about writing curriculum. At that time, we had the Curriculum Development Centre [CDC]. They would have a project going, so I would go and work and sit in these meetings. Having membership on the CDC subcommittee was important. I remember that the Aboriginal studies team at the Canberra region was meeting at that time and I can remember how

they'd written, 'Aboriginal Dreaming stories are like fairy stories'. (Kaye Price, interview, 2013)

The 1978 National Aboriginal Studies Seminar in Alice Springs had recommended that Aboriginal studies should be taught at all levels of education and embedded across the curriculum. The development of separate units and/or subjects was also recommended to ensure in-depth studies were undertaken (Schools Commission 1978). Similarly, the 1977 National Conference of Teachers of Aboriginal Children recommended that, 'Training institutions incorporate Aboriginal studies in all teacher education programmes as a fully integrated core element [and that] a working committee be established to examine the strategies involved' (Brumby & Green 1978, p. 56).

The 1981 draft statement by the NAEC and CASWG was used for consultation to allow both bodies to adopt a final policy position on embedding Aboriginal studies into the education curriculum for Indigenous and non-Indigenous students. The NAEC believed that Aboriginal studies should be part of an ongoing learning process throughout students' educational experience and not just isolated to a single unit of work:

> Aboriginal studies should never be seen as a simple unit of work which will be presented and completed in a given period. The area of Aboriginal studies must be seen as a continuous one which will involve all teachers and subject areas from early childhood education to tertiary. (CASWG 1982, p. 33)

The draft statement defined Aboriginal studies as having two important components:

(a) Develop an appreciation and understanding of cultural values;
(b) Explore the impact of the historical and cross-cultural contact and the effects this has had on contemporary Aboriginal life. (CASWG 1982, p. 34)

The draft statement also stipulated that Aboriginal and Torres Strait Islander peoples are best suited to pass on knowledge related to their own values and histories and, therefore, that teaching should be done by or in collaboration with Aboriginal and Torres Strait Islander people: 'We fought hard to get Aboriginal studies taught in the schools. So, we had Aboriginal Elders giving addresses in the schools. It was all new, novel, and exciting' (Pearl Duncan, interview, 2015). However, it was also a massive undertaking to have all Aboriginal studies taught by Aboriginal and Torres Strait Islander people:

> We would call ourselves the burned-out-blacks because, for starters, in some places, whether you like to admit it or not, there weren't Aboriginal people, so how can you get Aboriginal people to teach Aboriginal studies? And not all Aboriginal people know everything. (Kaye Price, interview, 2013)

The general lack of understanding of Aboriginal and Torres Strait Islander history and culture created tensions for Aboriginal and Torres Strait Islander students, which raised awareness of how important it was for educators to consider differences in lifestyles, values and practices:

> I think the emphasis to give a curriculum that would make Aboriginal people or make the population aware of where Aboriginal people fit into Australia was vital. I remember, in primary school, they started talking about things like Dick and Dora walking their dog on a chain, or on a lead. I said, what do they do this for? Because we don't — I had a dog and the dog had never been tied up in its life. Of course, the teacher then said to me, stop being disruptive. (Victor Forrest, interview, 2016)

A common debate was about whether schools were responsible for teaching Aboriginal studies to Aboriginal and Torres Strait Islander students. However, the NAEC was determined that Aboriginal and Torres Strait Islander people should have formal opportunities to learn about their identities and cultures, especially given the history of attempts at cultural genocide, and that some Aboriginal and Torres Strait Islander people struggled with their identity:

> The thing was, with Aboriginal studies, we would say everybody should do Aboriginal studies so they learn about the place and the people whose country they live in. And that was for non-Aboriginal people. And then

there's this culture and history, especially for us, growing up, and our history and our stories and how we do it, even Aboriginal people who think they don't know anything. When I was in charge of the Aboriginal and Torres Strait Islander Social Security central office, I ran a workshop for all the liaison officers in each state or major regional centre. We did it in New South Wales and most of the fellas in the group said they didn't know much. But when they started talking, they all had something different to offer; something that they knew or somebody that had an influence on them or somebody that they really valued and that was really interesting. Then the other thing that I did in that workshop, among other work-related sessions, is that we went to the New South Wales museum's warehouse. We had half a day to go up and look through the shelves, where they saw stuff that wasn't on display. The thing that impacted on me most was the scarred trees, something like a dozen scarred trees stuck away with the most beautiful geometric patterns you've ever seen. Everybody then was looking to see something that they can relate to. We only had half a day, but it really had a big impact on them. I like to think it had a good influence on them, because they were rapt in the course afterwards, but they were very wary at the beginning. That's all about them having their identity. (Eleanor Bourke, interview, 2013)

The 1982 *Report to the Australian Education Council*

The CASWG *Report to the Australian Education Council, March 1982* documented the audit of the quality and quantity of Aboriginal studies programs being offered and identified the following key issues: the extent of Aboriginal studies in schools; the policy aims and objectives of Aboriginal studies; the place of Aboriginal studies in school curriculum; the nature and content; staffing; material resources; and curriculum development.

A survey undertaken by the CASWG for the report had found that of the schools that responded, 13 per cent indicated that they had no related content at all; of the schools that did include Aboriginal studies, most content was concentrated between Years 3 and 6, with minimal inclusion in the other years. It was also evident that the content that was available was not taught as a separate curriculum; rather, it was embedded into social science and history studies (CASWG 1982, p. 110).

Some of the schools that had no content shared their reasons, which included not seeing relevance to the school environment; not having a high population of Aboriginal and Torres Strait Islander students; having a view that multicultural societies should teach unity and not single out ethnic groups; having a view that tribal schools have input from community and Elders; and pressures placed on the already expanded curriculum (CASWG 1982, p. 110). Racism was also cited as a reason for the lack of response by schools:

> Being a European-dominated and racist community, Aboriginal studies are not conducted at the school. Earlier attempts to introduce such activities resulted in unbelievable responses and pressures being brought to bear on the school and its staff. In the interests of survival no studies are conducted. (CASWG 1982, p. 111)

The CASWG report recommended that the Department of Aboriginal Affairs organise and fund a publicity campaign in collaboration with the NAEC to support the inclusion of Aboriginal studies in schools. It further recommended that consultation led by the NAEC and AECGs with Aboriginal and Torres Strait Islander communities needed to identify a community-led strategy to identify expectations related to the content and scope of Aboriginal studies. The Australian Education Council accepted the findings in the CASWG report shortly after it was tabled, endorsing the principle of integrating Aboriginal studies into the curriculum. By 1983, it seemed that most schools had attempted to embed Aboriginal studies at some level.

CHAPTER 8

Asserting a right to self-determination: the third term of the NAEC, 1983–85

> Aboriginal society has existed in Australia for over 40,000 years and provided for its members a unique social and educational system of learning . . . Nothing is more fundamental than the right of all Aboriginal children to an appropriate basic education, and the right of Aboriginal people to expect equity in education beyond the compulsory years of schooling. (Aboriginal Education Policy Task Force 1988, p. 1)

The years 1983 to 1985 saw a change of Australian government from a Liberal government to a Labor government. Throughout this period, the NAEC was named as principal adviser to the Minister for Education, Susan Ryan. This role increased the NAEC's responsibility for funding allocation and the national agenda. The NAEC had built respect and credibility with government leaders and was at the high point of its influence. It was starting to see results from its earlier work, which reflected the breadth and high level of work that was being undertaken.

During this term, the NAEC initiated a number of policy discussions and investigations that would be actioned in the next term of the NAEC. The voice of the NAEC as a primary adviser was very strong during this era and it continued to progress Aboriginal and Torres Strait

Islander people from a consultation role to that of genuine involvement in decision-making, including funding of Aboriginal and Torres Strait Islander education programs. Nonetheless, final responsibility for our own affairs was still to be achieved.

The third chairperson and members

In April 1983, Paul Hughes was appointed as the third chairperson of the NAEC. Concurrent with his appointment, which for the first time was on a full-time basis, a deputy chairperson positionced advertised and subsequently filled by Errol West.

Paul, a Yankunytjatjara/Narungga/Kaurna man, had already worked with the Department of Education and had also been an inaugural member of the NAEC. His experience and knowledge allowed him to consolidate the initial work of the NAEC and commence work towards longer-term strategies and policy positions. These were pinnacle points in the evolution of contemporary Aboriginal and Torres Strait Islander education.

An article in *Aboriginal Child at School* (Isles 1984), on role models in Aboriginal and Torres Strait Islander education, highlighted the importance of Paul's position as chairperson. The article describes the two exemption certificates hanging in Paul's office and the effects they have had on his life:

> The certificates declare that 'by reason of character and standard of intelligence and development', the subjects had earned unprovisional exemption and 'shall cease to be an Aborigine for the purpose of the said Act'.
>
> Paul Hughes, now chairman of the National Aboriginal Education Committee, received his certificate on 3 December 1952, when he was eight years old. His father, Tim, received his at the age of 38, after he had served in the AIF [Australian Imperial Force] during World War II and won the Military Medal during the Buna campaign in New Guinea. He served with the South Australian 2/10th infantry battalion.
>
> The Act has long since been repealed but Paul Hughes keeps the certificate as a reminder of being born 'a second class citizen' on the Point Pearce Aboriginal reserve. He grew up in Lucindale, a small farming

centre in [the] south-east of the state, where his father had been granted a Soldier Settler's farm on his return from the war. 'All of our people have something to prove; I suppose you could say it is simply two things. The first is that we are a people in our own right and the second is that we are second to none in our abilities if given a chance to do it.' (Isles 1984, pp. 7–8)

At the time of Paul's initial appointment as an inaugural member of the NAEC, he was an executive officer with the South Australian Department of Education. Paul reflects that most NAEC members were quite young considering the responsibility given to them:

> In '77, I was thirty-three when I first joined the committee, so under forty when I was chair. So people were [young] — we called Ethel Munn 'Mrs Munn' because we thought she was old, but she probably would have only been about fifty-two, fifty-three or something. Now as I approach being sixty-nine, fifty-three is a kid. (Paul Hughes, interview, 2013)

PAUL HUGHES

At the time of his appointment as chairperson, Paul was the director of Aboriginal Studies, director of the Teacher Education Centre and the co-ordinator of Aboriginal Teacher Education Programs at the South Australian College of Advanced Education. Prior to his membership of the NAEC, Paul had completed a Diploma of Teaching (Primary) at the Torrens College of Advanced Education and went on to

Figure 8.1. Paul Hughes (courtesy Kaye Price).

undertake an Advanced Diploma in Teaching (Aboriginal Studies) at the Adelaide College of Arts and Education. In 1979, he was the inaugural chairperson of the South Australian Aboriginal Education Consultative Committee (University of South Australia 2008). By the time he joined the NAEC, he had a broad range of educational experience nationally and internationally. Paul gained qualifications in community development at the Australian National University in 1974 before embarking on an international study tour of America and Canada to research Indian and Inuit teacher education programs. While he was chairperson, he was also appointed to a part-time position with the Schools Commission (Ryan 1983).

After his work with the NAEC, Paul graduated with a Master of Education from Harvard University. Paul was a professor at the University of South Australia at the time of his retirement. In recognition of his initial work with the NAEC, as well as his contribution to Aboriginal and Torres Strait Islander education over forty-three years, he was awarded an Honorary Doctorate of Letters from Flinders University. Paul's very significant contribution to Aboriginal and Torres Strait Islander education was also recognised when he was awarded a UNESCO Comenius Medal for Education Excellence, Citizen of Humanity, by the United Nations Human Rights Council and an Order of Australia in 1993. He is an emeritus professor of the University of South Australia (University of South Australia 2008). He continues to contribute to Aboriginal and Torres Strait Islander education through participation and leadership in committees, keynote addresses and publications, and through involvement in national strategies such as the More Aboriginal and Torres Strait Islander Teachers Initiative (MATSITI).

My most memorable moment was just being on the NAEC, being with the groups. Because it taught me what I know in terms of things over time. Admittedly, I'd been involved as the education officer for Aboriginal Affairs since 1972 here in South Australia. So, I'd had five years' experience running budgets and all the stuff here

> in South Australia, which was the biggest operation in the country at the time. So, I had a lot of experience, but getting with all the other mob, we just made it up as we went on. But getting together with other people and then trying to determine, well, what are we actually on about was the biggest deal of the whole lot. The times together were quite wonderful. We didn't have any opposition in the sense that it was all pretty much bipartisan. But under Susan Ryan was when it was allowed to grow the fastest and that was in the times of Australia when the whole business about self-determination and people's rights to be involved and do what they want to do were actually there, which made it a bit easier. So, the times were right for whatever we happened to be doing and we accidentally happened to be there. (Paul Hughes, interview, 2013)

Following her membership of the NAEC from 1979 to 1981, Kaye Price was appointed as executive officer of the NAEC from 1982 to 1984. Patsy Cameron recalls the first time that Kaye introduced herself to the NAEC at a meeting in Hobart in 1977. The local newspaper and radio station had reported on an NAEC meeting held in Tasmania:

> The article was talking about Aboriginal education in Tasmania, the neglect of Aboriginal kids in this state in terms of their education and what their aspirations and our aspirations were to be then. We also mentioned that we could only locate one Tasmanian Aboriginal teacher. That's when we first met Kaye Price. Kaye actually arrived at our accommodation that night . . . she said, 'Hey, here I am. I'm an Aboriginal teacher. I'm number two.' (Patsy Cameron, interview, 2013)

Kaye was nominated to the NAEC once Patsy's membership had expired. She was nominated by the Tasmanian Aboriginal Centre. Kaye recalls the first NAEC meeting she attended on Thursday Island in the Torres Strait:

> I'd lived in Tasmania all my life. I used to save up to go to Melbourne, so I could go to the art gallery once a year. And so, to go all the way from Hobart to Thursday Island was magic, because Patsy was also with me for

that meeting. As we went we collected people . . . John Thomas [NAEC member 1980] from Adelaide joined us in Melbourne and Hazel McKellar from Cunnamulla [in Queensland]. (Kaye Price, interview, 2013)

KAYE PRICE

When Kaye became a member of the NAEC, she was teaching in Hobart, having graduated with a Diploma of Teaching from the University of Tasmania. Throughout her career, Kaye continued building on her qualifications, completing a Bachelor of Education at Edith Cowan University, a Master of Education at the University of South Australia and, in 2007, a doctorate from the Australian National University. Kaye attributes much of her career aspirations to the NAEC:

Figure 8.2. Kaye Price, University of Tasmania, 2013 (photo: Leanne Holt).

I wouldn't be doing what I'm doing today if it hadn't been for the NAEC. I was a primary school teacher. I was going to do my time and become a principal and get a school near the sea. That was my aim in life. So, I'd have this school by the sea and then I'd retire, and I'd still be by the sea. That was my aim. You never thought about going on to Master's. (Kaye Price, interview, 2013)

After her term on the NAEC and her subsequent appointment as executive officer, Kaye Price accepted a role as section head of Aboriginal and Torres Strait Islander education at the Commonwealth Department of Education. She later went to the New South Wales Department of Education and completed short appointments with the NSWAECG before returning to Canberra to the Australian Capital Territory education department. Kaye moved into higher education, working as a lecturer, and was appointed as director of the Ngunnawal Centre, University of Canberra. She participated in major studies on Aboriginal education, published and edited many books and journal articles and, recently, has been a principal researcher in the MATSITI project with co-members of the NAEC Paul Hughes and Peter Buckskin.

At the same time as Kaye's appointment as executive officer, a research officer, Victor Forrest, also joined the NAEC secretariat. Victor, like Kaye, had just served a term as a member of the NAEC and was a representative of Western Australia when he took on the role of research officer.

The research officer was responsible for applying for grants, collating research for inquiries undertaken by the NAEC and reviewing submissions for Commonwealth grants:

> Part of my role was to review submissions for Commonwealth grants in the area where Aboriginal education, Aboriginal history or Aboriginal subjects were involved. I was the person who perused the application to see if, in fact, they were fair dinkum about doing something about

Figure 8.3. NAEC members, 1984 (NAEC archives).

Aboriginals. Making sure that the submission views were in line with the NAEC — not only regarding education for Aboriginal people but education of non-Aboriginal people to ensure they were looking at proper aspects of where improvements might be made for Aboriginal people. (Victor Forrest, interview, 2016)

VICTOR FORREST

Victor left his home on Mount Magnet Aboriginal Reserve in the Mid West region of Western Australia and moved to Perth at a young age: 'My last home with my parents was living on an Aboriginal Reserve at Mount Magnet. I left home with ten shillings in my pocket and a blanket' (Victor Forrest, interview, 2016). Victor realised very quickly that education was going to be an important aspect of his future:

I was virtually the third Aboriginal person to graduate from Curtin University — in those days, Western Australian Institute of Technology. So, education, I guess, was my way of looking at the world and saying, without the English language, without the white Australian education qualifications, Aboriginal people are doomed to rot in Hell for a very long time. Being a stubborn person, I thought, no. So, I went back to night school and that's how I got into education. Well, I finished a Bachelor of Arts degree at Curtin University and then I did a Graduate Diploma in Secondary Education. I was lecturing at Mount Lawley [CAE in Perth] in their Centre for Multicultural Studies. May O'Brien is a relative of mine and she was [a] member of the NAEC. At the same time, she was with Aboriginal Education, a section of the Western Australian Department of Education. So, when a vacancy arrived on the NAEC, I put in an application with mainly the support of people like May and Stephen Albert. Stephen had completed some of his early education in Perth, so I knew a lot of people involved in education. At that stage, the Western Australian Department of Education didn't have an Aboriginal Advisory Committee. From

[my] application, lo and behold, I was accepted and that's how I become a member. (Victor Forrest, interview, 2016)

Sometime after he resigned from the secretariat, Victor embarked on a law degree at the Australian National University. He graduated in 1993 and then, in 1994, graduated with a Regional Diploma in Legal Practice:

Now I'm admitted as a barrister and solicitor in the ACT and as a solicitor in New South Wales, and of course I'm on the roll on the High Court. People say to me, why did I do a law degree? I said, 'To keep myself out of jail and because of the high incarceration rate of Aboriginal people and Aboriginal children in Australia — education is the key.' (Victor Forrest, interview, 2016)

New specialist appointments to the NAEC were also identified, and Wendy Ludwig was appointed as a specialist in adult education. She continued as a member from 1983 to 1986.

WENDY LUDWIG

Wendy started teaching in 1980 at the Darwin Community College after completing a double diploma in community work and welfare work. While she was completing her diploma, she was funded by the Commonwealth Department of Education to attend the National Union of Students conference in Melbourne. It was here that she started developing her national networks with other educators, as it was at this conference that the National Aboriginal and Torres Strait Islander student union was proposed:

I met people like Michael Mansell, Mickey [Michael 'Mick'] Dodson and Jeannie Bell and we were hosted by Gary Foley. Bruce McGuiness and Stephen Albert were there too. (Wendy Ludwig, interview, 2016)

In 1981, she had the opportunity to attend the NAEC conference in Bendigo:

I attended an NAEC conference and was just blown away by all of these amazing people and being involved in so many different things. (Wendy Ludwig, interview, 2016)

Through her attendance and involvement in this conference and the networks she had established, she was nominated for a position on the NAEC:

I kept teaching and running a teacher ed enclave in what was then Darwin Institute. Darwin Community College had morphed into Darwin Institute of Technology, then University College of Queensland, to Northern Territory University and then Charles Darwin [University]. I resigned in 1989 and, in that time, I completed a degree and started a master's in education, again as an external student, juggling a child and work and study. I did my master's externally through Uni of New England and then I went to Queensland: twelve years as head of a faculty in a TAFE institute. (Wendy Ludwig, interview, 2016)

Following this role, she was appointed director of Employment Programs and worked with community organisations and long-term unemployed Aboriginal and Torres Strait Islander people in the areas of traineeships and cadets. It was a massive undertaking, working with staff from Palm Island up to Thursday Island, out to Doomadgee and to Mount Isa. Wendy later moved back to the Northern Territory and is currently Director of Operations at the Australian Centre for Indigenous Knowledges and Education at Charles Darwin University.

John Heath, a Biripai man, was appointed a member of the NAEC from 1984 to 1988.

JOHN HEATH

I was always interested in education — I was the third eldest of seven kids — the eldest boy with a Koori mother and white father. I enjoyed school and I did reasonably well. My parents separated for the last time towards the end of my Year 10, because of domestic violence and so on; it was all through our lives. I arranged to spend the last two years of my schooling with a mate of mine. They're not an Aboriginal family, but just in [a] housing commission area, so we shared the same little bedroom. I'm just relating that because it's an example of my determination to finish schooling. I was a recipient of a state bursary. In those days, they were payments to the disadvantaged people, and this was before ABSTUDY and ABSEC [Aboriginal Secondary Grants Program]. This provided further incentive to me, because I guess I felt that there was some belief in one's ability.

Figure 8.4. John Heath, 2018 (courtesy: University of New England).

I finished the HSC [Higher School Certificate] with fairly good results and I had this determination to teach, but I couldn't take up the teacher's scholarship because of the financial restrictions. It just wasn't enough when you didn't have a secure family base. At the end of 1969, I saw an ad in the paper — Aboriginal students who wanted to go to university could apply for ABSTUDY. This was a new scheme then; it had only been operating for one year, and so I applied and was awarded an Aboriginal study grant. In those days, university fees weren't free, so this study grant would pay for the fees and also give you a book allowance as a part-time student. I elected to do an arts degree [part-time while working as a cadet industrial engineer], and I structured it so that I could teach geography and economics. After graduating, I wanted to be a history and economics teacher but, in those days, you had the choice of either history and English, or geography and economics. I went on and did the DipEd [Diploma of Education], which meant I was a qualified secondary school teacher. After teaching at a Catholic college for eighteen months, I took up an appointment with Commonwealth education at ABSTUDY and ABSEC to administer both those programs.

Around the same time, the New South Wales Government had established an Aboriginal education advisory committee under some different name, but it had a few Aboriginal people on it. They then advertised in the press for Aboriginal educators who were interested to apply. You had to have the endorsement of an Aboriginal organisation, so the Awabakal [Aboriginal Co-operative] in Newcastle, of which I was a director and treasurer, nominated me. I became a member of that, which was the forerunner to the New South Wales AECG. I was then on the New South Wales AECG during the early stages of the NAEC, given that the AECG had emerged basically through the push of people like Stephen Albert. I left ABSTUDY in 1984 and took up a lecturing position at Newcastle College of Advanced Education . . . in those days, as with a lot of the other NAEC members I'm sure, we wore a lot of hats because we had to. At that stage in Newcastle, the only other Aboriginal person who was actively involved in Aboriginal advancement, or Aboriginal politics, who had a high-level formal education, was Bill Jonas [at the time, director, Newcastle Awabakal Aboriginal Co-op, before going on to be the Aboriginal and Torres Strait Islander Social Justice Commissioner]. Coincidently, Bill had been one of my teachers in secondary school. Then, through all of this, I was appointed to the NAEC. (John Heath, interview, 2016)

John still plays a significant role in education and Aboriginal and Torres Strait Islander affairs.

A change in government makes Aboriginal and Torres Strait Islander education a priority

The Labor Party, led by Bob Hawke, won the 1983 federal election. Continuing the commitment to self-determination for Aboriginal and Torres Strait Islander peoples, the party's policy statement (quoted in NAEC 1986b, p. 15) for the election declared:

> The aim of the Labor Government policies will be to ensure that . . . Aboriginals as a group have the possibility of self-determination. This will require structural change . . . Labor's program will be directed at creating a situation where Aboriginals can control basic services such as health, education, housing, so that they can come in a form and of a standard that meet Aboriginal needs as defined by Aboriginal people themselves.
>
> From the earliest attempts Government policies for Aboriginals have failed because they were not based on an understanding of Aboriginal culture and society and because Aboriginals were not involved in their formulation and did not want them. Programs in which Aboriginals determine their own needs and priorities are not only more equitable, they are more successful and cost effective.
>
> Labor's commitment to Aboriginal self-determination has two important implications for service policy. First the way federal funds are distributed is as important as what decisions are made. A program, however expertly devised, imposed on Aboriginals has very little chance of success. Aboriginals do not only want improved services but also control over them.

Under the new Labor government, Susan Ryan was appointed Minister for Education in 1983. Ryan was very committed to Aboriginal and Torres Strait Islander education and she recalls her first meeting with the NAEC, where she wanted to make a positive and respectful impression:

> I remember actually feeling a bit nervous about how it would go and whether they would accept my goodwill or whether they'd say this is all a waste of time: 'You guys never do anything.' People were saying, 'Oh, they're very tough,' but it turned out to be very professional. We talked about the aims and what we were going to do. In all these kinds of meetings, the language of the meeting can make a big difference to how everyone feels about it. I was very keen to demonstrate my respect and that this was a national committee of great significance to the government. But, on the other hand, you don't want to be pompous and sound as if you took yourself too seriously, but you certainly took them seriously. So, it was always a bit of a balance about language and so forth. But I remember saying to Peter Wilenski [Secretary, Department of Education] afterwards, 'Oh, that went well.' He said, 'Yes, minister.' He was relieved, too, because he was expecting some antagonism or something unrealistic like, we've got to have all this now otherwise we'll know you don't want to do anything. (Susan Ryan, interview, 2016)

Although the NAEC secretariat had been placed within the Department of Education, the change of government opened up renewed debate over its location. The NAEC and the Minister for Education wanted to ensure that Aboriginal and Torres Strait Islander education remained primarily in the education portfolio and not in the Department of Aboriginal Affairs. Charles (Charlie) Perkins had argued a case for Aboriginal and Torres Strait Islander education to be part of the wider Aboriginal affairs portfolio. The DAA funded early childhood and other special education programs, so it was a viable argument. Susan Ryan recalls the tension:

> Charlie wanted Aboriginal education to go to DAA and be in his domain. As much as I respected Charles, and I had known him for a very, very long time and I really respected him — I thought he was terrific and a great choice by Clyde [Holding, Minister for Aboriginal Affairs 1984–87] to make him head of the department — I said, 'Look, education is not like everything else. We've got to do it through the education bureaucracies and the other education ministers.' (Susan Ryan, interview, 2016)

In the end, it was concluded, with the agreement of the NAEC and the Minister for Education, that to get the attention and priorities it required, the NAEC should maintain its position in the education portfolio but act in an advisory capacity to the DAA:

> So, the transfer of Aboriginal funding came out of DAA, which I don't think Clyde [Holding] liked very much. I know that he didn't like it at all. To be part of that executive meeting in the Parliament House when Susan [Ryan] requested a meeting with the Minister for Aboriginal Affairs and the minister had to bring Charlie. Then they were given the instructions that this needs to be transferred and we had it signed off by the PM [prime minister]. So, to see that realised, I thought, 'Well, that's power.' (Peter Buckskin, interview, 2015)

The state challenges still remained; however, from a national perspective, Ryan was willing to do everything she could to ensure Aboriginal and Torres Strait Islander education was seen as a significant priority of the Australian Government. One of her strategies was to make it her business to meet with NAEC members when she was in their regions:

> It's not often that a minister will come and sit in your office and have a yarn, and that used to happen. We had regular meetings with the minister. We had regular meetings with Susan Ryan when she was minister and with John Dawkins [succeeded Susan Ryan]. We used to also have regular big meetings with the union. We knew everyone in the Australian Education Union then — they were, I think at the time, non-Aboriginal people. We'd have a meeting at ANU [Australian National University] with the NAEC, and the minister, such as John Dawkins, would come, or the shadow minister would come to those meetings. So, we must have been a pretty powerful group to have that happen. I suppose during the first five, six or seven years of the NAEC, there must've been an awful lot of goodwill. (Kaye Price, interview, 2013)

Susan Ryan claims it went beyond goodwill; it was a true reflection of the Labor government's commitment to ensuring Aboriginal and Torres Strait Islander education was a high priority:

> I had been Labor's shadow minister for Aboriginal Affairs from 1980 to 1983. So, in that time, I had come from kind of a standing start to being pretty well informed. I'd travelled a lot, particularly to remote

communities around the Kimberley and the Pilbara and Northern Territory. I had some contact with the urban Indigenous people and the regional services, but I had to educate myself about the conditions in the remote areas. So, when I became Minister for Education, I was determined to try and use that knowledge and awareness to make something happen in education. It fitted in with my central political philosophy, which is [that] education is the building block for everything else, whether it's women, whether it's migrant groups, whether it's Indigenous, whether it's children with disability — education is the thing that can overcome disadvantage. So, I decided to take the NAEC very seriously.

I remember having a discussion with the head of my department, a very well known policy thinker, Dr Peter Wilenski. He's just absolutely brilliant. He'd worked for Gough Whitlam as a young man when Gough was prime minister. I remember having the discussion about the NAEC, saying, 'It must be real, can't just be one of these groups we meet with occasionally.' Wilenski agreed with me because he was very committed to such things too. So I think that's how we started off. I was really in a good position because there were so many capable people on the NAEC. Paul Hughes, I thought, was absolutely brilliant. They were very experienced educators themselves, very successful, very effective. They really knew what they were talking about. So, I said, 'Okay, you advise me. As far as it's possible for me, I will accept that advice and implement it.' So, it started in a very positive and strong way. (Susan Ryan, interview, 2016)

The NAEC as principal adviser

The NAEC initially had been delegated an advisory capacity role to the Australian Government on Aboriginal and Torres Strait Islander education. In its new role as principal adviser, its level of influence was increased in determining government policy development and funding allocations. Being principal policy advisers completely changed the status of the NAEC:

> At one stage we were policy advisers. Then we formally got named as principal policy advisers. That's a big change . . . A policy adviser is one of a mob of people that they might want to talk to, including [the]

> Department of Aboriginal Affairs. The change came through most particularly at about the same time Susan Ryan got in and she made us the principal policy advisers. Now a principal policy adviser meant that you're even more principal than the Department of Aboriginal Affairs is, who was funding education. So that's a major sort of a change. John Parr was the head [Department of Education] when I was in there and he'd often come in and say, 'You're the principal policy advisers, what do we do now?' or 'We've got a problem here, what do you guys recommend?' (Paul Hughes, interview, 2013)

On 23 August 1983, Ryan announced, 'The government will enhance the capacity of the National Aboriginal Education Committee to enable it to carry out its role as the principal adviser on Aboriginal education . . . and the intention is to expand progressively the [NAEC's] functions' (NAEC 1986b, p. 15). A subsequent speech on behalf of the minister on 4 September 1983 declared, 'It is the ultimate aim of the Government to vest operational as well as policy responsibility for Aboriginal education in the National Aboriginal Education Committee' (NAEC 1986b, p. 16).

Throughout the 1980s, the NAEC provided comprehensive policy advice, information on programs, evaluation and research, as well as the allocation of resources across the nation. NAEC members ensured they were well prepared for any meetings with ministers or government officials, working out what questions needed to be asked and who was going to ask them. As time went on, the NAEC had built up a good level of knowledge on government systems, structures and politics, resulting in the confidence to make the most of its meetings:

> We used to have a rehearsal about who was going to say what and how you will say it. For example, we would get together before the DAA Superintendents' meeting. We rehearsed the whole thing; we probably were quite clever. We used to, I suppose, try to outmanoeuvre them. (Kaye Price, interview, 2013)

Susan Ryan relied heavily on the NAEC to provide the appropriate advice to ensure the engagement of parliamentary bipartisan support of Aboriginal and Torres Strait Islander education as a priority:

I was very grateful for the good open relationships. I really admired all those members, which is not true of every advisory committee a minister can have. But they were just excellent. I think the biggest value was putting Indigenous education as a top priority instead of a 'something else we have to worry about' kind of priority. Because of the standing of the NAEC and the quality of their ideas, it got a lot of attention; its importance was grasped for that period of time. It was a lot more than lip service. It was bipartisan, so it wasn't an area where I was attacked by the Opposition or anything like that. It really started when we were embedding objectives about Aboriginal education into teacher training and it became a major policy objective. We did that because of the calibre and the work of the NAEC. (Susan Ryan, interview, 2016)

Peter Buckskin recalls meeting Susan Ryan as one of his most memorable moments:

My most memorable moment was, I think, meeting Susan Ryan, shadow minister for Aboriginal Affairs, [in] one of the top boardrooms of the Woden tower. She came to see us just prior to the election. Even though I think we had strong support from some Liberal ministers, with my Labor leanings I was so impressed to meet Susan Ryan. I had heard about her. Teaching in Broome, I was a member of the Labor Party; I was junior vice-president. So, the then Opposition used to have forums for Northern Australia, which is anything over [the] 26th parallel, so they'd bring together the Labor constituents. Seeing a shadow person come ask us what we think the priorities are for a Hawke government and us influencing that; I think I did cartwheels nearly in my home community to find out on the night of the election that Labor had won. The next day, Susan became Minister for Education. We were so happy she was going to be minister, and so we just thought, 'Gee, you know, did we fall on our feet?' Again, she came straight back to us about the conversations she had whilst she was in Opposition; now she's minister, she kind of made it happen. To meet her in Opposition and then to meet her as a government minister was amazing. The . . . secretary of the department, Peter Wilenski, was all powerful. He would come to the NAEC and map out a relationship that was going to achieve the minister's agenda. She appointed me to the UNESCO [United Nations Educational, Scientific and Cultural Organization] Australia Commission, where I got to meet Gough Whitlam, who was our ambassador in Paris. So, that time was the most awesome time for me, when she appointed me to the UNESCO Commission. And to see that work, having the opportunities to get to Paris and, of course, to even meet the big man, God himself, Gough. But yeah, meeting Susan Ryan and the resulting outcomes of that relationship, not just with me but with the NAEC, was very memorable. (Peter Buckskin, interview, 2015)

The Commonwealth Department of Education and the DAA had close relationships with the NAEC, particularly in working together on policy and funding. With the establishment of the DAA in the early 1970s, Aboriginal education officers were established. Key people, such as the Aboriginal education officers, from both departments worked closely with the NAEC and sat in on certain parts of the NAEC meetings to provide input and to develop an understanding of the priorities and perspectives from an NAEC viewpoint:

> The Commonwealth education department were really supportive. There were Commonwealth education officers who worked directly with us. There were a number of them, and gradually more Indigenous than non-Indigenous — they worked profoundly positive[ly] with us. (John Lester, interview, 2016)

Although Aboriginal and Torres Strait Islander groups were quickly starting to emerge across the nation, the NAEC was the first one to be fully funded by the government to provide advice directly to the minister. The key was providing advice that had clear policy objectives that would be broadly understood. The policy directives had to be supported not just by Commonwealth departments but also state governments, educational institutions and related departments. Good relationships with all stakeholders were therefore integral to achieving progress.

In February 1984, the Commonwealth Minister for Education and the Minister for Aboriginal Affairs made a joint statement that the NAEC was to be involved in decision-making related to all aspects of Aboriginal and Torres Strait Islander education (NAEC 1984a). Additionally, to show the government's commitment, it announced the allocation of one hundred study awards with a living allowance of $150 per week for Aboriginal and Torres Strait Islander students over the age of twenty-five, which could be accessed in addition to the existing study grants (NAEC 1986b).

Increased power in determining funding priorities

Prior to the NAEC, the distribution of Commonwealth funding to the states and territories was based on applications that were largely influenced by state and territory interests and resources in Aboriginal and Torres Strait Islander education. South Australia was the first state to introduce a Department of Aboriginal Affairs and the presence of this office, with an Aboriginal appointment, had a big influence on the ongoing development of Aboriginal and Torres Strait Islander education programs. It also attracted significant funding. Paul Hughes was appointed as the first Aboriginal education officer:

> I was the only person outside of Canberra in a state office putting up schemes applying for money. We had the [Aboriginal] taskforce [South Australian Institute of Technology], we had the Aboriginal Community College and we had a couple of other bits and pieces around the place that were being funded. At one stage, as much as 28 per cent of the Commonwealth money came to South Australia . . . Gradually other states got their own offices but, for a long, long time, we held a quarter of the money here in South Australia. (Paul Hughes, interview, 2013)

The NAEC provided a more equitable solution to distributing monies from the Commonwealth. In the early stages of the NAEC, members were part of the discussions relating to the budget allocations and relevant programs, but as the NAEC evolved to become the principal adviser, there came a higher level of responsibility for making decisions related to the funding allocations. State committees and other stakeholders would nominate programs within their state or territory that required funding, along with justifications and priorities. The NAEC would assess all the proposals that were submitted from all states and territories. They would then prioritise the programs to be funded and determine the amount based on the national pool of funds available. The recommendations for funding distribution would then be made by the NAEC to the Commonwealth. Funding was distributed by both the Schools Commission and the Department of Aboriginal Affairs.

Given the number of valuable Aboriginal and Torres Strait Islander education programs being established, it was not possible to fund all of them at once. The NAEC therefore adopted a rotation system that would allow consideration of 'near-miss' programs in the next round. This provided the opportunity for more programs to receive funding. Even though this process was adopted, the programs were always recommended on a merit-based approach (Bob Morgan, interview, 2016).

The NAEC had high-level access to resources and information that allowed for the identification of programs that aligned with national and state priorities, as informed by the state and territory consultative committees and in consideration of special national programs:

> We used to run through the entire budgets. We got the entire proposed Cabinet in Confidence papers on budgets, which you'd never get nowadays. We knew the entire budget the DAA was planning to spend and we went through it with a fine-toothed comb and made recommendations, taking some off the top for national programs; deciding, for example, about the medical school — there were two universities in the running for that, Flinders and Newcastle. They were the two places that were proposing Aboriginal medical education at the time and we decided that the money should go to Newcastle. Other national projects that were being held around the place, the Aboriginal task force in Adelaide, things like that, we creamed them off the top. Even though we were all coming from different states and obviously wanted to get our own monies, we worked those things through and made decisions based on how [to] grow certain things and what needed to be done nationally. Then what was left over, and how would that be split up amongst the states? The states, because the consultative groups had discussions about what they were interested in as well, came down to the business of deciding what the priorities were for them. (Paul Hughes, interview, 2013)

One of the funding negotiations related to the development of the medical school at The University of Newcastle:

> The medical school, when they came to us and they wanted to start their medical programs, they came not to the NAEC, but to the AECG. The meeting that we had about that was up in Taree [New South Wales]. We had to endorse it before it went off to the NAEC and the federal government for funding. (Bob Morgan, interview, 2015)

To ensure there was an Aboriginal and Torres Strait Islander voice when discussing programs and other issues, the NAEC chairperson had membership on the Schools Commission board. This ensured that the messages and recommendations from the NAEC could be filtered through to other relevant discussions. In the end, the process resulted in a tripartite approach to funding allocations for Aboriginal and Torres Strait Islander education between the NAEC, the states/territories and the Commonwealth.

Initially, allocation of funding was relatively straightforward because there were fewer programs. However, as the priority of Aboriginal and Torres Strait Islander education strengthened and the funding grew, the politics and bureaucracy became more difficult. The funding became more competitive, resulting in tougher decisions being made, although there was a sense of equity and a strong belief in addressing disadvantage. It was accepted that, across Australia, most Aboriginal and Torres Strait Islander people were disadvantaged but, among those people, some were more disadvantaged than others. There were many considerations made when determining the allocation of funding; however, from an Aboriginal and Torres Strait Islander community perspective, the process undertaken by the NAEC provided a strong voice in the important process of decision-making.

CHAPTER 9

Setting strong priorities

> While white Australians may open their social and political arms to their black brothers, their economic sorting machine is certain to steer Aboriginals to the lower end of the employment spectrum. Such a process is linked with education, not so much in the effect that education has upon economic mobility, but through the educational barriers that prevent access to employment. (Hughes & Willmot 1982, p. 22)

The third term was a momentous time in the life of the NAEC. The NAEC saw the setting of strong priorities, resulting in real, tangible achievements in Aboriginal and Torres Strait Islander education and Aboriginal and Torres Strait Islander studies from early childhood through to higher education. One such priority was the need to increase Aboriginal and Torres Strait Islander participation in TAFE, particularly given concerns about the lack of progress in response to recommendations the ACG made in 1976 (NAEC Working Party 1984). Another priority was the significant policy target of 1000 Aboriginal and Torres Strait Islander teachers by 1990. A third priority was the development of support systems in tertiary institutions to help increase enrolments and retain Aboriginal and Torres Strait Islander students through to successful graduation. Additionally, this term saw the introduction of the concept of an Aboriginal and Torres Strait Islander pedagogy.

The 1984 *Technical and Further Education for Aborigines and Torres Strait Islanders: Participation and Self-Determination* report

In the mid-1970s, the *Aboriginal Access to and Use of Technical and Further Education* (ACG 1976) report had determined the need for more comprehensive research and advice regarding increasing Aboriginal and Torres Strait Islander participation in vocational education. Responding to this recommendation, the NAEC set up an NAEC TAFE Working Party (TAFEWP).

The TAFEWP was chaired by Eric Law, a member of the NAEC, and comprised expertise inside and outside the NAEC. The comprehensive TAFEWP report, *Technical and Further Education for Aborigines and Torres Strait Islanders: Participation and Self-Determination* (NAEC Working Party 1984), was the first step towards investigating the lack of Aboriginal and Torres Strait Islander students enrolling in TAFE. The paper was subsequently used for discussion and dialogue at a national conference held in Brisbane, 22–24 November 1984, and co-hosted by the NAEC and the TAFE Teachers Association.

The TAFEWP report aimed to provide an Aboriginal and Torres Strait Islander viewpoint and perspective that aligned with the government philosophy of consultation and self-determination. The TAFEWP believed that the TAFE system had shown little evidence of this:

> Despite statements of good intent about consultation and self-determination, unfortunately it has been the case at all levels, from the Commonwealth Government through to individual instructors, that non-Aboriginal people have generally given only lip service to this policy and have continued to make decisions affecting Aboriginal people, often with only scant regard for clearly stated Aboriginal wishes. (NAEC Working Party 1984, p. 6)

Figure 9.1. John Heath, Bob Morgan, Errol West and Bill Daniels (Department of Education) protest cuts to government funding for Aboriginal education at Sydney Technical College, 1986 (photo: Rick Stevens/Fairfax).

Although TAFE had been highlighted by both the ACG and the NAEC as an important sector, there was a continued belief by the Aboriginal people within the TAFE sector that schooling and higher education were prioritised in relation to resources and funding over TAFE:

> I've got to tell you for a long time that the VET [Vocational Education and Training] and the TAFE area were the poor cousins at the party. The absolute focus was at the schooling sector and the higher ed. sector. John Lester was one of the few people along with myself that hung in that VET space. Some of the activities or initiatives that were implemented and driven in the VET space really came as a result of agitation in terms of that broader kind of influence from people like John. (Wendy Ludwig, interview, 2016)

The TAFEWP emphasised the importance of recognising TAFE as an integral part of Aboriginal and Torres Strait Islander education, equal to the other sectors. It considered that TAFE was able to meet three fundamental needs of Aboriginal and Torres Strait Islander peoples in education:

- overcoming the inadequacy of the schooling which has been provided to Aborigines;
- providing an alternative for students who do not wish to continue school beyond the legal leaving age;
- providing the skills necessary for effective self-determination, particularly at a community level. (NAEC Working Party 1984, p. 9)

The TAFEWP further saw TAFE as vital in the advancement of Aboriginalisation. There was a feeling that Aboriginal and Torres Strait Islander peoples were having unreasonable expectations placed on them without being provided with the opportunity to develop their skills and qualifications effectively. Aboriginal and Torres Strait Islander peoples wanted an end result of being responsible for their own futures and actions. However, without appropriate development, the TAFEWP saw that this would remain a dream and that self-determination would remain an abstract phrase (NAEC Working Party 1984, p. 11).

The TAFEWP determined that there had been little evidence of any change based on the recommendations of the 1976 ACG report *Aboriginal Access to and Use of Technical and Further Education*. It was clear, however, that Aboriginal and Torres Strait Islander peoples saw TAFE as an essential education provider:

> To this day, I see that the VET environment is the springboard for so many of our people into employment, into further studies or [for] allowing people to gain a whole set of skills and knowledge that allow them to operate as better members of their family and community by being able to go to a shopping centre and read all the signs and in the shops being able to make sure they're not getting ripped off at the cash register; to have just those really basic fundamental skills for living in other communities and the current environments that we live in. (Wendy Ludwig, interview, 2016)

At an NAEC meeting in Darwin (15–19 July 1985), the outcomes of the TAFE study were discussed in addition to other reports from states and territories. The NAEC (1985a) press release for the meeting highlighted the concern and frustration delegates expressed relating to the slow progress of advancing Aboriginal and Torres Strait Islander education: 'They [educational outcomes] resemble those that are found in Third World countries. To have such a situation in Australia is intolerable' (NAEC 1985a, p. 1).

Susan Ryan also recalled experiencing Aboriginal and Torres Strait Islander people's frustrations and tensions relating to the slow progress:

> There was a very big conference that I went to up in Townsville. There were some people who weren't happy with anything, so it was a bit stormy. Again, I was a bit on my guard. They really wanted me to fight because, apart from the committee, there were a lot of other players who felt things weren't going fast enough for their views. Of course, there was quite a lot of competition to be on the committee. It was a bit of a turbulent atmosphere and I was a bit uneasy. But again, it seemed to go okay. (Susan Ryan, interview, 2016)

The meeting concluded with two major resolutions relating to responding to the needs of Aboriginal and Torres Strait Islander communities through TAFE services, as well as an extensive three-year study on the concept of Aboriginal and Torres Strait Islander pedagogy (NAEC 1985a).

1000 Aboriginal teachers by 1990

One of the NAEC's major policy initiatives was the 1000 Aboriginal teachers by 1990 initiative. The target, which was a key recommendation in the Hughes and Willmot (1979) NAEC submission to the National Inquiry into Teacher Education (NITE), was endorsed in the Auchmuty (1980) report, resulting in it becoming a focused priority for responding to the critical need for Aboriginal and Torres Strait Islander teachers nationally. The initiative had a conservative target, with the figure of parity more than double this figure. The number of qualified Aboriginal and Torres Strait Islander teachers had already grown from seventy-two in 1977 to 220 in 1982 (NAEC 1986a). In 1982, the national target had been distributed into state targets determined by the Aboriginal and Torres Strait Islander population and geographic spread (Table 9.1).

Table 9.1. Aboriginal and Torres Strait Islander teacher targets by state and territory, 1982 (NAEC 1986a, p. 13).

STATE	STATE TARGET	ACTUAL NUMBER
New South Wales	258	58
Victoria	80	27
Queensland	263	71
South Australia	70	13
Western Australia	173	43
Tasmania	16	1
Northern Territory	137	3
Australian Capital Territory	3	4
Total	**1000**	**220**

The Australian Government's 1984–87 triennium report on Aboriginal and Torres Strait Islander education (NAEC 1984a) flagged the 1000 Aboriginal teachers by 1990 initiative as the major priority. This initiative was anticipated to increase Aboriginal and Torres Strait Islander school student outcomes and overcome other issues such as student attendance rates. Colin Bourke provides an example of the educational issues in the Northern Territory that resulted from poor teacher quality:

> The lack of commitment of the education departments, especially in the Northern Territory, was terrible. They just hired anybody to teach. Teacher training was pathetic and the whole emphasis really was providing white programs and wondering why black kids didn't do any good. That's why we pushed so hard for teacher training of Indigenous people. (Colin Bourke, interview, 2013)

The NAEC raised an additional proposal for a national teaching service. This initiative was proposed as a means of attracting high-calibre teachers to schools with high Aboriginal and Torres Strait Islander enrolment rates, particularly regional and remote schools. Susan Ryan was very supportive of such a proposal but was unable to get enough government backing for it to come to fruition:

> A lot of the NAEC members were teachers who had a teacher background or a teacher training background, so together, we understood the needs. At one stage we considered the idea of having a national teaching service, which people could apply to come [to] from any of the state teaching services, but specifically to go and teach in Indigenous schools in the more remote areas. People would join the service for a period of time, maybe ... a five or ten-year commitment, but they would be very high-calibre teachers. Because, to tell you the truth ... when you travelled around the remote areas, where there were schools ... the calibre of the teachers was often not good. Some of the teachers were great, but a lot of the teachers were kind of dropouts; there was a lot of goodwill, but no concept of what the challenge was to get these kids from the desert and give them enough education so that they could have choices about their lives. So,

Figure 9.2. NAEC chairperson Paul Huges with Sue Hawley (centre) and executive officer Kaye Price, 1983 policy summit, Goulburn (courtesy *Goulburn Post*).

we were very concerned about teacher quality. We developed this idea, but it didn't proceed. The state departments [of education], of course, didn't like anything called national. I mean, it would have been a massive thing to set up. The Commonwealth would have had to fund the extra costs. I think the idea was, for example, if you came out of the New South Wales teaching service to join this service for ten years, that the supplementary costs would be borne by the Commonwealth but maybe the states would continue paying your base salary. But we couldn't take it forward and it never happened. (Susan Ryan, interview, 2016)

At the time, Hughes and Willmot (1982) raised a concern relating to the social and economic advancement of Aboriginal and Torres Strait Islander peoples, and suggested that the increase in Aboriginal and Torres Strait Islander people in professions such as teaching would contribute to the economic and social advancement of Aboriginal and Torres Strait Islander communities, both in gaining their own educational qualifications and empowering students to continue to engage in education.

Hughes and Willmot (1982) concluded that the employment of Aboriginal and Torres Strait Islander teacher aides had been one of the most successful strategies so far in improving the educational outcomes of students. However, the employment of 1000 Aboriginal and Torres Strait Islander teachers by 1990 was seen as critical in taking the inclusion of Aboriginal and Torres Strait Islander peoples in education to the next level: 'As far as Aboriginal children are concerned, the thousand teachers will have a profound effect on their self-image and on their aspirations towards finding a place in Australian society' (Hughes & Willmot 1982, p. 22).

In 1983, the NAEC convened the eighth National Aboriginal Education Conference at Riverina CAE, Goulburn, New South Wales. The conference, titled 'NAEC Summit — Policy Development', ran over 3–9 September and focused on the 1000 Aboriginal teachers by 1990 initiative. One hundred Aboriginal and Torres Strait Islander people had been selected to attend the summit, with twenty participants each from the early childhood, primary, secondary, TAFE and university sectors. This representation provided the opportunity for a broad range of voices from each sector to contribute to discussions and agendas: 'That was proper consultation, in my view. We ran two conferences doing that' (Paul Hughes, interview, 2013). In addition to Aboriginal and Torres Strait Islander educators and experts, representation was encouraged from tertiary institutions and relevant government agencies.

The aim of the conference was to discuss the draft policy statement on the training of Aboriginal and Torres Strait Islander teachers developed by Hughes, Forrest and Sherwood in consultation with the wider NAEC Committee (NAEC 1986a). As a result of the conference and wider consultation, the NAEC determined that the current programs offered to increase teacher education outcomes would at best result in the completed training of 500 Aboriginal teachers by 1990. To harness formal support from the government towards achieving the 1000 Aboriginal teachers' initiative, the NAEC tabled the *Policy Statement on Teacher Education for Aborigines and Torres Strait Islanders* (NAEC 1986a) with the Department of Education. The target created a shared vision for the NAEC, government and tertiary institutions and provided the opportunity for much-needed discussion and action: 'The teacher project was the biggest success of the whole lot. The selling of policy about Aboriginal involvement, the creation of structures, and to get people involved in the discussions, was a big deal' (Paul Hughes, interview, 2013).

The goal of seeing 1000 Aboriginal and Torres Strait Islander teachers graduate by 1990 was reached in its target year of 1990 — a real achievement for the NAEC; however, many did not end up in the classroom:

> Unfortunately, our 1000 teachers were got, but not all of them stayed teaching. They all went off into various other walks of life in quite large numbers, which is good in the long run for Indigenous affairs, but it wasn't having an impact in the schools that we'd hoped it would have. (Colin Bourke, interview, 2013)

> With the 1000 teachers, we were trying to grow people in terms of knowledge, so we got more of our own people educated to be able to educate the next lot, and so on. But, now, it's actually following that through in some sort of detail. But it's understandable when you look back on it. If you get somebody with a qualification, a teacher's qualification, they're

going to get snapped up to do other things, because nobody else had anything. That led to a whole pile of other teacher education–type programs and so on and eventually led to that whole business of any person turning up at a university automatically being given a per capita amount of money that allowed for the development of enclaves, that later became support centres and became collections of people. (Paul Hughes, interview, 2013)

The 1985 *Support Systems for Aboriginal Students in Higher Education Institutions* report

The 1000 Aboriginal teachers by 1990 initiative stimulated much movement during the third term of the NAEC. Emphasis was placed on the development of enclaves in universities to create safe spaces as a major resource to ensure access, retention and success of Aboriginal and Torres Strait Islander students.

In 1985, the Commonwealth Tertiary Education Commission, in consultation with the NAEC, commissioned a study into support mechanisms in tertiary institutions. The study was led by Deirdre Jordan and its report, *Support Systems for Aboriginal Students in Higher Education Institutions*, was published in December 1985 (Jordan & Howard 1985). The study subsequently informed policy-making and funding decisions.

Teacher training programs for Aboriginal and Torres Strait Islander peoples had commenced in the mid-1970s, before the introduction of the 1000 Aboriginal teachers by 1990 initiative. The three existing programs referred to in the Hughes and Willmot (1979) NITE submission were assessed as good practice to be expanded. The teacher training programs were primarily supported by university enclaves and it was determined that the enclaves played a significant role in attracting, retaining and graduating Aboriginal and Torres Strait Islander teacher education students (Jordan & Howard 1985, p. 34).

The existing Aboriginal and Torres Strait Islander teacher education programs had been introduced as part of affirmative action programs. In 1976, the Mount Lawley campus of the Western Australian CAE (now

Figure 9.3. Students of Monash University's Orientation Scheme for Aborigines, 1987 (courtesy: Monash University).

Edith Cowan University) introduced the first Aboriginal and Islander Tertiary Education Program (AITEP) to encourage access to the diploma of teaching (primary) program through a special entry pathway. This was soon followed in 1977 by special programs developed by the Townsville CAE (now James Cook University), the CAE having been established in 1973, and The Torrens CAE (now the University of South Australia) in 1978. The South Australian Institute of Technology (amalgamated later with the CAE to form the University of South Australia) had already introduced a South Australian Aboriginal task force in 1973, which was attracting Aboriginal and Torres Strait Islander students from across Australia. Specific Aboriginal and Torres Strait Islander entry programs, including enclaves, were gradually being introduced to provide personal, social and academic support (Jordan & Howard 1985, p. 39):

> People like Paul [Hughes] and others in the NAEC had been involved in developing the Aboriginal task force for the South Australian Institute of Technology, the AITEP Aboriginal Teacher Education Programs

that took off in Townsville, Mount Lawley here in Western Australia. They influenced it when they were doing work around the . . . Schools Commission working groups . . . prior to the inception of the NAEC. So, you had those people getting together as a loose collective of people that then started to be the very first members of the NAEC. Some only did one or two terms, but it got voices in the higher education sector because they were connected with the [Commonwealth] Aboriginal Affairs department and others were working in the Department of Education at the time. They were able to assist the government in setting up things like the task force to increase the access and numbers of Aboriginal people around teaching, social work and public administration. (Peter Buckskin, interview, 2015)

Special entry programs were crucial to meeting the target of 1000 Aboriginal and Torres Strait Islander teachers by 1990. The school system had poor outcomes in relation to Aboriginal and Torres Strait Islander peoples, resulting in most not receiving a Year 12 certificate (Jordan & Howard 1985). Additionally, only small numbers of Aboriginal and Torres Strait Islander people had graduated from tertiary programs, creating a lack of awareness or aspiration for tertiary study:

We weren't getting our people through Year 12, so we just teased [adjusted] the entry. We said when our people are older, they are wiser, they will study harder. So, we tried this special entry and we were getting everybody to do that. (Stephen Albert, interview, 2012)

The special entry programs primarily focused on mature age students (Jordan & Howard 1985). The entry programs considered other attributes, in addition to academic qualifications, that would contribute to success in tertiary programs. In some instances, they included extended time for completion, academic preparation courses and tutoring (Jordan & Howard 1985, p. 46). Once special entry programs were adopted, it became obvious that further support services would be required to ensure students succeeded in unfamiliar tertiary learning environments. Exposure to a Western-dominant learning environment resulted in students feeling isolated. Having students with lower schooling levels and personal environments that were not conducive to tertiary study created the impetus for a space on campus that would counteract these challenges.

Hughes and Willmot (1979) had referred to these spaces as 'enclaves' in their *Report to the NAEC: The Education and Employment of Aboriginal and Torres Strait Islander Teachers*. The NAEC *Aborigines & Tertiary Education: A Framework for the 1985–1987 Triennium* report to the Minister for Education defined them as a place 'where Aboriginal students enrolled in standard courses within institutions are given additional support appropriate to their culture, lifestyles and educational background' (NAEC 1984a, p. 6). The report also noted the success that enclave programs had already achieved and, although wanting to maintain the momentum in teacher education, also encouraged institutions to roll out enclave programs to wider disciplines (NAEC 1984a):

> Enclaves were for all the students to go but, in the first instance, we were encouraging people into teacher training. But when other students were doing things like law, they used our resource, they came to our library, and that was putting a hub in all the universities. That was the creation of a place where people could come and feel comfortable, and so that when they would come to their lectures, they would do the same lectures, they had the same tutors, they came out with the same qualification. And that's the standard we wanted all the time. (Stephen Albert, interview, 2012)

One outcome proposed by Jordan and Howard (1985) was to change the naming of 'enclaves' to 'support systems'. This was based on the restrictions placed on the perception of services provided by an enclave, as well as identifying a name that would allow future growth. The study also proposed that institutions needed to maintain contact with the NAEC in establishing support systems, and it strongly recommended that institutions and the government should ensure adequate funding and resourcing of support systems (Jordan & Howard 1985, p. 52). It was recommended that institutions: appoint staff under the same guidelines and conditions as other institutional academic and administrative staff, and develop strategies to increase future opportunities and grow the Aboriginal and Torres Strait Islander tertiary workforce; provide a culturally appropriate space;

offer a broad range of student services to respond to personal, academic, financial and cultural needs; and implement an appropriate evaluation and review process developed in consultation with the NAEC (Jordan & Howard 1985, p. 57).

By 1985, when the study was undertaken, the majority of states and territories had support systems for Aboriginal and Torres Strait Islander students and, as a result, the enrolments of Aboriginal and Torres Strait Islander students at these institutions increased substantially. Aboriginal and Torres Strait Islander students increased from eighty-five Indigenous students before the introduction of enclaves to 551 after the implementation of enclaves or support systems. As the CAEs were amalgamated with universities in the mid to late 1980s, the enclaves and support systems automatically became part of the university structures.

The NAEC recommended to the Australian Government that an allocation of funding was needed to allow negotiation with all tertiary institutions across Australia about the adoption of enclave programs or student support systems. NAEC members were delegated to carry out these negotiations with CAEs and universities, in collaboration with the AECGs:

> The 1000 teachers by 1990 became the catchcry of the movement and it opened up tertiary education — CAEs and universities — for Aboriginal people. I became the NAEC tertiary education person. My role was to negotiate with all the universities around setting up programs and, because we controlled the funding, if you didn't think they were genuine, I would either recommend that they be supported or not. Then the members would debate that around the table. We were articulating aspirations and ideas that [have] since [become] realities — including these spaces at universities. We used to call them enclaves and, for all intents and purposes, that [is] what they were. They were surrounded by an often alien and sometimes antagonistic group of people. Some of the universities didn't want us to be a part of their system; but for the fact that we funded them, they wouldn't have used their own funding. Every university, the NAEC would have to negotiate mostly around that notion of 1000 teachers. But all the universities had to be convinced that what we were proposing didn't threaten their standards. (Bob Morgan, interview, 2015)

Towards an Aboriginal pedagogy and epistemology: the final NAEC conference

The last conference, and probably the most talked about, was the ninth conference, 'NAEC: Epistemology and Pedagogy', held in 1985. It was held at the Wirrina Conference Centre in South Australia under the chairmanship of Paul Hughes. The conference was attended by more than 200 participants and Paul provided the opening speech:

> I made a speech saying if we're going to be in education, we may want to talk some of the language — curriculum, epistemology, pedagogy and so on. The skits that were done at the Thursday night dinner were quite marvellous and wonderful. But people got rolling; people got talking about a whole pile of things. So we were building a national movement by people getting together. But they were all different people all the time, so it took a long while and it just happened that way. Those things were very important, the social bits and pieces and get-togethers. (Paul Hughes, interview, 2013)

The conference provided a safe space for Aboriginal and Torres Strait Islander peoples to discuss their priorities, values, philosophies and practices. It was also a safe space for learning new knowledges, sharing experiences and articulating views:

> It was the first time that a lot of discussion was held around the notion of pedagogy and epistemology. A lot of people that attended had no idea what that meant, so they were talking about 'patting doggies' and all this type of stuff. We just laughed; it was good laughter. No one was trying to be intellectually superior, but we were just saying that we were doing this stuff in our own way. White fellas talk and call it pedagogy and epistemology. Well, that's just another way of talking about the way that we create knowledge. How we do it sitting around a campfire, or we're talking about it in our yarning circles, and all that type of stuff. It's the same thing, just a different name. So, we got into those discussions and they were great. (Bob Morgan, interview, 2015)

Prior to the conference, Paul Hughes (1984) published a paper titled 'A call for an Aboriginal pedagogy'. The paper provided a good preamble for the conference, discussing the challenges to date of the education system in its failure to recognise the differences between Indigenous and Western epistemologies, which continued to result in detrimental educational experiences for Aboriginal and Torres Strait Islander peoples:

> We reject the common belief that it is our society's fault that we have not succeeded. That thinking is a classic 'deficit hypothesis' . . . We contend — in academic terms — that the Western systems are based on an epistemology that is not in any significant way an Aboriginal epistemological base and therefore inappropriate for Aborigines. (Hughes 1984, p. 20)

Hughes suggested that teachers needed to have a greater understanding of the diverse aspects of Aboriginal and Torres Strait Islander communities and traditional pedagogy. Western knowledges needed to be combined with Aboriginal and Torres Strait Islander knowledges, drawing on the strengths of students, including spatial ways of learning. The paper highly recommended that teachers should work much more closely with Aboriginal and Torres Strait Islander teacher aides in setting culturally appropriate curriculum and methods of teaching. The paper concluded:

> The NAEC strongly urges dialogue and involvement between schools and Aboriginal communities. We envisage an Australia which finds its true heart and soul by a discovery of Australia's Indigenous culture. We urge manifestations of Aboriginality in all Australian schools . . . Only when educators are able to provide an education system in tune with our culture will we be able to take our place with dignity as the descendants of the original inhabitants of this country. We firmly believe that only when this country accepts and understands Aboriginal and Torres Strait Island[er] peoples, past and present — only then will Australia achieve a true nationhood. The NAEC is more than willing to play its part in achieving that goal. (Hughes 1984, p. 22)

The conferences were forums that created both an awareness of the NAEC and its priorities among the wider community and a strong network for the NAEC to ensure effective consultation and inclusion. They assisted in building a national movement for Aboriginal and Torres Strait Islander education. One of the main challenges of the NAEC conferences was that participants varied each year, so that at times it was difficult to maintain good momentum or consistency in discussion. However, overall, they were extremely successful forums that were re-established after the NAEC was disbanded:

> To be able to hear what other people were doing but also to have a collective response to particular issues and have an agreed position on particular things; an agreed set of targets that you could then go back to your various institutions and say, 'At the national conference, this is a priority that was set by the Aboriginal people from across the country. This is where we want to go. This is what we want to see.' You had a Commonwealth Government that was prepared to put dollars into it and enter into negotiations at a state and territory level with the particular agencies around implementing targets, priorities and strategies. The national conference was good in that sense. It was also back in those days where there wasn't that many of us around, so the people that were involved in all of those different levels of the education and training journey were fairly thinly dispersed and fighting big battles, doing breakthrough stuff that had never been done before. And so that was pretty hectic, so having an opportunity once a year to get together with your own mob was just so important for us as Indigenous people. To collectively get together and just share stories and recharge your batteries and support each other and have a good balance between serious business and fun, singing and dancing. All of those other things that are really important for our survival and have a balance across all of those different aspects of our lives — that was really important to us as well. (Wendy Ludwig, interview, 2016)

This term of the NAEC initiated a number of policy discussions and investigations that would be actioned in the next term. The fresh water and salt water had merged. A healthy and sustainable environment had been achieved. The challenge now would be to keep the environment nourished to ensure it remained healthy and did not stagnate.

CHAPTER 10

Consolidating Aboriginal education policy: the final term of the NAEC, 1986–89

> The true essence of Aboriginal education is the right of Aboriginal people to imagine our own 'dreaming' and to have access to the skills, knowledge and wisdom to help to not only define this 'dreaming', but also to capture it and to make it happen. (Bob Morgan, interview, 2016)

The third term of the NAEC had seen its status transition from a broad advisory committee to principal adviser to the Commonwealth Minister for Education. This paved the way for the next level of advancement towards the development of policy statements and guidelines that would provide a strong foundation to move Aboriginal and Torres Strait Islander education agendas forward.

In its fourth and final term, the NAEC, in consultation with community, developed a range of polices from early childhood to higher education to inform current practice; these policies would also be used by the Aboriginal Education Policy Task Force in providing recommendations towards a national Aboriginal education policy.

The fourth chairperson

At the end of 1985 and leading up to the recruitment of the fourth chairperson, the Commonwealth Minister for Education floated the idea with the NAEC to appoint a female chairperson:

> Senator Ryan, who was the minister, didn't want to appoint a male, as there had already been three male chairs. A subcommittee of the women [NAEC] went to visit Susan Ryan and said, 'No, we just want to find who is the best person for the job, male or female.' That's how Errol [West] won the job. (Paul Hughes, interview, 2013)

In conjunction with Errol West's appointment as the fourth NAEC chairperson, Lynette Crocker was appointed as the first female deputy chairperson. Errol West had been the deputy chairperson in the previous term of the NAEC:

> Errol West was born in Launceston, Tasmania on 20.6.1947. His traditional lineage is [the] Emeratta tribe of Northern Tasmania. His spirit to be was created on the islands of his ancestors who were annihilated, and the remaining descendants were dispossessed in the Bass Strait area. Errol received only five years of formal education . . . in numerous schools on the islands and mainland of Tasmania. He accompanied his mother and father as they followed the cycle of seasonal work open to Aborigines in the late forties and early fifties. With the support and constant encouragement of his family, he re-entered education and studied to be a primary school teacher. (Williams 2013, p. 51)

ERROL WEST

Errol West (2000) introduces himself, in the third person, in his doctoral thesis:

The primary storyteller is a late middle-aged male, who spent his formative years living on a government mission, on Cape Barren Island. He went to segregated primary schools and never formally completed education above grade six in the government schooling system, and was never enrolled into secondary schooling, either systematic or non-systematic. Since those days, he has successfully completed a Diploma in Primary Teaching, converted a Bachelor of Education to a master's degree (by research) and is currently a doctoral candidate, which is how I finally met him. (West 2000, p. 18)

Figure 10.1. Errol West (NAEC archives).

Aboriginal people of Tasmania were not eradicated, as misguidedly recorded by some early historians, although the cultural genocide that was inflicted on their people has had long-term effects, as it has for Aboriginal and Torres Strait Islander peoples across the whole of Australia. This is highlighted in Errol's statement above in which he credits the journey of his doctorate as a means to explore or find himself. He has now rejoined the spirit world.

As a young man in the early 1970s, Errol West wrote a poem, 'The Moon Birds of Big Dog Island', that illuminates harm as a result of cultural dislocation and identity. It illustrates how Errol, as an Aboriginal man, through his own identity, was passionate about Aboriginal education and the advancement of Aboriginal people:

There is no one to teach me the songs that bring the Moon
Bird, the fish or any other things that make me what I am.
No old woman to mend my spirit by preaching my culture to me
—No old man with the knowledge to paint my being.
The spectre of the past is what dwells within —
I search my memory of early days to try to make my presence real,

significant, whole.

I use my childhood memories of places, people and words to re-create my identity. (West, cited in Scutter 2001)

After the NAEC, Errol's academic work became nationally and internationally recognised, primarily in the fields of Aboriginal and Torres Strait Islander studies, curriculum development, and Indigenous methodologies and pedagogies. Errol held senior academic appointments at numerous universities, including James Cook University and the Australian National University and, finally, as Professor of Aboriginal Studies at Southern Cross University. He was unwavering in his passion to ensure social, restorative justice and the recognition of Aboriginal and Torres Strait Islander sovereignty.

The 1986 Policy Statement on Teacher Education for Aborigines and Torres Strait Islanders

The NAEC, when we first did our write-ups in 1986, we wrote about teacher education for one of the policy documents, the other policy document was about higher education and another was about TAFE. So, we talked about that whole further education of Aboriginal peoples, and part of that was to say, you've got to expand into a whole range of things. (Paul Hughes, interview, 2013)

The NAEC *Policy Statement on Teacher Education for Aborigines and Torres Strait Islanders* (hereafter, the Policy Statement on Teacher Education) made the point that effective education would require different kinds of thinking and practice to that which had hitherto been considered normal: 'It is the opinion of the National Aboriginal Education Committee that Aboriginal society is very different from non-Aboriginal society and applying normal Western methods does not always work' (NAEC 1986a, p. 11).

The variations in Aboriginal and Torres Strait Islander societies were categorised in a way that was similar to that in the EEATSIT report (Hughes & Willmot 1979, p. 145), namely traditional, rural non-traditional, urban and urban dispersed societies. The Policy Statement on Teacher Education suggested that teachers who came from a similar background to the children they taught would ensure relevant and effective teaching methods and content. Having teachers from similar backgrounds was seen to be:

> Necessary in order for the teachers to understand the values, lifestyles, languages and cultural methods for the children and their community. Such teachers working with the institutions of western society are invaluable to devising appropriate and effective bicultural education. (NAEC 1986a, p. 11)

To attain the objective of training more Aboriginal and Torres Strait Islander teachers from across all the community categories outlined by Hughes and Willmot (1979), more targeted teacher education programs needed to be established. The Policy Statement on Teacher Education used successful and proven international examples in Indigenous teacher education as a basis for determining good practice. The international programs provided evidence of success through special entry programs; specifically designed and delivered courses; allocation of funding to Indigenous education strategies; and an overall commitment by and support from government agencies. Another successful strategy was the provision of off-campus teacher training where Indigenous students could remain in their own communities. The Policy Statement on Teacher Education highlighted the importance of specialised approaches to both on-campus and off-campus teacher training options (NAEC 1986a).

The Policy Statement on Teacher Education also extended the initial calculations, which stated that to achieve good representation, there needed to be an extra 2964 Aboriginal and Torres Strait Islander teachers trained on top of the estimated 5518 teachers identified by the NAEC in 1982 (NAEC 1986a, p. 2) . The already ambitious target of 1000 Aboriginal and Torres Strait Islander teachers by 1990 required action to increase the access and retention of Aboriginal and Torres Strait Islander teaching students in tertiary institutions:

> Paul [Hughes] had this clear commitment to increase the numbers of Aboriginal teachers to go into university spaces or Colleges of Advanced Education. Clearly, they were models that other people replicated in other disciplines, in a sense. Then those Indigenous student support groups grew into centres, faculties, schools. There was a movement of the model. (Peter Buckskin, interview, 2015)

In relation to enclaves, the Policy Statement on Teacher Education stated that there must be a minimum of ten Aboriginal and Torres Strait Islander students for an enclave to become effective. Having a group of students studying together was seen as important because 'Enclave students feel far more at ease within the alien and somewhat disturbing environment of a college because they are in the company of other Aborigines' (NAEC 1986a, p. 14). The statement also declared that a larger group of Aboriginal and Torres Strait Islander students would provide peer support and encouragement to each other, bringing with them a range of backgrounds and experiences that would complement the support the staff of the enclave offered.

Another key feature of the enclave structure highlighted in the Policy Statement on Teacher Education was that the students needed to be enrolled in standard teacher education programs that would result in full teaching qualifications. Furthermore, even though an enclave program provided the opportunity to enter tertiary studies via a special entry route, Aboriginal and Torres Strait Islander students who entered university through a mainstream competitive entry process would still have access to the enclave. The statement argued that the enclaves created an important opportunity for the employment of Aboriginal and Torres Strait Islander staff who could share their professional perspectives and experiences within the institution (NAEC 1986a, p. 3).

> We brought in the pre-tertiary courses. We wanted the teachers, but we found that the teachers weren't qualified to enter tertiary. So, we got the support systems going in the universities, or CAEs in those days. We

got pre-tertiary courses in there, and that gave them entry to university, to teacher training . . . because they just weren't there. They just weren't educated. First of all, we started up the enclaves and then we started up the pre-tertiary courses. (Pearl Duncan, interview, 2015)

The NAEC (1986a) identified two approaches to training teachers in traditional communities. First, Batchelor College, in conjunction with the Darwin Community College in the Northern Territory, had developed a three-year Remote Area Teaching Education Program in which a large component was delivered onsite within communities. Although it attracted criticism from non-Indigenous teachers in regard to the quality of outcomes (Wendy Ludwig, interview, 2016), the NAEC recognised it as an innovative program that had not been attempted in any other state:

> To go to [a conference in] Melbourne and go to Swinburne and see this whole class of black people sitting together was just mind blowing for us. We went back to Darwin and we were talking to some of the Elders in the community . . . and telling them about what we saw in Melbourne with this whole group of students. We were talking about the content of the course that they were doing as well and that Koori studies was really important. We were talking about how amazing it would be to have a similar kind of thing happening in Darwin. The purpose of the Koori education program at Swinburne was also about getting people into not only study, but into jobs and things. That was the impetus for us to start up that first course in 1980. (Wendy Ludwig, interview, 2016)

The other community-based teacher training program was developed by independent Aboriginal and Torres Strait Islander schools as a type of in-service training for their traditional Aboriginal and Torres Strait Islander teachers. At first it was an informal arrangement to assist in up-skilling the teachers. However, after good results were achieved, a full-time teacher was appointed to train and supervise the training of teachers. The schools attempted to negotiate the use of this program to achieve more formal qualifications through the Darwin Community College.

In the *Education for Aborigines* (ACG 1975, p. 17) report, the ACG had highlighted the issue of untrained teachers in schools in the Torres Strait, and had recommended training Torres Strait Islander teachers and placing these schools under the jurisdiction of the Queensland Department of Education. A program had since been established for Torres Strait Islander teachers to travel to Cairns for intensive courses. However, the move to the Queensland curriculum came with challenges:

> I went to Murray Island and we met with community there and we found that people from the Torres Strait were being provided with teacher training. It was really what you would call a 'sandwich' course that they taught there, and then they would go to Cairns to do some weeks of training and then back. But that training only allowed them to teach in the Torres Strait; they couldn't teach anywhere else. We found that they had to follow the Queensland curriculum strictly, so that on 7 April, they will be doing this out of *Spell Well*. It was irrelevant to those kids on Murray Island. It was interesting too what it was actually like for a Torres Strait Islander person where the teachers did not recognise that the language they were speaking wasn't a first language. Those kids on Murray Island, they spoke their own language, but they were learning in English out of this *Spell Well* book. That was new to me and I think new to other people, how irrelevant the curriculum was . . . for our kids, Aboriginal kids and Torres Strait kids. There was this prescribed curriculum and that's what they were supposed to teach and that's, of course, what they were tested on. It seemed to me to be just wrong. (Kaye Price, interview, 2012)

The NAEC urged the Australian Government and Australian tertiary institutions to consider the development of appropriate programs to train Aboriginal teacher aides and assistants:

> Teacher aides and teaching assistants play vital roles but are restricted to assisting non-Aboriginal teachers and do not have the status or responsibilities of teachers. Consequently, with the exception of independent Aboriginal community schools, school planning and implementation are carried out by teachers who are 'outsiders' to each Aboriginal community. (NAEC 1986a, p. 20)

The offering of off-campus teacher education options, where Aboriginal and Torres Strait Islander aides and assistants could remain connected to their communities and cultural environments while gaining a credential, was believed to be a route towards increasing the participation and successful completion of teaching qualifications. The NAEC appealed to tertiary institutions to incorporate content in courses that related to Aboriginal and Torres Strait Islander people teaching in non-urban communities:

> The Committee believes that for a teacher to be successful in what is a different set of cultural mores and values within Aboriginal society, a teacher must be intimately aware of those mores and values. Aboriginal people are best suited to this situation. Current teacher programs fail to provide teachers with the understanding and skills necessary to teach in these areas. (NAEC 1986a, p. 16)

The 1986 *Policy Statement on Tertiary Education for Aborigines and Torres Strait Islanders*

In 1986, the introduction of the *Policy Statement on Tertiary Education for Aborigines and Torres Strait Islanders* (hereafter, the Policy Statement on Tertiary Education) (NAEC 1986b, p. 19) highlighted that 799 Aboriginal and Torres Strait Islander students were enrolled in programs in universities or CAEs at the beginning of the year, with the retention of 617 by the end of the year. Of these students, 285 were enrolled in courses other than teaching, with the majority being mature age students. The statement indicated the need for 3630 Aboriginal and Torres Strait Islander students to be enrolled to achieve parity with non-Indigenous students (NAEC 1986b, p. 19).

At the time the Policy Statement on Tertiary Education was developed, it was becoming obvious that Aboriginal and Torres Strait Islander teaching graduates were not being retained in the classroom. Only 50 per cent of Aboriginal and Torres Strait Islander teachers were retained in the classroom: 'The table incorporates the fact that approximately half the Aboriginal qualified teachers have left classroom teaching and consequently 2000 graduates are required' (NAEC 1986b, p. 21). The Policy Statement on Tertiary Education (NAEC 1986b, p. 21) set these estimates, noting a requirement of between 476 and 758 new enrolments each year dependent on a variable retention rate of between 50 and 80 per cent.

The NAEC ensured that there remained a strong government focus on teacher training to meet the targets set:

> Higher education was such a big focus when the teacher education policy was announced — pushed things into higher education and, when the teachers were trained, we did get the 1000 trained, but they didn't end up working in the schools; they ended up getting jobs in government. So, there was an impact there from those people being wherever they were, perhaps working in the universities, going into the centres. So, it was a different outcome from what was intended. (Eleanor Bourke, interview, 2013)

The Policy Statement on Tertiary Education focused on expanding the discipline of law and medicine to Aboriginal and Torres Strait Islander students. In 1983, only seven Aboriginal and Torres Strait Islander graduates were in law and two Aboriginal and Torres Strait Islander graduates were in medicine. The law graduates had come from The University of New South Wales and the medical graduates from The University of Newcastle. The NAEC determined that, under the current environment, it would take significant time to realise the impacts of these initiatives in law and medicine. The Policy Statement on Tertiary Education recommended that in negotiating the increase in enclaves, particular attention also needed to be given to programs supporting enrolments in these two disciplines. In the short term, funding was allocated towards specialised enclaves, one in eastern Australian and one in Western Australia:

> It must be remembered that Aboriginal customary law and traditional medical practices are of at the least equal importance in the lives of many Aboriginal people. There is increasing recognition by non-Aboriginal society of the validity of these forms of traditional learning and any program of special measures for Aborigines in tertiary education must include the facility to provide resources for these forms of learning. (NAEC 1986b, p. 24)

However, the Policy Statement on Tertiary Education explained that as the awareness of the current enclaves grew, an influx of applications from prospective Aboriginal and Torres Strait Islander students was already putting a strain on financial and staffing resources. This needed immediate attention:

> A framework must be established which enables institutions to cater adequately for the increased interest in higher education by Aborigines. The current situation is that a new enclave ... generates a demand which often cannot be met. People with the ability who were initially not given the opportunity to complete their schooling are forced to wait, perhaps a number of years. (NAEC 1986b, p. 27)

The Policy Statement on Tertiary Education affirmed that Aboriginal and Torres Strait Islander–specific bridging programs that were run through enclaves were successful; however, the strong view of the NAEC was that, in the longer term, Aboriginal and Torres Strait Islander students should be encouraged to enrol in standard courses (NAEC 1986b, p. 27).

The NAEC (1986b) also criticised the neglect of research and evaluation in Aboriginal and Torres Strait Islander education. It was recommended that research centres be established and funded:

> There is an increasing need for incorporating Aboriginal perspectives and approaches into various fields but few resources have been provided to 'develop and extend the art' in different fields. These Centres would be Centres of teaching and research in various aspects of Aboriginal Affairs ... outside the standard Western curricula. (NAEC 1986b, p. 36)

An education in Aboriginal studies would also be relevant for those teaching the programs:

> When I was studying law in the '90s, one lecturer had the audacity to say to the lecture theatre, 'When Australia was settled, we brought all the laws from England to Australia.' I interrupted and said, 'I can't believe this, Indigenous people, we had our own laws, our own language and our own culture long before you invaded us.' He was a little bit taken back and said, 'Yes, yes, I apologise, Aboriginal people were here.' But it shows that even in tertiary institutions, like the law school, and quite an

esteemed law school — it's not as if they've got fools there — but they were still teaching this sort of thing. (Victor Forrest, interview, 2016)

The number of Aboriginal and Torres Strait Islander organisations was rapidly increasing and there was a need for Aboriginal and Torres Strait Islander people to have the appropriate managerial skills to lead them and ensure these organisations were sustainable. Tertiary courses with a focus on these areas had already commenced but they needed to be expanded. The introduction of the first Aboriginal and Torres Strait Islander program run by the Darwin Community College, the Certificate in General Studies for Aborigines, was a good example of a course that opened up opportunities for Aboriginal and Torres Strait Islander people to embark on tertiary studies in business and management:

> It was a ground-breaking course that a whole heap of people in the community had spent the previous four or five years negotiating with the community college hierarchy around introducing . . . It was the first ever Indigenous-specific course to be run in that institution. We had to deal with all of the negative kind of comments about apartheid in reverse and 'It's a Mickey Mouse course' and 'It's not going to be anywhere near the equivalent of mainstream courses' and all of that stuff. The course came about as a result of the fact that we had lots and lots of our people sitting in low-level positions within the public service, both the NT and Commonwealth public service, and the need to increase the amount of Aboriginal people in higher-level positions. Also, the reality — that is still very much true today — that not a lot of our people were completing Year 12. (Wendy Ludwig, interview, 2016)

The Policy Statement on Tertiary Education concluded:

> All tertiary institutions should adopt, as policy, special entry requirements; recognise that measures to assist Aborigines operating within their institutions are part of their responsibility for the operation of special programs; and should ensure that Aborigines participate in the general operation of the institutions, especially by employing Aboriginal people and appointing Aborigines to the governing bodies of institutions.

Education institutions should also have a policy of encouraging faculties to improve their courses by incorporating units and material reflecting Aboriginal learning and perspectives; in particular, to include units and materials reflecting Aboriginal values and needs where this will help to prepare teachers who will later teach Aboriginal children. (NAEC 1986b, p. 39)

The Aboriginal and Torres Strait Islander Pedagogy Project

The Aboriginal and Torres Strait Islander Pedagogy Project was a joint initiative of the NAEC, the Commonwealth Curriculum Development Centre, and the state and territory AECGs. The aim of the project was to review, identify and promote appropriate Aboriginal and Torres Strait Islander teaching and learning approaches and establish curriculum materials that would facilitate student learning at all levels of education (NAEC & CDC 1986). In determining the aim of appropriate pedagogy for Aboriginal and Torres Strait Islander students, the NAEC stated, 'An appropriate pedagogy should contain all the diverse elements that impact upon the learning of Aboriginal and Torres Strait Islander children' (NAEC & CDC 1986, p. 3).

The NAEC voiced concerns about the current school environment:

> The learning environment, which includes the school curriculum, its organisation, management and the hidden overt signals about what is acceptable and what is not has been traditionally viewed as foreign to Aboriginal and Torres Strait Islander students, their parents and community. (NAEC & CDC 1986, p. 3)

The research for the project included the distribution of discussion papers, commissioned action research undertaken in each state and territory, and the distribution of a questionnaire. However, generally there was a lack of information available to lead these types of projects and initiatives:

> Initially it was historical Aboriginal studies, post-colonisation. By the end of the NAEC, people started to get into the business of expanding

about Aboriginal knowledges and what people did inside of cultures and so on. Then the gradual movement of Aboriginal studies into Aboriginal perspectives, taking the information and putting it across the curriculum. Those things grew out of the NAEC, because we'd always said that there were different forms of Aboriginal studies: one was to know about the study as a whole and [another] was to have perspectives about it incorporated across the curriculum. Then the third arm of everything was the whole discussion about what sort of pedagogy do you need. I'm sure we spent a lot more time looking at information coming forward about bits and pieces, but nobody had done a whole lot of particular research about the best way to teach Aboriginal studies or the best way to teach Aboriginal kids. (Paul Hughes, interview, 2013)

The outcome of the project was the development of an Aboriginal and Torres Strait Islander Resource (NAEC & CDC 1986) that aimed to contribute to the improvement of teaching practices in schools and other educational institutions. The resource was launched by the Curriculum Development Centre in 1991 and included materials on both traditional and contemporary perspectives on Aboriginal and Torres Strait Islander studies, as well as examples and guidelines for the delivery of appropriate pedagogy (NAEC & CDC 1986).

The 1989 *National Policy Guidelines for Early Childhood Education*

In 1985, the NAEC appointed an Early Childhood Working Party to contribute to the development of Aboriginal and Torres Strait Islander early childhood education policy guidelines. The working party was chaired by Paul Hughes and consisted of Oriel Green, the early childhood specialist appointed to the NAEC; three members from the early childhood sections of various state departments of education; five further NAEC members; and one member of the NAEC secretariat.

Early in 1989, the NAEC published the *National Policy Guidelines for Early Childhood Education*. The aim of the document was to provide advice on developing an integrated system that would meet the needs of Aboriginal and Torres Strait Islander families and communities. The policy document was developed for the use of early childhood services and other stakeholders involved in the sector.

John Dawkins, Minister for Employment, Education and Training at the time, stated in the preface to the document, 'The position represented in this document is that Aboriginal [early childhood education] services should be delivered within a broader framework that actively promotes the emotional and psychological well-being of young Aboriginal people in Australia' (NAEC 1989, p. 2). Errol West, NAEC chairperson, and Lynette Crocker, deputy chairperson, further elaborated on behalf of the NAEC and the working party:

> We hope this document will enable educators and administrators to understand the importance of Early Childhood Education which recognises and utilises the cultural background and knowledge systems of young Aboriginal and Torres Strait Islander children. We believe that such understanding is essential to effect relevant and satisfactory learning and development for our children in the educative process. (NAEC 1989, p. 3)

To capture the holistic experience of early childhood, including the transition from preschool to primary school, the working party elected to focus the paper on birth to eight years of age instead of the usual birth to five years. The working party had considered that birth to eight years was a time when development and attitudes towards education were vitally important. It was seen as integral that parents, community and educators work together to ensure that strong skills and attributes were developed to link classroom environments with children's identity and Indigeneity.

The NAEC (1989) considered that early childhood education was the foundational platform on which future educational success would be built for Aboriginal and Torres Strait Islander children. It was clear from evidence the Commonwealth Department of Education collected that Aboriginal and Torres Strait Islander children were not achieving success in the school system:

> While the problem of school failure has not yet been solved, the NAEC believe this situation can be reversed by the provision of appropriate, quality and culturally relevant Early Childhood Education.
>
> The NAEC believes that positive educational experiences for Aboriginal and Torres Strait Islander children in early childhood must build on the strengths and cultural traits they possess. This enables the maintenance and development of their cultural heritage, language and identity. (NAEC 1989, p. 6)

The working party believed that a major strategy for achieving better outcomes was to have Aboriginal and Torres Strait Islander people contribute to decision-making in early childhood education. This included all levels of the sector such as administration, policy development and, especially, teaching:

> The Indigenous teachers had to be part of the classroom instead of sharpening the pencil and doing other things, odd things. They had to be in the classroom and listening to students read and helping them to recognise words and, especially [in] early childhood, [this] is a must. That's where the learning starts and it's very important. Once the teachers get in the classroom, they had to be very cluey in their head what they needed to teach. For example, just don't think about, we do English all the time. Most of our Territory kids have English as the second language or third language even. Yeah, so [we] need to make it more easy access material for the students to work off and to see. If you talk about this, they wouldn't even think about what it is. It's a picture of some sort of colour. They might say the colour, they know what this is, but they have to see visual in front of them, not just told or written on the board. (Didimain Uibo, interview, 2014)

The NAEC advised that early childhood education must promote the holistic needs and wellbeing of Aboriginal and Torres Strait Islander children physically, emotionally, spiritually and cognitively (NAEC 1989, p. 9). It emphasised that education should ensure children maintain a positive self-image and self-concepts related to identity and culture. Children needed to have the opportunity to extend their linguistic skills and be in an environment that involved group, parent and community development.

The teaching of Aboriginal and Torres Strait Islander studies and the recognition of diverse Aboriginal and Torres Strait Islander cultures was also seen as an important aspect of the early childhood education experience.

The NAEC delivered a suite of exceptionally well-informed and well-developed policies from early childhood through to higher education, including the targeting of teacher training, early childhood, and an Aboriginal and Torres Strait Islander pedagogy. These policies were developed with a high level of consultation from Aboriginal and Torres Strait Islander communities and stakeholders nationally. They continued the push towards self-determination, calling for increased Aboriginal and Torres Strait Islander involvement in decision-making at all levels of education.

CHAPTER 11

The NAEC's final story

> So much has grown out of what we did — and there are a lot of us over the years, when you think of an eighteen-member committee and what's grown out of that. So much has grown out of what we did — and there are a lot of us over the years, when you think of an eighteen-member committee and what's grown out of that. The AEP [Aboriginal Education Policy] was implemented in 1989 . . . all of that came out of the NAEC. (Kaye Price, 2013)

The final stage of the NAEC saw the legislating of the Aboriginal Education Joint Policy Statement, which was a landmark in advancing Aboriginal and Torres Strait Islander education. However, many viewed it as a joint agreement between Commonwealth and state and territory governments, and not as a compact with Aboriginal and Torres Strait Islander communities. It was yet to be seen if the implementation strategy would maintain the same level of inclusion of Aboriginal and Torres Strait Islander peoples in determining the future of Aboriginal and Torres Strait Islander education.

This was the last term of the NAEC. The government no longer saw the need for its continuation and opted instead for internal bureaucratic structures. However, the NAEC had developed structural mechanisms that were built on relationships and networks that represented real community input into decision-making for Aboriginal and Torres Strait Islander education. While the new policy direction would maintain a practical future for Aboriginal and Torres Strait Islander education, the question remained about its ability to contribute to the self-empowerment of Aboriginal and Torres Strait Islander peoples and responsibility for our own futures.

The 1988 *Report of the Aboriginal Education Policy Task Force*

In April 1988, the Australian Government Minister for Employment, Education and Training, John Dawkins, and the Minister for Aboriginal Affairs, Gerry Hand, appointed an Aboriginal Education Policy Task Force. The task force, chaired by Paul Hughes, a former chairperson of the NAEC, was given the responsibility to develop a national Aboriginal and Torres Strait Islander education policy. Gerry Hand announced the establishment of the task force, stating: 'We have had enough enquiries into Aboriginal education . . . what we need now is action' (DEET 1988, p. 2).

As educational policies evolved, the Australian Government was drawing distinctions between Commonwealth and national policies, as articulated in 1987 with the National Policy for the Education of Girls in Australian Schools:

> There is a necessary distinction between Commonwealth and national policies in education. Commonwealth policies relate specifically to the objectives of the Commonwealth Government, such as those addressed through the Commonwealth's general resources programs and its specific purpose programs. In contrast, a national policy in education addresses matters of concern to the nation as a whole in which a comprehensive approach to policy development and implementation is adopted by school and system authorities across the nation. A national policy, based on principles of collaboration and partnership, necessarily involves commitment and agreement from the various parties responsible for schooling, including Commonwealth, State and Territory governments and non-government school authorities. (Schools Commission 1987, p. 11)

The Australian Government determined that a national Aboriginal and Torres Strait Islander education policy was needed to lead Aboriginal and Torres Strait Islander education into the future. The work of the NAEC, in collaboration with the AECGs, strongly contributed to the work of the task force: 'We ended up setting up a framework for a national policy, and the NAEC had a fair bit to do with that' (Laurie Padmore, interview, 2013).

Major policy documents from the past two terms of the NAEC proved particularly useful. There was, however, some disappointment in the NAEC executive about the organisation being overlooked to undertake the work allocated to the task force:

> Paul [Hughes], who got invited to chair a task force, included a number of ex-members of the NAEC ... At the time, I think Errol [West] and others felt there wasn't due respect paid for the movement and, if anything, those Aboriginal people should have referred that work to the NAEC. I understand, probably we had different types of roles to play, but I'm sure Errol felt, 'No, that was our job.' I thought, well, the NAEC will have an opportunity to respond to the report, and we did. We had [the] opportunity to be interviewed or write our own submissions to the task force. And I don't think the outcome, in terms of establishing the AEP [Aboriginal Education Policy] and then [the] whole suite of programs

Figure 11.1. Paul Hughes (right), chairperson of the National Education Policy Task Force, with Gerry Hand, Minister for Aboriginal Affairs, 1988 (DEET 1988, p. 2).

that supported the policy to give it life, would have been different if the NAEC did it themselves. We all came from that shared understanding, because we were such a small cohort of people and, as I said, it was green pastures, because there was nothing. (Peter Buckskin, interview, 2015)

Paul Hughes perceived the need to create a consolidated policy on Aboriginal and Torres Strait Islander education that the government would accept and that would link in with the government's budgeting structure:

> A lot of the policies that have been developed have been written from a philosophical viewpoint. They don't necessarily fit into the bureaucratic funding structure . . . A lot of the developments in Aboriginal education in this country have been the result of the work of the NAEC and the Aboriginal education consultative network. It has provided a way for people to get involved in the decision-making process and it's done a lot to push the cause and open up the debate . . . One of our problems is that we don't have a negotiated State–Commonwealth agreement in Aboriginal education that allows for confident, long-term budget and program processes. (DEET 1988, p. 2)

The Aboriginal Education Policy Task Force reinforced that Aboriginal and Torres Strait Islander peoples experienced a continued disadvantage in education. It explained that although there seemed to have been a significant increase in outcomes over the past twenty years, this resulted from a low starting point (Aboriginal Education Policy Taskforce 1988, p. 15). The 1986 education participation rates demonstrated the continued crisis of Aboriginal and Torres Strait Islander education (Table 11.1).

The Aboriginal Education Policy Task Force (1988) identified, through the previous commissioned reports and NAEC policy documents, that Aboriginal and Torres Strait Islander peoples place a high importance on education. However, barriers affecting the participation and success of Aboriginal and Torres Strait Islander students in education continued to occur, including:

- racial discrimination which serves to exacerbate the educational disadvantage faced by many Aboriginal people;

- social and cultural alienation which is experienced both in local communities and in schooling;
- economic disadvantage and poorer living standards which inhibit Aboriginal participation and impede successful completion of an education;
- geographical isolation which is experienced by the one-third of the Aboriginal population who live in Aboriginal townships, homeland communities or other small townships across the nation with less than 1000 inhabitants, and which are not as well provided for educationally as larger centres of population; and
- lack of co-ordination among services at various levels of government which effectively isolates many Aboriginal people from available education programs. (Aboriginal Education Policy Task Force 1988, p. 16)

The task force highlighted five comprehensive objectives that would overarch the recommendations towards a national Aboriginal and Torres Strait Islander education policy. The objectives were based on principles of self-determination and self-management by Aboriginal and Torres Strait Islander peoples in education. The objectives were:

- to achieve equity in the provision of education to all Aboriginal children, young people and adults by the year 2000;
- to assist Aboriginal parents and communities to be fully involved in the planning and provision of education for themselves and their children;
- to achieve parity in participation rates by Aboriginal people with those of other Australians in all stages of education;
- to achieve positive educational outcomes for Aboriginal people in schooling and tertiary education; and
- to improve the provision of education services across the nation at the local level. (Aboriginal Education Policy Task Force 1988, pp. 16–17)

The task force was given two months to complete the report and, in July 1988, the report was presented to the ministers with fifty-nine recommendations. The recommendations set the following priorities: Aboriginal community involvement; increased participation; positive educational outcomes; improving local provisions; strategies for schooling in all sectors of education, including early childhood, primary and secondary, tertiary education and higher education; and governance (Aboriginal Education Policy Task Force 1988, p. 19).

Table 11.1. Education participation rates, 1986 (Aboriginal Education Policy Task Force 1988, p. 9).

AGE GROUP	ABORIGINAL PEOPLE (PER CENT)	ALL AUSTRALIANS (PER CENT)
5–9 years (a)	88.2	99.0 (b)
10–15 years (a)	83.1	98.3
16–17 years	31.6	74.5
18–20 years	7.5	41.4
21–24 years	4.1	20.4
25 years and over	2.7	(c)

a) The education participation rates for those aged 5 to 9 years include school and preschool participation; for those aged 10 to 15 years, they include school participation only. The rates for all other age groups show participation in schooling, TAFE and higher education.
b) Estimated
c) For the age group 25–64 years only

The launch of the Aboriginal Education Policy

In October 1988, the Minister for Education, Employment and Training announced that, informed by the Aboriginal Education Policy Task Force (1988) report, the Commonwealth and the states and territories would develop a National Aboriginal and Torres Strait Islander Education Joint Policy Statement. This policy was to guide the progress of Aboriginal and Torres Strait Islander education into the future.

A Commonwealth Working Group was established to work towards the development of the joint policy statement. The working group was chaired by Mike Gallagher, first assistant secretary of Community and Aboriginal Programs, Division of the Department of Employment, Education and Training. To work in collaboration with the working group, an Aboriginal and Torres Strait Islander reference group was established. This was led by

Figure 11.2. Painting featured on the cover of the *National Review of Education for Aboriginal and Torres Strait Islander Peoples: Final Report*: 'The painting . . . is by Sarah Napangati Bruno, Paul Tjampitjinpa Bruno, Monica Nangala Robinson and Victor Tjungurrayi Robinson from Walungurru (Kintore), Northern Territory. It tells the story of the Pintupi people's experience of education and their hopes for the future in education' (Yunupingu 1995, p. i).

Lynette Crocker, the final chairperson of the NAEC, and Eleanor Bourke, deputy chairperson of the NAEC, with members from all AECGs across Australia. The reference group was to ensure Aboriginal and Torres Strait Islander input was maintained throughout the development of the joint policy statement (Department of Education 1989).

The draft joint policy statement was distributed to all relevant Commonwealth and state and territory departments of education for their comments and endorsement, before being tabled in the Australian Government Cabinet of Ministers. Although all departments provided positive input and endorsement, the Commonwealth Department of Aboriginal Affairs commented:

> While the draft policy paper alludes to the importance of Aboriginal involvement in the processes of educational decision-making, there is no clear indication of the strategies to achieve this aspect of the policy objective. The Department is fully aware of the call by Aboriginals throughout Australia for a comprehensive Commonwealth Education Policy . . . The proposal does no more than outline a policy and strategy for achieving educational outcomes in the Aboriginal community consistent with that available to all other Australians. (Department of Education 1989, Attach. C)

On 26 October 1989, the Minister for Employment, Education and Training launched the National Aboriginal and Torres Strait Islander Education Policy (DEET 1989, p. 2). The policy outlined twenty-one goals defined across four main themes: involvement, access, participation and outcomes.

The implementation of the joint policy statement put a strong emphasis on the involvement of Aboriginal and Torres Strait Islander people:

> For Aboriginal education purposes the effectiveness of schools, colleges and other educational institutions depends in large part on the degree to which Aboriginal people are involved in the process of educational decision-making. Without parental and community involvement there can be no guarantee that students will attend, that the curriculum will be relevant and that learning outcomes will be achieved. Aboriginal youth are also more likely to stay on and succeed at school when they see and have contact with Aboriginal people in professional roles in school, and are exposed to Aboriginal role models. (DEET 1989, p. 10)

Criticism of the joint policy statement

There was a lot of support from Aboriginal and Torres Strait Islander communities for a consolidated policy that would hold the Commonwealth and states and territories accountable for the ongoing commitment to Aboriginal and Torres Strait Islander education. However, there was also criticism relating to the final joint policy statement. The original task force report stated that:

> Equality for Aborigines in education is essential to the economic, social and cultural development of Aboriginal communities. Perhaps the most challenging issue of all is to ensure education is available to all Aboriginal people in a manner that reinforces rather than suppresses their unique cultural identity . . . Therefore the Government must commit itself to providing education opportunities to Aboriginal people regardless of where they live, and in a manner that is appropriate to the diverse cultural and social situations in which they live. (Aboriginal Education Policy Task Force 1988, p. 2)

In contrast, the launch and implementation documents for the National Aboriginal Education Policy summarised the visions of the task force as 'a concerted effort to achieve broad equity between Aboriginal people and other Australians in access, participation and outcomes in all stages of education' (Aboriginal Education Policy Task Force 1988, p. 2).

Bob Morgan, a member of the task force, as well as Herbert (Nugget) Coombs, a Labor Party policy writer on Aboriginal affairs, publicly described the policy as assimilationist (Coombs 1994, p. 171). Eleanor Bourke supported their arguments on the basis of the definition of assimilation and because the plan did not reflect some of the main points raised by the task force:

> The policy has been summarised into twenty-one goals. They deal with Aboriginal involvement, access, equity and outcomes. There is little emphasis on curriculum development or on matters Aboriginal. It offers little support for the maintenance and continued use of Aboriginal language and Aboriginal students appreciating their history, cultures and identity. The major thrust of the policy is to have Aboriginal students achieve the same as non-Aborigines. (Bourke 1991, p. 16)

Bob Morgan explained his angst regarding the department's interpretation of the task force report:

> The first report [original report tabled from the task force] that came from the task force was in my opinion very innovative and creative and, again, seminal. It was recommending things that hadn't even been thought of before. We bravely put that report together. The first report

wasn't acceptable to the department, so the department then decided that it wanted another report. I remember, because I was very vocal about the right of the task force. We were trying to assert our own vision and our own set of recommendations to achieve that vision. So, I was ropeable about the fact that the department wanted us to rewrite or water down the report. I wanted no part of that . . . I remember they had this one guy and another Aboriginal guy; they invited me to lunch. They said, 'Well, Bob, you seem to be the voice of opposition to everything inside the department and they're scared of what you're doing. So, can we maybe talk about your opposition to them?' And I did. They tried to convince me that it wasn't proper for me as the president of the AECG [NSW] and as a member of the task force to disagree. I said, 'No, I'm not going to agree with that; I think that what you're proposing flies in the face of all the things that I believe in and all the things that the NAEC stands for.' This was around independence and autonomy and the right to self-determination and all that stuff. I then refused to be a part of the official launch because they did proceed to put it together in another report and with a series of recommendations, which I didn't agree with. So, I boycotted the launch. I didn't want to be a part of it. It didn't make any difference — they went ahead and did it — but, for me, I felt really good about the fact that I stood by my principles.

Some of the other members also had very similar views — I used to have a great rapport with [Galarrwuy] Yunupingu, because he was also part of the task force [in 1994, he led the national review of Aboriginal and Torres Strait Islander Education]. I think he was a principal at one of the schools. He knew the stuff that I was promoting and objecting to was virtually what they were trying to do in those schools in the Northern Territory. A couple of the other people that were a part of the task force . . . intuitively knew that they were being conned by the government and the department. You've got to remember, this is after the NAEC had started to be disestablished, so the NAEC didn't exist to be able to fight those battles. So, as for the task force, the two reports, they're a bit like chalk and cheese. It was written in a way that made it more acceptable and probably sellable, if you want to put it that way. Whereas, I thought the whole notion of a task force was to be independent and to put forward the type of vision that we wanted. We wanted accountability. (Bob Morgan, interview, 2015)

Recommendations for combating racism in higher education

The increased participation of Aboriginal and Torres Strait Islander people in tertiary education was accompanied by increased reports of racism (NAEC Working Party on Racism in Higher Education 1989). The NAEC believed that if Aboriginal and Torres Strait Islander peoples were going to move forward within Western educational institutions, attention needed to be given to combating such racism. The NAEC Working Party on Racism in Higher Education was established in response, and one of the last contributions of the NAEC was a paper that dealt with combating racism in tertiary institutions (NAEC Working Party on Racism in Higher Education 1989). Paul Hughes pointed out there was not a lot of literature to go on:

> There was little research and papers on the best way to deal with racism. All those sorts of things were in their infancy in terms of anybody else making comment about them or researching them in various sorts of ways. So, it wasn't just a matter of making it up as we went along; we didn't have much to use to make up or to go on. We looked in general at social science and the activist movement in America, but most particularly — most of our educational thinking pretty much came out of the Canadian experience of [Indigenous] education. (Paul Hughes, interview, 2016)

The NAEC Working Party on Racism in Higher Education (1989) paper stated that racism manifested itself in racial prejudice, racial discrimination and institutional racism. The paper clarified the definitions of these different types of racism and provided advice on how to respond to racist actions. The paper gave examples of institutional racism such as:

- Courses in Australian literature which do not include any Aboriginal or Torres Strait Islander literature.
- Courses in Australian history which exclude Aboriginal or Torres Strait Islander perspectives.
- Sociology courses which deny the legitimacy of Aboriginal or Torres Strait Islander family structures. (NAEC Working Party on Racism in Higher Education 1989, p. 5)

The working party clearly articulated the institutions' responsibilities for ensuring a racism-free environment for Aboriginal and Torres Strait Islander students, staff and communities.

The final phase of the NAEC

Lynette Crocker, a Kaurna woman from South Australia, was working in Victoria at the Department of Education when she was appointed to the NAEC in 1986. Having been deputy chairperson under Errol West, she became the final chairperson of the NAEC in 1989 at the conclusion of Errol's term. Her role was mainly to finalise the operations of the NAEC and ensure an appropriate transition of business to other departments.

Eleanor Bourke was appointed deputy chairperson to assist with the abolishment of the NAEC. Eleanor was appointed to the NAEC in 1979 for two years and was then reappointed in 1985, continuing through to the conclusion of the NAEC.

ELEANOR BOURKE

A descendant of the Wergaia and Wamba Wamba peoples, Eleanor was working for the Commonwealth Department of Aboriginal Affairs at the time of her first appointment to the NAEC. She was the first woman in Victoria to be appointed to the NAEC and came from a community background:

I didn't have an educational background. I trained as a journalist, so I came from a community perspective. But because of the consultative groups starting in Victoria, I got more engaged in education because I worked for Aboriginal Affairs and got nominated onto the consultative group by Aboriginal Affairs. (Eleanor Bourke, interview, 2013)

Eleanor had a successful career in Aboriginal affairs, working in various roles as an Aboriginal adviser to the department, as director of the

> *Aboriginal and Torres Strait Islander Service in the Commonwealth Department of Social Security and as senior Aboriginal adviser for the Office of the Status of Women, Department of Prime Minister and Cabinet. Although her early career was not in education, she later held significant positions in higher education, including as director of the Aboriginal Research Institute, as associate professor in Aboriginal Education at the University of South Australia and as chair of Aboriginal Indigenous Studies and director, Aboriginal Programs, at Monash University. On her retirement, she was appointed to an adjunct professor role at Monash University. Throughout her time on the NAEC and post the NAEC, she maintained a strong passion for curriculum development in Aboriginal and Torres Strait Islander studies.*

The movement to abolish the NAEC can be traced to the Aboriginal Education Policy Task Force report, which had stipulated:

> Whilst recognising that the Aboriginal and Torres Strait Islander Commission will also be involved in education, the Task Force recommends a separate advisory or consultative structure to the Minister, the National Board of Employment, Education and Training and the Department of Employment, Education and Training be established to continue work developed by the National Aboriginal Education Committee and the National Aboriginal Employment and Training Committee. It is essential that a formal voice be available to the Commonwealth if it is to see through the objectives and strategies proposed in this report. (Aboriginal Education Policy Task Force 1988, p. 18)

Although the task force had recommended the continued presence of a national Aboriginal and Torres Strait Islander advisory committee as an important mechanism for appropriate consultation, at the conclusion of Errol West's appointment as NAEC chairperson, the Commonwealth Minister for Employment, Education and Training, John Dawkins, announced that in light of the introduction of the Aboriginal and Torres Strait Islander Commission (ATSIC), the NAEC would be abolished on 31 December 1988 (West 1988).

> There was no national voice that could challenge anything; I thought the demise of the NAEC was one of the worst things that's ever happened in this country and forever I'll lament the fact that we've not replaced the NAEC with a community-based national organisation. We have a number of models but [they] don't come anywhere near what the NAEC was, except the federation of AECG, which existed for a little while. (Bob Morgan, interview, 2015)

Peter Buckskin reflected that the employment of senior Aboriginal and Torres Strait Islander people across all areas of government had created the impression that there was no longer a need for an Aboriginal and Torres Strait Islander committee:

> I think by the end of the NAEC's influence, the challenge was maintaining its voice when more of us were developing our competencies and our capabilities and started to win Aboriginal jobs in the bureaucracies. We became the superintendents, we became the directors and suddenly there was this Aboriginal advisory group there from the minister and government's perspective. Then the government was saying, 'Well, we've got our own Aboriginal voices in the departments, do you need those other people?' So, the challenge was . . . to understand people's roles and functions and that you needed both an internal and external voice. (Peter Buckskin, interview, 2015)

The NAEC was formally abolished in December 1988, the final month of the bicentenary of Australian white settlement. Minimal appointments were retained to ensure appropriate transitions were finalised in 1989.

* * *

Over a short period of time, the fresh water had run so fast that it joined with the salt water with such force that it started to flow out into the ocean. Although, this would result in definite advantages for Aboriginal and Torres Strait Islander peoples, the salt water in the ocean remains dominant, asserting power and control over Aboriginal and Torres Strait Islander voices.

CHAPTER 12

The river continues to flow: a celebration of leadership and legacy

> I guess I attribute a lot of the privileges . . . that we enjoy today to that seminal period in my history. The NAEC did so many great things. We had more power in those days. So, as a group of educational leaders, it was quite profound what we were able to do at that time. Keeping in mind that we were all raw and we were all relatively young as well. We quite often didn't know what we were doing. But the good thing about it was that no one else did either. So, we could argue whatever we wanted and dress it up as if it was an authority, because it came from us. It was, I guess, a manifestation of the principle of self-determination, which I've always believed in, and it worked. (Bob Morgan, interview, 2015)

The NAEC was active from 1977 to 1989, during which time it successfully set the agenda for Aboriginal and Torres Strait Islander education policy development in Australia. It is easy to attribute this success to the Australian Government, which introduced the 'self-determination' policy (Altman, Biddle & Hunter 2005) and initiated the appointment of the NAEC; however, the journey had started long before the NAEC was established. Aboriginal and Torres Strait Islander peoples had been actively and publicly advocating and fighting for their right to be recognised as citizens in their own country since the 1920s (Maynard 1997). With more than 150 years of oppression, it was time that justice was served and Aboriginal and Torres Strait Islander peoples were given the right to education and economic development. By the time of the establishment of the NAEC, the Australian Government could no longer ignore the long struggle. The NAEC members took up the efforts of their forefathers and mothers and connected Aboriginal and Torres Strait Islander peoples across the country to commence healing and the building of relationships that would open up a space for Aboriginal and Torres Strait Islander peoples in the Western educational arena. The inclusion of a national voice was the key factor in the NAEC's success. The NAEC made a significant contribution to the development of Aboriginal and Torres Strait Islander education policy in Australia, through Aboriginal and Torres Strait Islander voices, for the guidance of future educators and leaders. Without knowing our past, we cannot truly define our futures.

An empowered space in education

> What the NAEC did was to expose hundreds of people — hundreds of Aboriginal people and non-Aboriginal people — to Aboriginal education. It allowed lots of people to have that experience who wouldn't have had it. It allowed so many people to have an input. (Kaye Price, interview, 2013)

The NAEC created a truly national forum for people to start to think seriously about Aboriginal and Torres Strait Islander education. Aboriginal and Torres Strait Islander people from across Australia, including small and remote communities, were invited to participate in discussions that would lead to national decisions about the future of Aboriginal and Torres Strait Islander education. The NAEC opened up an empowered space for building capacities and capabilities for Aboriginal and Torres Strait Islander peoples that resulted in increased employment, particularly inside government agencies, and this permeated to create greater Aboriginal and Torres Strait Islander influence on policy from the inside out. As a result of creating this space, access to education was opened up and attitudes in governments started to change.

The NAEC developed clear objectives and guidelines that reflected values and philosophies from an Aboriginal and Torres Strait Islander viewpoint. This was a major strength of the NAEC and it led to substantial policy development in the areas of Aboriginal and Torres Strait Islander studies, the presence of Aboriginal and Torres Strait Islander teachers in schools, Aboriginal and Torres Strait Islander employment, and access and success across all educational sectors from early childhood to higher education. The NAEC members were not inhibited by Western epistemology or in its way of thinking about the education of Aboriginal and Torres Strait Islander peoples. They progressed a unique agenda that no other group had done before. The NAEC shared a vision to achieve better outcomes for Aboriginal and Torres Strait Islander peoples and communities, and it did this by genuinely bringing these communities with it on the journey.

> The NAEC gave us the opportunity to influence decision-making on how we could develop our own models of education and insert our voices into the mix, to moving beyond what I had termed the 'guest' paradigm. Capacity strengthening... recognises that communities have got inherently a strength that makes them survivors, and integral to the development of a future generation that's proud of our identity and our heritage. (Bob Morgan, interview, 2015)

A central focus of the NAEC was to raise the credibility of Aboriginal and Torres Strait Islander voices in educational decision-making. Throughout the history of Aboriginal and Torres Strait Islander education policy, the NAEC had the highest national level of participation from Aboriginal and Torres Strait Islander people and involvement in influencing policy development. The development of a committee structure across all states and territories provided clear lines of consultation with Aboriginal and Torres Strait Islander communities nationally. The NAEC empowered these communities to provide culturally appropriate forums that stimulated the creation of future visions for Aboriginal and Torres Strait Islander peoples in education and assisted with the production of numerous evidence-based research papers that informed policy.

The community empowerment that the NAEC instilled focused on giving people a new sense of purpose and new sense of capacity. There was a need to heal communities from the past atrocities that had excluded them from education. A new era was introduced, where people's voices were heard and respected for the knowledge and experiences they contributed towards the advancement of education. The NAEC provided a platform for communities to better appreciate how their voices could contribute to educational decision-making and to the development of a clear and positive direction for national Aboriginal and Torres Strait Islander education. The collaboration between the NAEC and the AECGs resulted in that enthusiasm circulating through to the grassroots level, to parents, students and community members.

The AECGs continued post-NAEC as peak advisory groups to state and territory education departments. The AECG structure was integral to the NAEC in ensuring that the voices of Aboriginal and Torres Strait Islander Elders, parents, education professionals, teacher aides and teachers were heard. The current AECGs have a strong focus on school education and maintaining a close relationship with the state departments of education:

> I always thought it was great to have an AECG, because you worked together. You just had different roles to play. I think some AECGs have done well — the ones that are still in place because they've mastered that capacity to build confidence in the community and continue to do that and show the value that they add to the department. (Peter Buckskin, interview, 2015)

The increase in participation in education

> I really do think that a lot of the strategies that we put in place, the policies and what have you, have led to an amazing increase in Aboriginal graduates, undergraduates, postgraduates; and the increase in Aboriginal teachers around the country. We have such a national approach to music, the arts, our histories. It is an amazing, big community of ours, dynamic yet diverse. So, I saw the NAEC being that universal voice. (Patsy Cameron, interview, 2013)

The NAEC encouraged programs and initiatives to increase the access, participation and success of Aboriginal and Torres Strait Islander students from early childhood through to higher education. Government reports undertaken after the disbandment of the NAEC, such as the Yunupingu (1995) review report and the Ministerial Council on Education, Employment, Training and Youth Affairs (MCEETYA) (2000) report, attributed the ongoing increase in Aboriginal and Torres Strait Islander education outcomes to the implementation of the Aboriginal Education Policy, which was largely influenced by the work of the NAEC. In 2020, the Aboriginal Education Policy continues to guide Aboriginal and Torres Strait Islander education strategies, action plans and evaluation in collaboration with federal and state government education departments, educational institutions and the surviving AECGs. Research by Malin and Maidment (2003) confirms the strengths of the work of the NAEC and the introduction of the Aboriginal Education Policy for producing longer-term results in the participation of Aboriginal and Torres Strait Islander peoples in education.

In the decade following the disbandment of the NAEC, growth in school enrolments continued, with an increase of 40 per cent between 1991 and 1998 (MCEETYA 2000, p. 5). However, MCEETYA also highlighted that the participation of Aboriginal and Torres Strait Islander children at primary school level was 83 per cent in 1996 compared to the 89 per cent participation rate of non-Indigenous children, and that the secondary school rate of Aboriginal and Torres Strait Islander students represented a significant challenge with an increase from 54 per cent in 1986 to 60 per cent in 1996 (compared to 84 per cent for non-Indigenous students) (MCEETYA 2000, p. 5).

The Aboriginal Education Policy Task Force (1988, p. 9) reported that in 1969 less than one hundred Aboriginal and Torres Strait Islander students were enrolled in tertiary education, which by 1986 had increased to 4800 enrolments across TAFE and higher education. The MCEETYA (2000, p. 5) report, moreover, detailed that from 1994 to 1998 enrolments in vocational education nearly doubled. The VET sector offers an important educational platform for Aboriginal and Torres Strait Islander peoples and the NAEC ensured that it became a focal point as a critical education provider.

Rigney (2001) credits the NAEC with playing an integral role in the access and participation of Aboriginal and Torres Strait Islander peoples in higher education. The 1000 Aboriginal teachers by 1990 initiative opened up universities and CAEs to Aboriginal and Torres Strait Islander students and communities. Hughes and Willmot (1979) reported, in their submission to NITE, that in 1977, there were seventy-two qualified Aboriginal and Torres Strait Islander teachers. The introduction of enclaves and other specific entry programs contributed to the growth in the number of qualified Aboriginal and Torres Strait Islander teachers to 220 in 1982 (Hughes & Willmot 1982, p. 46).

The enclave movement in tertiary institutions was encouraged and supported by the NAEC. The Jordan and Howard report (1985) noted that, by 1984, fourteen Aboriginal enclave programs had been introduced nationally. Prior to these enclaves, only eighty-five Aboriginal and Torres Strait Islander students were recorded in higher education institutions (Jordan & Howard 1985, p. 2). This increased by more than 500 per cent to 551 after the enclave programs were introduced (Jordan & Howard 1985, p. 2). By 1988 there were forty-two Aboriginal and Torres Strait Islander enclave programs in tertiary institutions across all states and territories (Bin-Sallik 2003). From 1991 to 1998, there was a 60 per cent increase in higher education enrolments (MCEETYA 2000).

Even after the introduction of enclaves, the number of Aboriginal and Torres Strait Islander people working in the enclaves was minimal, particularly at senior levels. Jordan and Howard (1985) emphasised the need for Aboriginalisation of staff in enclaves. The enclaves have now developed into Aboriginal and Torres Strait Islander student, academic and research higher education centres, primarily staffed by Aboriginal and Torres Strait Islander people. Colin Bourke and Bob Morgan, drawing on their experiences during and post the NAEC, state that the challenge now is in increasing the employment of Aboriginal and Torres Strait Islander people outside of the Aboriginal and Torres Strait Islander centres. This is considered critical to encouraging a whole-of-university approach that continues to simultaneously respect the expertise and knowledges of Aboriginal and Torres Strait Islander peoples and the need for continued spaces within institutions to empower that expertise and knowledge while broadening the roles of Aboriginal and Torres Strait Islander people in universities (Colin Bourke, interview, 2013).

The NAEC opened the doors to higher education for Aboriginal and Torres Strait Islander students, primarily through the 1000 Aboriginal teachers by 1990 initiative. By maintaining the essence of this initiative of providing a culturally inclusive environment that contributes to building the capacity of Aboriginal and Torres Strait Islander students and communities within higher education, success in tertiary education will continue to grow. In 2013, there were 13,576 Aboriginal enrolments in universities and 1859 completions in the same year (Department of Education and Training 2014):

> My favourite moment wasn't during the NAEC. I think my favourite moment was when I was away from it and I was at a conference, me and Chubby [Keith] Hall. I was on a panel and the students had to say who they are and what they do, and this girl would come and say, 'I'm such and such, I'm doing my studies to become a doctor . . .'; or another one, 'I'm such and such, I'm an undergraduate student for law.' Me and Chubby Hall looked at each and said, 'Jiminy Cricket, bro, NAEC,' and then we looked at each other and said, 'Did we really do this?' The penny dropped. All of a sudden, there were all these people coming in and they were in tertiary education, in all these different disciplines. I think that's when the penny dropped for me. I thought, 'WOW! Did I really do that?' and we said, 'Yeah, [we're] super.' (Stephen Albert, interview, 2012)

Patsy Cameron also notes feeling this sense of achievement:

> I think to see some of the workshops, the young ones and the not-so-young ones that have come on, to see the increase in confidence of our young people that have gone through the education system, from early primary now to university, that is incredible. I think that has been something that, especially even in Tasmania, for me working at the university, doing an undergraduate degree myself, and then doing a master's degree, to witness those programs that have helped — that are in place to help with

the young ones as they progress through their studies and through the school systems. I think that's rewarding. (Patsy Cameron, interview, 2013)

Since the foundational work of the NAEC, there has been a continued increase in the participation of Aboriginal and Torres Strait Islander peoples in all areas of education (Department of Education and Training 2014). Despite this, major disparities still exist between Indigenous and non-Indigenous people in education. For example, a 2012 Australian Government report, *Review of Higher Education Access and Outcomes for Aboriginal and Torres Strait Islander People*, stated, 'Despite significant progress in recent decades, Aboriginal and Torres Strait Islander people remain significantly under-represented in Australian universities' (Behrendt et al. 2012, p. 4).

Given that we, as Aboriginal and Torres Strait Islander peoples, commenced our educational journey significantly behind the Western educational outcome 'starting line', concerted attention is needed to ensure social justice is achieved. As emphasised continually by the NAEC, this requires Aboriginal and Torres Strait Islander peoples to be centrally involved in consultation and decision-making.

Aboriginal and Torres Strait Islander employment

> [Aboriginal and Torres Strait Islander people] bring with them a whole range of . . . experiences, skills and expertise, and the dilemma for those people around the expectation as you become more and more senior in [an] organisation, the Aboriginal [and] Islander connection becomes less important. It's about you toeing the line in terms of the organisation, whether that's government or universities or private business or whatever. How we remain true to our communities and our families [is the dilemma]. (Wendy Ludwig, interview, 2016)

When, soon after its inception, the NAEC introduced the concept of Aboriginalisation, the vision was to move Aboriginal and Torres Strait Islander people from advisory positions to roles with substantial involvement and responsibility. To achieve this vision, the NAEC recognised that

Aboriginal and Torres Strait Islander people needed to be employed in senior government roles. The 1000 Aboriginal teachers by 1990 initiative had two outcomes. First, it generated a great increase in the participation of Aboriginal and Torres Strait Islander people in tertiary education, leading to their graduation as fully qualified teachers. Second, and less anticipated, it provided Aboriginal and Torres Strait Islander graduates who were employable within government departments. When assessing whether the strategies of the NAEC contributed to Aboriginalisation, whether in schools or in government departments, it was clear there was a positive impact on the employment of Aboriginal and Torres Strait Islander people, including those who rose to positions of influence.

By June 1996, the number of Aboriginal and Torres Strait Islander staff employed in the Australian Public Service had risen to 3390, which was 2.63 per cent of the total workforce (Larkin 2013, p. 138). The employment of Aboriginal and Torres Strait Islander staff peaked in 1999 and then, by 2011, had declined to 3236, calculated as 2.1 per cent of the overall Australian Public Service workforce (Larkin 2013, p. 132). This decline has been attributed to ongoing racism (Larkin 2013).

The NAEC developed clear policy positions that committed the government to employment targets, and it negotiated employment strategies to meet these targets. In the decade immediately following the NAEC, there was a demonstrated success in Aboriginalisation; however, this appears to have subsequently declined.

Aboriginal and Torres Strait Islander leadership and mentorship

> The NAEC's biggest contribution has been to mentor young people like myself, and for us to observe and learn, and model on the good work that they were doing. (Peter Buckskin, interview, 2015)

The contributors in this book determined that a noteworthy impact of the NAEC was the mentorship provided to other NAEC members and community people. The collaboration with hundreds of Aboriginal and

Torres Strait Islander people across the country created hope and aspiration. The members of the NAEC, as demonstrated in their biographies, all continued in leadership roles in education or in their communities. They primarily attribute their success to the professional and personal development, networking and other opportunities experienced during their appointment to the NAEC.

The leadership displayed by the NAEC demonstrated to Aboriginal and Torres Strait Islander peoples and communities the possibility of achieving professional status as educators and leaders. The provision of role models for the next generation was an important part of the NAEC's success. The networks that were established through forums, meetings and the AECGs provided an enduring platform for a collective vision to put possibilities into action.

The NAEC members were mostly very young and early in their careers. The members were assigned a huge responsibility and unprecedented access to senior government officials in the portfolios of education and Aboriginal affairs. The accomplishments over the four terms and the knowledge the members imparted had a significant impact on Aboriginal and Torres Strait Islander education. The cross-fertilisation of ideas and networks between the NAEC and the AECGs resulted in the development of structures and processes that produced fundamental role models and mentors. Consequently, mentoring moved beyond the members of the NAEC to the broader national communities to empower future leadership.

Aboriginal and Torres Strait Islander curriculum

The NAEC had great challenges to overcome, especially given the discrimination and barriers in place when it was embedded in educational institutions and society more broadly. Achieving the goal of integrating Aboriginal and Torres Strait Islander heritage and history into curriculum, especially higher education, was difficult. The journey of the NAEC shows resilience and determination, driven by the passion and dedication of our communities.

By working within the Schools Commission, the NAEC was able to forge strong relationships with the Curriculum Development Centre. This relationship resulted in a position on the Curriculum Development Centre Advisory Board. The ongoing connections led to joint projects between the NAEC and the Curriculum Development Centre, including an investigation into the inclusion of Aboriginal and Torres Strait Islander studies in the school curriculum; the audit and development of appropriate resources for Aboriginal and Torres Strait Islander studies; and a ground-breaking study on Aboriginal and Torres Strait Islander pedagogy (NAEC & CDC 1986).

Prior to the NAEC, there was very little taught in schools on Aboriginal and Torres Strait Islander studies and many of the textbooks and resources were culturally inappropriate and lacked accuracy. One of the NAEC's first priorities in relation to Aboriginal and Torres Strait Islander studies involved an audit of resources. The contribution of the NAEC in this area was significant in prompting national action on the appropriate teaching of Aboriginal and Torres Strait Islander studies. The focus on strengthening Aboriginal and Torres Strait Islander studies led to a significant contribution in the production of principles for the provision of the culturally appropriate curriculum that is evident in today's national school curriculum.

Furthermore, in most universities, Aboriginal and Torres Strait Islander studies is a core requirement of teacher and medical education, and increasingly in other professional degree programs. Progress has been slow and challenges remain, but the legacy of the NAEC endures. The NAEC provided the foundation that resulted in a momentous shift. It produced publications that promoted an understanding of the benefits of Aboriginal and Torres Strait Islander studies based on the principles of a more inclusive society and the need to overcome racial and cultural ignorance.

National policy development

In lots of ways, it made government look good because, even now, we talk about the high unemployment rates, this, that and the other. So, education, once it became the focus, fitted . . . in with what the federal government wanted to do. It suited their philosophy and they also were able to say to the states, we'll give you more money for the education for Aboriginal people if you do this. Of course, it was a nice position to be in. (Victor Forrest, interview, 2016)

The NAEC provided a positive direction that would translate into better futures and opportunities for Aboriginal and Torres Strait Islander peoples through education. The Australian Government had made a commitment to advancing outcomes for Aboriginal and Torres Strait Islander peoples, and the work of the NAEC enabled it to implement policies with clear visions and outcomes.

The NAEC was highly respected by both sides of government, allowing it to play a strong political role in advocating for better educational opportunities for Aboriginal and Torres Strait Islander peoples. This assisted in laying the foundations for the Aboriginal Education Policy Task Force and the subsequent Aboriginal Education Policy, which, as did all the policies tabled by the NAEC, received bilateral support in parliament.

The introduction of the Aboriginal Education Policy provided a framework that would guide Aboriginal and Torres Strait Islander education into the future. Five years after the implementation of the Aboriginal Education Policy, the *National Review of Education for Aboriginal and Torres Strait Islander Peoples: Final Report* (Yunupingu 1995, p. 6) reviewed its progress and impact: 'The joint policy is helping to build an Australian culture in which there is greater recognition of, and respect for, Aboriginality, and a greater awareness of, and sensitivity to, the aspirations and concerns of Aboriginal and Torres Strait Islanders.'

The report affirmed that the joint policy was having an impact in the improvement of outcomes in Aboriginal and Torres Strait Islander education. However, it criticised the loss of voice to the broader Aboriginal and Torres Strait Islander community and remarked that, without Aboriginal and Torres Strait Islander people in positions of influence, their voices were no longer being heard. Furthermore, it noted that the joint policy did not include Aboriginal and Torres Strait Islander people as joint partners or signatories. The review recommended that the Australian Government needed to appoint a new national body to direct Aboriginal education and that the national conferences should be re-instated (Yunupingu 1995, p. 7).

The *National Review of Education for Aboriginal and Torres Strait Islander Peoples* (Yunupingu 1995), which encompassed all educational sectors, was the last national review of Aboriginal and Torres Strait Islander education led by Aboriginal and Torres Strait Islander people. Since then, there have been individual state reviews or reviews on separate sectors of Aboriginal and Torres Strait Islander education but none has provided a consolidated, holistic viewpoint on the national position of the kind that was at the core of the NAEC's work.

The aims and philosophies that were a key part of the NAEC policy document (NAEC 1985b) were not fully reflected or defined in the Aboriginal Education Policy and were therefore invisible for new educators and leaders. Some members of the NAEC believed that it should have positioned itself in a monitoring and evaluation role to ensure the successful integration of the Aboriginal Education Policy and its related policies. However, this was a role that was, instead, conferred on the Aboriginal and Torres Strait Islander Commission (ATSIC), which was introduced in 1990. ATSIC was a government body wherein Aboriginal and Torres Strait Islander peoples could be involved in decision-making. In 2005, ATSIC was disbanded. This removed significant Aboriginal and Torres Strait Islander voices from government without a similar structure to replace it.

It could be argued that since the disestablishment of the NAEC, there has been a continual decline in genuine consultation between the Australian Government and communities, with no mechanism that informs the educational sector from early childhood to higher education. Additionally, although there has been a steady increase in statistical outcomes in some indicators of Aboriginal and Torres Strait Islander education, it is evident there has also been a decline in the impacts on educational and employment outcomes that encompass the values, the philosophies and the dreaming of Aboriginal and Torres Strait Islander peoples. For Aboriginal and Torres Strait Islander peoples, connectivity and relationality is integral to a continued future of self-determination and maintaining culture. Patsy Cameron's reflection captures the essence of many of the stories shared by the contributors:

> The NAEC actually allowed me to broaden my horizons. It just gave me such an incredible journey that took me out into the rest of this land. I think it just gave me that experience that I could not have gained in any other way to see something across the national spectrum of Aboriginal Australia in terms of education. The collegiality, that closeness and that sheer respect based on integrity, that respect of each other that I can't really explain, but it's something I'll never forget. Each one of them . . . was just the springboard of giving me the room to think, to actually then go on and do the things that I've done. It actually is the springboard of thinking, seeing and doing something that's not just for a small group. It's to look at something across the expanse of it all. The journey has been incredible, and it still is. The journey continues. On occasions when I can go through the photos and just reflect on those times, it does bring back those amazing memories. Then to see the next generation and the next generation, two generations of deadly young people coming through and achieving some of those aims that we were only dreaming of then. (Patsy Cameron, interview, 2013)

Legacy and advice

The contributors to this book were each asked what advice and legacy they would like to pass down to future generations. The following are some of their responses. Their advice for future Aboriginal and Torres Strait Islander educators and leaders articulates the importance of being strong and true to yourself as an Aboriginal and/or Torres Strait Islander person and to your communities, and the importance of recognising and respectfully acknowledging our histories and the hard work of those who have walked before us. The Aboriginal and Torres Strait Islander men and women responsible for our histories in providing strong foundations in Aboriginal and Torres Strait Islander education policy in this contemporary world have shared their stories. They are now ready to hand over the baton and allow the current and upcoming Aboriginal and Torres Strait

Islander educators and leaders to take hold of it and make their own stories, which, forty years from now, can inspire and lead the following generation.

Stephen Albert

Nobody can cut us down if we just keep on growing. So that's the message that I want to use . . . we been at that game since a long time ago and we've improved so don't despair, let's keep on improving. Since thirty years ago, a lot of Australians and white people have changed their attitude, and because of the change of that attitude, that's why we were able to change; we need to continue this. Two hundred years of nothing, forty years of something really good, and then what the other forty years going to bring us, or what the next two hundred years going to bring us? And I'll leave that up to somebody else to answer that. But the thing is, what I wanted to prove is that the government must have Indigenous involvement; that's the thing I want to improve. Without the involvement, we wouldn't've got any of this; it's that simple. But the thing is, the government keep on changing their policies and they keep on changing and cutting our staff slowly and slowly. (Stephen Albert, interview, 2012)

Kaye Price

People started to think seriously about Aboriginal education. People started to include Aboriginal and Torres Strait Islander people; we had a presence within the education system. We did so much in that ten years. We need to remember there was nothing and now, look, within that time, what there was and what we've got since . . .

It is so important that we continue to graduate Aboriginal teachers; however, it's one thing to have graduates . . . but they need to really appreciate what has been done . . . and their understanding of where we are [history], the [community] philosophies that were developed [by the NAEC], they [Aboriginal education students and the education sector] talk about ground roots communications and the principles behind Aboriginal and Torres Strait Islander education – but do they really understand and appreciate it? (Kaye Price, interview, 2013)

Patsy Cameron

There's still a long way to go, because I really do think the focus now needs to be on going back to understanding our history and the histories of Australia. I don't think there's enough known within our own community, as well as the wider community, about the history of this land. I still think there's a lot that can be done in order to address the issues that people like Marcia Langton [Aboriginal scholar and activist] raise. I think there is still a lot of work to do, but we've come a long way, I have no doubt about that. I think a lot of it's because of the groundwork that was done by the NAEC over that period of time and the people that were involved. I still participate in talking to principals and key educators in the public sector, the Catholic and the private sectors. There's still a lot of work to do in closing the gap of Aboriginal education right across Australia. That's where I think the NAEC notion of having an overarching body of people from around the country with all the expertise, that was what was special about the NAEC. The collective expertise of people right across the sectors of education made it such a powerful committee. That's what's missing, I think. There are committees that deal with higher education. There are small bodies that deal with other areas of education. I think [the] NAEC and the overarching vision that was able to be discussed at that level was just something . . . it's now a great loss. (Patsy Cameron, interview, 2013)

Lillian Holt

To me, education is about the total person, and it's about awareness, it's about attitudes, and I think most people are just skilled and qualified. There's a tertiary education report[3] that came out in . . . the early 1990s and they talked about the danger of turning out skilled barbarians. You know, people who knew what their job was and didn't have the faintest clue about themselves and others. I think the truly educated person is someone who knows themselves. I've met so many people in society, and it's a white fella society; it's a very Western way of looking at things. To me, yeah, they have a lot of head knowledge, but I think you've got to have the head and the heart, and sometimes the greatest journey is from the head to the heart. (Lillian Holt, interview, 2013)

---

3   Report unspecified.

Paul Hughes

The best advice I can give is to establish an agenda and follow it through. Recognise that all of these things take yonks to happen and that talking them through is a long, slow process, simply because education is societal — it takes societal growth, and that's not simple. When having discussions, try and find a way of basing your discussions on evidence and, in the end, try and develop an actual way of doing something about it. Many of the things you have to do to fix something are really high-level stuff. It's no good deluding yourself that someone's going to fix something, or it'll fix itself, because it doesn't happen that way. This whole business of working things through is a long-term sort of thing and we've mucked it up by stopping our growth and development ourselves; government's done that as well. But you would think your own mob of people, like villages in the old days, recognised that they had to grow and continue to work out ways of changing things; we didn't do that as a group. When I hear about people arguing about each other on boards, I don't think that helps a lot. It's not working as a community. (Paul Hughes, interview, 2013)

Colin Bourke

I don't think we at the NAEC saw the proliferation of people studying across all the programs to the extent it has occurred. What we did see, and it hasn't happened, is the need for a stronger emphasis on Indigenous culture and education as an Aborigine. I think that's quite weak, even though I don't think we saw the strength that has come out in Aboriginal situations like language. Language is now spoken in nearly every conference. We never envisaged welcomes to the country. I don't think we envisaged Indigenous dancing like it is and the way it's spread. The actual strength of Indigenous culture in the community today is not reflected in the educational institutions. Perhaps we thought if we pushed the education barrier for Aboriginal studies and Aboriginal culture and those things, languages and other things will come from there; but they haven't, they've come from the community outside of the education system. We saw the education system as a vehicle. It hasn't proved to be. So that's disappointing, in a way. I think the lack of formal programs which are Indigenous today — and I'm speaking about my experience of

Monash [University] — we don't have every teacher in Australia having Aboriginal studies as part of their program. We don't have Aboriginal languages taught in schools. They don't get taught in universities much either now, if at all, but they are taught within community organisations to some degree. I don't know how well it's done, or much about it, except I know that people I dealt with, they had no language and now have got language. So that's something that's happened outside the education portfolio. It should have been within the education portfolio, really. So, I mean in one way now, from 1977, Aboriginal culture has permeated society more, but it hasn't done it in the education system where it needs to happen. (Colin Bourke, interview, 2013)

Eleanor Bourke

Every university has a presence now, which . . . remains as a testament to what the vision was. What bothers me about that, though, is there is some sort of expectation from younger people that there are things in place and they are there for them just to take for granted. We've got a new responsibility. We need to be teaching about what's happened in recent times as part of Aboriginal studies; the way we've got ourselves into the system and how hard it was, how fragile it is and how important it is to keep that going; not just something that is just there. Young ones need to understand that they have a similar responsibility that's passed on to maintain standards and maintain the position, not to lose it, but to carry it on. There is a real conversation to be had in white Australia, because they're comfortable, they don't want to be disturbed, and anything we do sort of ruffles their feathers. So, I think that'll always be there. You only have to look where the power rests — white males mainly.

The important thing is to be true to yourself and to really understand your people and place. I mean, if you're strong on that, nobody can touch you in anything, in my view. If you're strong and proud, doesn't matter what people say. Then you can explain it and talk to others and keep that pride happening. To me, that's the most important thing; you can do your research, get information off your families. Sometimes you don't even know what you've got and then it means something later on. I've done this myself; I got a lot of material out of the archives. I had enough information from my grandmother to actually be able to identify family members in the protectorate papers, which sort of showed me where they were being moved and how they were being dealt with. Even though their surnames weren't in it, their first names were there, and they were being moved from one place to another. I was able to say, well, a lot of the things I've been told are true; the detail mightn't be there, but it made me stronger, because what my grandmother said about who we were was right. But what she went through, and she didn't give up on her identity, even though she was frustrated that we didn't seem to have an educational base, but she was still really proud and strong, and she influenced a whole lot of her grandchildren in that way. I think that's the biggest thing, people can be proud of themselves by understanding their own culture and place. It's much easier to pass it on and it's easy to stand up to challenges. (Eleanor Bourke, interview, 2013)

Pearl Duncan

You can't evade hard work. There might be shortcuts but, in the long run, it is dedication and hard work. I really don't think anything's handed to you on a plate, on a silver platter. You do get opportunities, there's no doubt about that, and you've got to be awake enough to recognise your opportunities. You don't let a good opportunity slip by. It all boils down to dedication and hard work and making the right decisions. Education is a right, not a privilege. (Pearl Duncan, interview, 2015)

Laurie Padmore

Well, don't be afraid to really have a go. You've got to trust the people that you work with and. if you've got no confidence, you'll get it. You'll get it because you learn off each other. I could say I was the most grass-roots person that you could ever get. I never had a clue, even though I did work, and I was working in education. When Aboriginal education started here, I was the second officer in the state. I didn't have a clue, I didn't know any Aboriginal families — didn't know any of them. So, I joined the Tasmanian Aboriginal Centre; it was a good organisation, but sort of changed over the years. The thing that I do see is that I do admire some of these people. They're angry people, because they've lost so much. They've got to really understand — they don't have to be really angry to achieve what you want to achieve. I've done this without stirring anything up. You know? I've just utilised the resources. Try to utilise people — get them to believe in the ideas that I believe — common-sense kind of stuff. I used to visit the people around — you visit, and you get ideas from parents. What do you reckon should happen? They are the teachers, really. I would say the community, the parents, the teachers out there, I'd go and ask them a question: 'What do you think should be changed? Is there anything that could make it any better for our kids?' They'd come up with some ideas — some brilliant ideas. You're always learning, you're never too old to learn, and that's one thing I did learn through the NAEC, I did learn about education. That education, not only universal but in Aboriginal education, you don't have any limits. It's an ongoing process that you have. You don't have levels like, say, in academia; you have levels that you've got to reach. Aboriginal education, you don't have to have that. You just keep going, and that's what I like about it. There's still a lot of work. (Laurie Padmore, interview, 2013)

May O'Brien[4]

We need to continue to grow our own capacity. We just grew white fellas' capacity. We didn't push hard enough for our jobs and things, I think. That's where a lot of white fellas went in, and we liked them being there, because they were supporting the cause. But then they were the ones that got all the jobs. Yeah, that's a big, big problem now at this stage . . . I think some of that self-doubt and not believing in yourself has got a lot to do with that, as well, and we need to do a lot of capacity building. The idea that kids won't do things and say it's 'shame', thinking that's okay, that it's part of our culture to be shamed. Well, it's not. It's not part of our culture. But our kids have grown up thinking that it is part of who we are. Not allowing the kids to say, 'I'm not confident with that' or 'I'm nervous'. I think that's one of our points that we need to deal with, because our kids, sometimes they go, 'Oh, no, I can't do that or say that.' You can say that, you can do that. A lot of them now, they need a lot of encouragement, because a lot of people still think that our kids can't do it. We've got to help them. We've got to let them use their own heads. (May O'Brien, interview, 2014)

---

4 Carol Garlett also contributed to this conversation.

Rex Granites

[Speaks in Warlpiri language] What I said was, you're listening, you're going to be listening of what I've done in the past of me being in the National Aboriginal Consultative Committee, which meant for the education of our people; I was part of that and it got me to where I started talking about the education forever, that can be. But it was through the national Indigenous groups of our people, the Aboriginal people, we're talking about these issues that nowadays the younger people aren't really listening to. All I say, you've got to start listening to the right people when they're trying to teach you in ceremonies or other things, start listening or else you'll never be who you are. You'll be down the streets, be bumped around by so many people that you don't know. I was lucky that [when] I grew in a way that got myself into strife with grog and alcohol, it only took me one week to turn over, not with white programs or the government money or anything like that. I turned away with what knowledge I had from my community and the Country and how I connected myself to that. You look at the change what happened to the people. Now we still getting it, we're going to try and get back, it was a new page, all we've got through with our cultural knowledge and understanding. They can't do it; we can do it. (Rex Granites, interview, 2014)

Didimain Uibo

Education is the key. Keep doing what you have been taught from your school days and what you have learnt. Continue what you want to learn about. If you are a teacher, the students who you are going to be teaching, you need to give them high-quality education, so they can be able to use it for their own children. Every school — every kid should go to school. Without that school learning, there will be nothing. (Didimain Uibo, interview, 2014)

Bob Morgan

One of the messages that I would give to younger, emerging scholars and leaders is to never forget their connectedness to Country and to community. But they should see their participation in these sorts of endeavours as a privilege, not a right. I despair sometimes when I see some of our people — both some of our academics and some of our students — operating as if this is a right because they don't understand the actions that were fought to create the privilege that they now enjoy. I'm proud of the fact that we're producing so many great thinkers and great leaders that are going to lead the next generation. I would hope, though, that that generation never forgets the history of the NAEC, and some of the stuff that happened before the NAEC as well, of course.

But you understand that we can never be anything but who we are. So, if you want to be an academic, only an academic, well work in the Academy and you can be an academic. But if you want to be an Aboriginal or Torres Strait Islander or Indigenous academic, that's something totally different. People need to understand what that means and then to dedicate their careers to celebrating the uniqueness of that. So, my message to you and some of those people that are coming through is to be proud of the fact that you come from one of, if not the, longest surviving and continuing cultures on this planet. No one else can claim that. Understand what that means in real terms, not just in historical terms. Be dignified in the way in which you assert your rights and your freedoms to be Aboriginal, be a Torres Strait Islander, be Indigenous. Never settle for just being someone else's guest. Understand that you've got that history, that thousands and thousands and thousands of years of unconventional tradition that we should be utilising today to grow our own. There are some young ones that are here that I am so excited about. I think they will be the next leaders. A true leader is someone that can not only articulate and lead and . . . add vision, but they're also gifted in how they bring people with them. So, it's about being proud, being grounded in your identity and your culture. Not a sort of notion of cultural imperialism where we are superior to everyone else, but just to acknowledge that we're different. Not better, not worse, but different, and how does that manifest in our thinking and in our leadership skills? The fact that we're doing things now by incorporating Elders into the decision-making processes. Somewhere, the voices of those that have gone before must be acknowledged and celebrated in the way in which we create a vision for the future. That's about honouring, it's about acknowledgment and it's about respect, and it's about being grounded in something that essentially makes you who you are. (Bob Morgan, interview, 2015)

Peter Buckskin

The NAEC clearly demonstrated the power of Indigenous voices, and when you work together as a collective, as we did, with mutual respect, understanding the boundaries, you can really achieve. I thought the processes that we adopted and the way we wanted to work together in terms of that respect for each other . . . even when there were tensions, at the end of the day we dealt with it to make sure whatever [was] going to happen, happened. So, we were all there together, all reflecting on the work of the NAEC. It shows that we can have a voice. And it mentored so many emerging people like myself; I wouldn't probably be here if it wasn't for the NAEC, in this role. I have a lot of respect for the people that were part of the journey. That's why I hope I give respect for other younger people, because there's got to be the point of transition to a new leadership group. I think that's why I believe NATSIHEC [National Aboriginal and Torres Strait Islander Higher Education Consortium, national committee in 2020] can be so powerful. If we operate in that type of framework and context, we will have done our jobs. (Peter Buckskin, interview, 2015)

John Lester

The saddest thing I've seen, and memorable, I've referred to it in my own thesis, [is] it never ceases to amaze me that we go into a community as NAEC, or the AECG, and every community would proudly bring out their preschool kids. They'd come and perform in front of you. They'd do an amazing performance. They would be happy, they would be laughing and they would be into it. It would be exciting. The kids were beaming. I'll never forget that picture of that little Aboriginal kid that's pointing and dressed up and dancing. The sense of pride in who he was. You'd see that, and then the only thing I could think — and it led me to start thinking about my own PhD — along the way, what do schools do to these kids? They've got so much enthusiasm. They love doing cultural stuff; they're right into it. My thesis indicates that they're about five when they arrive at school, and it takes that lifetime again, and they've switched off school. So, within five years of being in school all that stuff is knocked out of them, all that enthusiasm. (John Lester, interview, 2015)

John Heath

The legacy of the NAEC was the programs . . . some of which still exist today. They are part of the history of Aboriginal education and Aboriginal development in this country, which is an important legacy to understand. The fact that the NAEC established an understanding of the value of Aboriginal community advisory bodies was also important. That's a legacy that people should bear in mind; however, whenever you're in an advisory committee, that's all that you'll be, and your voice can be heeded or ignored. I also think we've lost a bit in that there was Aboriginal education that was focused [on] Aboriginal children. But then there was Aboriginal studies that was for non-Aboriginals — there was a real separation. White educators said to me, 'Well, Aboriginal education is for Aboriginal students, it's only for Aboriginal students.' My response was, 'No, that's not what we're talking about.' That helped me in my understanding of the need to try to clarify what we were talking about. Unfortunately, we are still having some of these conversations and the same debates. It really shows in some ways where we have failed as educators to educate. Failed where we've got our own people, who should be further along in their thinking, reinventing the wheel type of thing. Because they haven't learnt from what we did, or what we said. (John Heath, interview, 2016)

Victor Forrest

Sadly, the history hasn't been recorded and it's a history that has to be told. It's a story that has to be told. I don't think many Australians, both black and white, realised just what was happening at that stage in terms of education. Today is a very, very different scenario. When I see private schools having scholarships for Aboriginal kids to go in to, it was way beyond my wildest dream when I was a child to be granted a scholarship. I think I was encouraged to leave school when I did, at the age of thirteen. I think they thought, well, that's another one we don't have to worry about. But these days, when I see the growing numbers [of] Aboriginal people going to universities, or higher education, this is going to have an impact on the broader community. When you have success breeding success, it can only multiply. I guess if I was providing advice to an Aboriginal undergraduate, I'd encourage them to not only succeed in what they were doing but also to go beyond just the basic degree and become involved in such a level that whatever their chosen profession is, also make an impact on that. People became aware that Aboriginal people can get into leadership roles and saw Aboriginal people in prominent positions; it made an impact. Soon Aboriginal men and women were heading up academic departments, which I think has certainly broken down barriers, and breaking down the barriers that non-Aboriginal people have put up, rather than vice versa. (Victor Forrest, interview, 2016)

Wendy Ludwig

... I think it's really important that people do have access to their history and we continue to say, and we've said forever, that you can't deal with the present and go into the future without taking the past with you, and using that as a foundation to give you the strength to be able to do what needs to be done. I think that people need to immerse themselves in the history of where we've come from and the intent of people involved in those times and what the legacies are — what our responsibilities and obligations are to that, and how, in the context of the work that people are going to do, how do they contribute to the wellbeing of Aboriginal people collectively? I think, given the nature of the environment that we operate in and the use and reliance on technology to assist and support people studying, it really feeds in and plays into that individualistic ... way of operating, which is something that we have fought against in the education system forever. If you go back and have a look at the old documents coming out of NAEC, it's always about our kids in schools — primary schools, high schools, in the VET system, at university, having places and having spaces for us to be together, to stay strong. That's always been the case. Since the beginning of time, when we were all created, it was about communal ... support and community infrastructure and staying strong and being immersed and connected and all those kinds of things. That's even more important now and we've had to fight really strongly against being busted up and dispersed. (Wendy Ludwig, interview, 2016)

CONCLUSION

The NAEC has made a significant contribution to the development of Aboriginal and Torres Strait Islander education policy in Australia. As a group, its membership combined academic, professional, cultural and community knowledge, and this expertise put Aboriginal and Torres Strait Islander education on the centre stage. The NAEC developed a corpus of robust educational research and policy publications that had not existed before. The scope and scale of the NAEC contribution was a first within the history of contemporary Aboriginal education.

Forty years is a short time in the history of Aboriginal and Torres Strait Islander peoples. Although we have seen significant improvements initiated by the work of the NAEC, there are still challenges. These are no longer the same challenges that our people endured prior to the 1970s, but they are new challenges with some of the old flavours of assimilation, integration and racism. We now witness the continued challenge of maintaining a space and a voice in the Australian education system. Since the era of the NAEC, never has there been an independent body with a consolidated viewpoint spanning all levels of education nationally. Nor has there been the level of collectiveness and shared vision that the NAEC created.

Acknowledgment needs to be given to the Aboriginal and Torres Strait Islander men and women who have made a significant contribution to the journey of Aboriginal and Torres Strait Islander education over the past forty years and beyond. The Aboriginal Education Policy Task Force

(1988, p. 2) believed that 'equality for Aborigines in education is essential to the economic, social and cultural development of Aboriginal communities'. This belief continues to guide our resilience in leadership and governance now and into the future.

Although there has been clear advancement for access to and participation in education for Aboriginal and Torres Strait Islander peoples, lots of work remains to be done and attitudes need to be changed. Aboriginal and Torres Strait Islander educators and leaders need to maintain their voice and ensure the inclusion of the voices of Aboriginal and Torres Strait Islander communities in decision-making. We must not be lost in the crevices of a Western education system. Continuing the legacy of the NAEC, we must be seen and respected for the knowledges, experiences and perspectives that we bring to education and that will lead to the self-empowerment of Aboriginal and Torres Strait Islander peoples and communities, as well as the wider Australian society.

> Two hundred years of nothing; forty years of something really good.
> (Stephen Albert, interview, 2012)

APPENDIX A

NAEC membership

First term, 1977–80

NAME	REPRESENTATION	YEARS
Stephen Albert	Inaugural Chairperson	1977–80
Paul Hughes	SA Department of Aboriginal Affairs	1977–80
May O'Brien	WA Department of Education	1977–80
Vera Farrell (Budby)	WA Pre-school Education	1977–80
Phil Stewart	Qld Department of Education	1977–80
Robert (Bob) Morgan	New South Wales	1979–80
Kevin Gilbert	NSW Department of Aboriginal Affairs	1977–80
Barbara Kennedy	NSW Department of Education	1977–80
Colin Bourke	Victoria, Monash University	1977–80
Len Malone	Qld, Palm Island Schools	1977–80
Jim Hamilton	Qld Department of Education	1977–80
Isobelle Norvill	SA Department of Community Welfare	1977–80
Les Tucker	WA Department of Education	1977–80
Patsy Cameron	Tasmania, Community Worker	1977–80
Desmond White	NT Department of Education	1977–80
George Passi	Torres Strait Islands Department of Education	1977–80
John Budby	Qld Department of Education	1977–80
Natascha McNamara	SA Technical and Further Education	1977–80
Margaret Valadian	Tertiary Education	1977–80
W Nguakyukwokka	Northern Territory	1978–79
Kevin Rogers	NT Primary Education	1978–79
Eric Craigie	New South Wales	1978–79

Second term, 1980–83

NAME	REPRESENTATION	YEARS
John Budby	Chairperson, Second Term	1980–83
Stephen Albert	Continuing Member, WA	1980–83
Paul Hughes	Continuing Member, SA	1980–81
May O'Brien	Continuing Member, WA	1980–81
Vera Farrell (Budby)	Continuing Member, WA	1980
Phil Stewart	Continuing Member, NT	1980
Robert (Bob) Morgan	NSWAECG	1980–83
Eleanor Bourke	Victorian AECG	1980–81
Kaye Price	TASAECG	1980–81
Eddie Mabo	Torres Strait Islands	1980–81
Esther Bevan	Western Australia	1980–81
Elizabeth McCann	Queensland	1980
Hazel McKellar	Queensland	1980–81
John Thomas	South Australia	1980
Alfie Bamblett	TAFE	1980
George Tongerie	South Australia	1980–81
Victor Forrest	Western Australia	1981–83
Raelene Hudson	South Australia	1980–83
John Lester	Primary Teacher	1980–83
Eve Fesl	Language Development	1981–83
Oriel Murphy	Queensland AECG	1980–83
Maurie Ryan	Northern Territory	1980–83
Didimain Uibo	NTAECG	1980–83
Pearl Duncan	Primary Education	1980–83
Laurie Padmore	TASAECG	1981–83
Peter Buckskin	SAAECG	1981–83
Mary Atkinson	Victorian AECG	1981–83
Glen Miller	Queensland	1981–82
Robin Granites	Northern Territory	1980
Eric Hampton	Queensland AECG	1980–83

NAME	REPRESENTATION	YEARS
Les Hegarty	Queensland AECG	1980–82
Patsy Williamson	Traditional member	1981–83
Sepi Woosup	Queensland AECG	1981–83
Pat (Julia) Williamson	Northern Territory	1981–82

Third term, 1983–85

NAME	POSITION	YEARS
Paul Hughes	Chairperson, Third Term	1983–85
Errol West	Deputy chairperson	Full Term
Stephen Albert	Member	1986
Rex Granites	Traditional member	1983–84
Robert (Bob) Morgan	NSWAECG	1983–85
Eleanor Bourke	Victorian AECG	1985
Eve Fesl	Language Development	1983–84
Didimain Uibo	NTAECG	1983–84
Laurie Padmore	TASAECG	1983–84
Eric Law	TAFE	1983–85
Oriel Green	WAAECG	1983–85
Rex Garlett	WAAECG	1983–85
Ethel Munn	Early Childhood	1983–85
Peter Buckskin	SAAECG	1984–85
John Heath	NSWAECG	1984–85
Davina Tyrell	Curriculum Development	1983–85
Mary Atkinson	Victorian AECG	1984–85
Wendy Clinch	SAAECG	1983–85
Charles (Chicka) Dixon	New South Wales	1983
Helena Gulash	Primary/Secondary Education	1983–85
Wendy Ludwig	Adult Education	1983–85
Sepi Woosup	Queensland AECG	1984–85

Final term, 1986–89

NAME	POSITION	YEARS
Errol West	Chairperson	1986–88
Lynette Crocker	Deputy chairperson Chairperson	1986–88 1989
Eleanor Bourke	Victorian AECG Deputy chairperson	1988 1989
Bob Morgan	NSWAECG	1986–88
Eric Law	TAFE	1986–89
Oriel Green	Early Childhood	1986–89
Rex Garlett	WAAECG	1986–88
Ethel Munn	Queensland	1986–89
Ken Wyatt	Primary	1986–89
Les Hegarty	Queensland AECG	1988
Peter Buckskin	SAAECG	1986–88
John Heath	NSWAECG	1986–88
Lillian Holt	Tertiary	1986–88
Davina Tyrell	Curriculum Development	1986–89
William Baird	NTAECG	1986–89
Mary Atkinson	Victorian AECG	1986–88
Trevor Adamson	Traditional member	1986–89
Julius Billy	Queensland	1986–87
Helena Gulash	Primary/Secondary Education	1986
Janis Koolmatrie	SAAECG	1986–89
Wendy Ludwig	Adult Education	1986
Alma Stackhouse	TASAECG	1986–88
Kevin Rogers	Primary School	1986–88
Michael Torres	WAAECG	1986–89
Patricia Townsend	Feppi NTAECG	1986–88

APPENDIX B

Timeline of reports

1979	The Education and Employment of Aboriginal and Torres Strait Islander Teachers report
1980	Rationale, Aims and Objectives in Aboriginal Education
1982	Aboriginal studies report
1984	Funding Priorities in Aboriginal and Torres Strait Islander Education
1984	Technical and Further Education for Aboriginal and Torres Strait Islanders: Participation and Self-Determination
1985	Philosophy, Aims and Policy Guidelines for Aboriginal and Torres Strait Islander Education
1985	NAEC Commissioned report: Support Systems for Aboriginal Students in Higher Education Institutions
1986	1000 Aboriginal teachers by 1990
1986	Policy Statement on Teacher Education for Aboriginal and Torres Strait Islanders
1986	Policy Statement on Tertiary Education for Aboriginal and Torres Strait Islanders
1986	Aboriginal and Torres Strait Islander Pedagogy Project
1989	National Policy Guidelines for Early Childhood Education
1989	Aboriginal and Torres Strait Islander Education Joint Policy Statement

REFERENCES

Aboriginal Education Policy Task Force 1988, *Report of the Aboriginal Education Policy Task Force*, Australian Government Publishing Service, Canberra.

ACG (Aboriginal Consultative Group) 1975, *Education for Aborigines: Report to the Schools Commission*, Schools Commission, Canberra.

—— 1976, *Aboriginal Access to and Use of Technical and Further Education*, Technical and Further Education Commission, Canberra.

Albert, S 1977, 'National Aboriginal Education Committee', paper presented at the Preparing Teachers for Aboriginal Education National Conference, 28–31 August, Mount Lawley College, Perth.

—— 1978, 'Education of Aborigines criticised', *Northern Territory Teachers Federation Newsletter*, vol. 3, no. 7, p. 4.

—— 1979, 'Aboriginal Sunday', *Aboriginal Child at School*, vol. 7, no. 4, pp. 19–23.

Altman, JC, Biddle, N & Hunter, BH 2005, 'A historical perspective on Indigenous socioeconomic outcomes in Australia, 1971–2001', *Australian Economic History Review*, vol. 45, no. 3, pp. 273–95.

Auchmuty, J 1980, *Report of the National Inquiry into Teacher Education*, Australian Government Publishing Service, Canberra.

Beaton, G 1978, 'Aboriginal education in Victoria: new directions: 1975–?', *Aboriginal Child at School*, vol. 6, no. 5, pp. 2–6.

Behrendt, L, Larkin, S, Griew, R & Kelly, P 2012, *Review of Higher Education Access and Outcomes for Aboriginal and Torres Strait Islander people*, Australian Government, Canberra.

Bin-Sallik, M 2003, 'Cultural safety: let's name it!', *Australian Journal of Indigenous Education,* vol. 32, no. 1, pp. 21–8.

Bonner, N 1976, *The Environmental Conditions of Aborigines and Torres Strait Islanders and the Preservation of their Sacred Sites: Report from the Senate Select Committee on Aborigines and Torres Strait Islanders*, Government Printer, Canberra.

Bourke, C 1991, *Creating the Future from the Past: Aboriginal curriculum*, University of Queensland Press, St Lucia, Qld.

Brumby, E & Green, N 1978, 'Preparing teachers for Aboriginal education: report on the national conference, August 28–31, 1977',

Aboriginal Child at School, vol. 6, no. 2, pp. 55–61.

Budby, J 1980a, *Handbook: Operational Plan 1980-1983 of the National Aboriginal Education Committee*, Department of Education, Canberra.

—— 1980b, 'The new chairman of the National Aboriginal Education Committee', *Aboriginal Child at School*, vol. 8, no. 2, pp. 3–12.

Cameron, P & Miller, L 2011, 'Reclaiming history for Aboriginal governance: Tasmanian stories' in S Maddison & M Brigg (eds), *Unsettling the Settler State: Creativity and resistance in Indigenous settler-state governance*, Federation Press, Melbourne, pp. 32–50.

Carrick, J 1977, 'National Aboriginal Education Committee', *Aboriginal Child at School*, vol. 5, no. 2, pp. 3–6.

CASWG (Commonwealth Aboriginal Studies Working Group) 1982, *Report to the Australian Education Council, March 1982*, Australian Government Publishing Service, Canberra.

Coombs, HC 1984, *Aboriginal Autonomy*, Cambridge University Press, Cambridge, p. 171.

DEET (Department of Employment, Education and Training) 1988, 'Aboriginal Education Task Force asked to report urgently', *Aboriginal Employment and Education News*, June, 18, p. 2.

—— 1989, *National Aboriginal and Torres Strait Islander Education Policy: Implementation*, Department of Employment, Education and Training, Canberra.

Department of Education (Cth) 1976, *Submission No 419: National Committee on Aboriginal Education — Decision 1247 (Amended)*, National Archives of Australia, Canberra, Series A12909, Item 7426593.

—— *Cabinet Submission 6577: National Aboriginal and Torres Strait Islander Education Policy — Decisions 12855/ER and 13063*, National Archives of Australia, Canberra, Series A14039, Item 31430749.

Department of Education and Training 2014, *Selected Higher Education Statistics — 2014 Student Data*, viewed 8 April 2016, <www.education.gov.au/selected-higher-education-statistics-2014-student-data>.

Departmental Advisory Group on Aboriginal Education 1982, 'Aims in Aboriginal education', paper.

Duncan, Pearl 2014, 'The role of Aboriginal humour in cultural survival and resistance', doctoral thesis, University of Queensland, viewed 13 July 2020, <www.austlit.edu.au/austlit/page/8366368>.

Fife, W 1980a, 'Chairman of National Aboriginal Education Committee appointed', press release, 8 April, viewed 16 March 2016, <http://parlinfo.aph.gov.au/parlInfo/download/media/pressrel/HPR06003233>.

—— 1980b, 'Multicultural place for Aboriginals too', press release, 47/80, 1 September, viewed 16 March 2016, <http://parlinfo.aph.gov.au/parlInfo/download/media/pressrel/HPR06003274>.

Hughes, P 1984, 'A call for an Aboriginal pedagogy', *The Australian Teacher*, 9, pp. 20–2.

Hughes, P & Willmot, E 1979, *Report to the NAEC: The education and employment of Aboriginal and Torres Strait Islander teachers*, National Aboriginal Education Committee, Canberra.

—— 1982, 'A thousand Aboriginal teachers by 1990' in J Sherwood (ed.), *Aboriginal Education: Issues and innovations*, Creative Research, Perth, pp. 45–9.

Isles, T 1984, 'Trail-blazing for Aboriginal education', *Aboriginal Child at School*, vol. 12, no. 2, pp. 6–18.

Jordan, DF & Howard, SM 1985, *Support Systems for Aboriginal Students in Higher Education Institutions*, Tertiary Education Authority of South Australia, Adelaide.

Karmel, P 1973, *Schools in Australia: Report of the Interim Committee for the Australian Schools Commission*, Australian Government Publishing Service, Canberra.

Larkin, S 2013, Race matters: Indigenous employment in the Australian Public Service, doctoral dissertation, Queensland University of Technology, Brisbane.

Maddison, S 2009, *Black Politics: Inside the complexity of Aboriginal political culture*, Allen & Unwin, Crows Nest, NSW.

Malin, M & Maidment, D 2003, 'Education, Indigenous survival and well-being: emerging ideas and programs', *Australian Journal of Indigenous Education*, vol. 32, pp. 85–100.

Maynard, J 1997, 'Fred Maynard and the Australian Aboriginal Progressive Association (AAPA): one god, one aim, one destiny',

Aboriginal History, vol. 21, pp. 1–13.

McConnochie, KR 1982, 'Aborigines and Australian education: historical perspectives' in J Sherwood (ed.), *Aboriginal Education: Issues and innovations*, Creative Research, Perth, pp. 33–43.

MCEETYA (Ministerial Council on Education, Employment, Training and Youth Affairs) 2000, *Report of MCEETYA Task Force on Indigenous Education*, MCEETYA, Canberra.

NAEC (National Aboriginal Education Committee) 1977, *Black Community School Study*, Department of Education, Canberra.

—— 1980a, Briefing document prepared for the Meeting of State Superintendents, National Aboriginal Education Committee, State Consultative Group Representatives, Southern Teachers' Centre, Hobart.

—— 1980b, *Rationale, Aims and Objectives in Aboriginal Education*, Department of Education, Canberra.

—— 1981, 'Report: Fifth National Aboriginal Education Conference', *Aboriginal Child at School*, vol. 9, no. 5, pp. 6–19.

—— 1984a, *Aborigines & Tertiary Education: A framework for the 1985-1987 triennium*, Department of Education, Canberra.

—— 1984b, *Funding Priorities in Aboriginal and Torres Strait Islander Education: First report of the Working Party on Aboriginal and Torres Strait Islander Education*, NAEC and Commonwealth Schools Commission, Canberra.

—— 1985a, 'National Aboriginal Education Committee', press release, The Committee, Woden, ACT.

—— 1985b, *Philosophy, Aims and Policy Guidelines for Aboriginal and Torres Strait Islander Education*, Australian Government Publishing Service, Canberra.

—— 1986a, *Policy Statement on Teacher Education for Aborigines and Torres Strait Islanders*, Australian Government Publishing Service, Canberra.

—— 1986b, *Policy Statement on Tertiary Education for Aborigines and Torres Strait Islanders*, Australian Government Publishing Service, Canberra.

—— 1989, *National Policy Guidelines for Early Childhood Education*, Australian Government Publishing Service, Canberra.

NAEC & CDC (Curriculum Development Centre) 1986, *Aboriginal and Torres Strait Islander Pedagogy Project: A joint project*, Australian Government Publishing Service, Canberra.

NAEC Working Party 1984, *Technical and Further Education for Aborigines and Torres Strait Islanders: Participation and self-determination*, Australian Government Publishing Service, Canberra.

NAEC Working Party on Racism in Higher Education 1989, *Combating Racism in Tertiary Institutions*, South Australian College of Advanced Education, Adelaide.

National Aboriginal and Torres Strait Islander Higher Education Conference 1992, *Towards 2000: maintaining the momentum: National Aboriginal and Torres Strait Islander Higher Education Conference, Hervey Bay, Queensland, 6–11 December 1992*, Kumari Ngurpai Lag Higher Education Centre, University of Southern Queensland, Toowoomba, p. 1.

Naylor, R & James, R 2015, 'Systematic equity challenges: an overview of the role of Australian universities in student equity and social inclusion. In M Shah, A Bennett & E Southgate (eds), *Widening Higher Education Participation: A global perspective*, Elsevier, Oxford, UK, pp. 1–14.

NSWAECG (New South Wales Aboriginal Education Consultative Group) 2015, 'History', NSWAECG, viewed 3 March 2016, <www.aecg.nsw.edu.au/about/history>.

Ohlsson, T 1977, 'One people, one voice: Stephen Albert and the National Aboriginal Education Committee', *Australian Institute of Aboriginal Studies Newsletter*, 16, pp. 10–15.

Parbury, N 1991, *Survival: A history of Aboriginal life in New South Wales*, NSW Department of Aboriginal Affairs, Surry Hills, NSW.

Reynolds, M 1981, 'The Black Community School in Townsville', *Social Alternatives*, vol. 2, no. 2, pp. 64–8.

Rigney, LI 2001, 'A first perspective of Indigenous Australian participation in science: framing Indigenous research towards Indigenous Australian intellectual sovereignty', *Kaurna Higher Education Journal*, no. 7, pp. 1–13.

Ryan, S 1983, 'Chairman of the National Aboriginal Education Committee: Mr Paul Hughes', *Aboriginal Child at School*, vol. 11, no.

4, pp. 3–4.

SAAECG (South Australian Aboriginal Education Consultative Group) 1983, 'Rationale, aims and objectives for Aboriginal education in South Australia', *Aboriginal Child at School*, vol. 11, no. 4, pp. 21–37.

Sackville, R 1975, *Law and Poverty in Australia: Second main report, October 1975*, Commission of Inquiry into Poverty, Australian Government Publishing Service, Canberra.

Schools Commission 1975, 'Education for Aborigines' (Schools Commission report for the triennium 1976–78: Chapter 9), *Aboriginal Child at School*, vol. 3, no. 3, pp. 42–54.

—— 1978, 'Report, papers and recommendations', paper presented at the National Aboriginal Studies Seminar, 24–27 July, Alice Springs, NT.

—— 1987, 'National policy for the education of girls in Australian schools: the Commonwealth's contribution', vol. iv, p. 13, Canberra.

Schwab, RG 1995, *Twenty Years of Policy Recommendations for Indigenous Education: Overview and Research Implications*, Centre for Aboriginal Economic Policy Research, Australian National University, Canberra.

Scutter, H 2001, 'Writing the childhood self: Australian Aboriginal autobiographies, memoirs, and testimonies', *The Lion and the Unicorn*, vol. 25, no. 2, pp. 226–41.

University of South Australia 2008, *Citation for Professor Paul Hughes, AM FACE*, viewed 20 March 2016, <http://w3.unisa.edu.au/unicouncil/honorary_awards/citations/emeritus_prof/Paul%20Hughes_FINAL.pdf>

West, EG 1988, 'Aboriginal and Islander education consultative groups', *The Australian Teacher*, 21 (October), pp. 22–5.

—— 2000, An alternative to existing Australian research and teaching models: the Japanangka teaching and research paradigm; an Australian Aboriginal model, doctoral dissertation, Southern Cross University, Lismore, NSW.

Williams, L 2013, People, places and pathways in NSW Aboriginal education: the impact of Aboriginal community on education provision in NSW, doctoral dissertation, University of Newcastle.

Yunupingu, M 1995, *National Review of Education for Aboriginal and*

Torres Strait Islander Peoples: Final report, Australian Government Publishing Service, Canberra.

INDEX

Note: Bolded numbers indicate photographs.

1000 Aboriginal Teachers by 1990 Initiative, 41, 73, 75, 78, 99, 102, 138, 142–47, 149, 151, 159, 164, 191–92, 194.

Aboriginal and Torres Strait Islander Commission, 86, 184, 198.
Aboriginal Consultative Group, 1, 3, 9, **10**, 11, 14–20, 45–46, 48, 109–10, 138–41, 161.
Aboriginal Education Consultative Committee, 10, 119.
Aboriginal Education Consultative Group, xxiii, 26, 36, 42, 45–53, 55–57, 59–60, 62–64, 72, 82–84, 86–87, 92, 98–99, 105, 115, 122, 127, 137, 151, 167, 174, 178, 181, 185, 189–90, 195, 208.
Aboriginal Education Policy, 4, 51, 116, 155, 172–77, 180, 184, 190, 197–98, 211.
ACG, *see Aboriginal Consultative Group*.
ACT, *see Australian Capital Territory*.
AECG, *see Aboriginal Education Consultative Group*.
Albert, Stephen, xix, 1–2, 6, 11, 21–22, **23**, 24–25, 29–31, 33–34, 36–38, **39**, 40, 46–47, **57**, 69, 72, 74, 76, 78, 80, 85, 89, 99–101, 123–24, 127, 149–50, 192, 200, 212.
Atkinson, Mary, **90**.
ATSIC, *see Aboriginal and Torres Strait Islander Commission*.
Australian Capital Territory, vi, 55–56, 97, 122, 143.

Beazley, Kim, 7, 11.
Black Community School, 31, 39, 66–71.
Bonner, Neville, 111.

Bourke, Colin, vi, xix, 11, 24–25, 36, **39**, 40, 43, 69, 75, 96, 102–3, **104**, 105, 143, 146, 191–92, 202–3.
Bourke, Eleanor, vi, xix, 40, 51, 58, 80, 98, 109–10, 114, 164, 178, 180, 183, 203–4.
Buckskin, Peter, vii, xx, 8, 54, 58, 65, 71, 77, **84**, 85–88, 90, 100–1, 122, 130, 133–34, 149, 160, 175, 185, 189, 194, 208.
Budby, John, vii, 29, 43, 69, 72, 79–83, **89**, **90**, 96, 98, 111.
Burney, Linda, 85.

Cameron, Patsy, vi, xx, 24, 32–33, **34**, 35–36, 38, **39**, 55, 69, 87–88, 120, 189, 192–93, 199, 201.
Carrick, John, 18, 21, 23, 25, 37, 97.
CDC, *see Curriculum Development Centre*.
Crocker, Lynette, 156, 169, 178, 183.
Curriculum Development Centre, 26, 31, 111, 167–68, 196.

Dawkins, John, 108, 130, 169, 173, 184.
Duncan, Pearl, v, xx, 41, 44, 61, 90–92, 100, 113, 161, 204.

EEATSIT, see *Report to the NAEC: The Education and Employment of Aboriginal and Torres Strait Islander Teacher*.

Fife, Wallace, 66, 77, 80.
Forrest, Victor (Vic), xx, 75–76, 80–81, 88, **90**, 113, 122–24, 146, 166, 197, 209–10.

Gallagher, Mike, 177.
Garlett, Carol, **13**, 205.

Granites, Rex, xxi, 10, **14**, 15, 19, 59, 89, 94, 206.

Hall, Keith, 50, 192.
Hampton, Eric, **90**.
Hand, Gerry, v, 29, 38, 95, 110, 129, 173, **174**, 199.
Hawke, Robert (Bob), 128, 133.
Heath, John, xxi, 49, 71, 125, **126**, 127–28, **140**, 209.
Holt, Lillian, xxi, 26–29, 43, 201.
Hughes, Paul, vii, xxi, 29, 41, 43, 54, 62–64, 69, 73, 75, 85, 86, 88, 93, 101, 107, 117, **118**, 119–20, 122, 131–32, 135–36, **144**, 146–48, 152–53, 156, 158, 160, 168, 173, **174**, 175, 182, 202.

Jonas, Bill, 127.
Jordan, Dierdre, 77, 147–151, 191.

Langton, Marcia, 201.
Lester, John, xxii, 49–50, 63, 92–93, **94**, 134, 140, 208.
Ludwig, Wendy, xxii, 53–54, 124–25, 140–41, 154, 161, 166, 193, 210.

Mabo, Eddie, vii, 39, 68–69, 71.
Maynard, Roy, 88.
McKellar, Hazel, vii, 41, 121.
McNamara, Natascha, 10, 19, **57**, 85, 101.
Morgan, Rober (Bob), xxii, 37, 41, **42**, 43, 47, 49, 51, 60, 62, 83–84, 92, 105, 136–37, **140**, 151–52, 155, 180–81, 185–86, 188, 191, 206–7.

National Policy Guidelines for Early Childhood Education, 168.
National Review of Education for Aboriginal and Torres Strait Islander Peoples, 178, 197–98.

New South Wales, xvii, xix–xxii, 37, 42–43, 49–51, 64, 66, 90–94, 114, 121, 124, 127, 137, 143, 145, 164.
Northern Territory, xxi–xxiii, 14, 31–32, 53–54, 72, 74, 80, 94–95, 98, 108, 125, 131, 143, 161, 178, 181.

O'Brien, May, vii, xxii, 10, 11–12, **13**, 14, 19–20, 26, 41, 56, 59–60, 84–85, 101, 123, 205.
O'Shane, Pat, 50.

Padmore, Laurie, x, xxii, 80–81, 87–88, **90**, 174, 204–5.
Passi, George, 40, 69.
Perkins, Charles, 24–25, 125, 129.
Perron, Marshall, 72.
Philosophy, Aims and Policy Guidelines for Aboriginal and Torres Strait Islander Education, 52, 105–6, 108.
Policy Statement on Teacher Education for Aborigines and Torres Strait Islanders, 146, 158.
Price, Kaye, v–viii, xxiii, 30, 32–33, 39–41, **57**, 74–75, 85, 87, 111–13, 118, 120, **121**, 122, 130, 132, **144**, 162, 172, 187, 200.

Queensland, xx–xxiii, 10, 27–29, 31, 41, 46, 48, 62, 67, 69, 80, 82–83, 87, 90–92, 98, 100, 121, 125, 143, 162.

Rationale, Aims and Objectives in Aboriginal Education 1980, 52, 66, 74, 96, 102.
Report to the Australian Education Council, 114.
Report to the NAEC: The Education and Employment of Aboriginal and Torres Strait Islander Teachers, 73–75, 150, 159.
Ryan, Maurie, 76, 88, 94.

Ryan, Susan, xix, xxiii, 87, 98, 107–8, 116, 120, 128–34, 142, 144–45, 156.

Schools Commission, 7–9, 11, 15, 18, 25–26, 45–46, 48, 52, 63, 68–69, 71, 97, 107, 112, 119, 136–37, 149, 173, 196.
South Australia, xxi, 23, 52–53, 62, 85–86, 105, 117–19, 135, 148.
Support Systems for Aboriginal Students in Higher Education Institutions, 147, 151.

TAFE, *see Technical and Further Education.*
Tasmania, vi, xxii–xxiii, 32–33, 35–36, 38, 55, 80, 87–88, 111, 120, 204.
Technical and Further Education, xxii, 18–19, 21, 63, 94, 97, 125, 138–42, 145, 158, 177, 190.
Tongerie, George, 86.
Tripcony, Penny, 100.

Uibo, Didimain, vii, xxiii, 32, 45, 55, 94–95, 170, 206.

Valadian, Margaret, 10, 12, 19, **57**, 85, 101.
Victoria, 40, 48–49, 55, 100, 105.

West, Errol, vi, vii, 46, 53–54, 56, 72, 98, 117, 123, **140**, 156, **157**, 158, 169, 174, 183–84.
Western Australia, 13–14, 56, 77, 123, 147.
Whitlam, Gough, 2, 7, 11, 18, 131, 134.
Wilenski, Peter, 129, 131, 133.
Williamson, Eric, 90.
Willmot, Eric, **10**, 25, 41, 43, 73–77, 138, 142, 145, 147, 150, 159, 191.

ABOUT THE AUTHOR

Leanne Holt (née Lilley) is a Worimi woman from coastal New South Wales, Australia. She has worked in Aboriginal and Torres Strait Islander higher education for over twenty years, and is currently the Pro Vice-Chancellor (Indigenous Strategy) at Macquarie University. She is currently the President of the National Aboriginal and Torres Strait Islander Higher Education Consortium and deputy co-chair of the World Indigenous Nations Higher Education Consortium.